LECTURES ON SOCIAL LIFE AND THE THREEFOLD SOCIAL ORGANISM

RUDOLF STEINER

The Liberation of the Human Being
as the Basis for Social Reorganisation

Old thinking and new social will

Nine public lectures,
held between 11 March and 10 November 1919 in
Basel, Bern, and Winterthur

2023

ANTHROPOSOPHICAL PUBLICATIONS
FREMONT, MICHIGAN U.S.A.

Translation by Ernesta Carsten-Krüger

Cover designed by James D. Stewart

Rudolf Steiner Portrait on Back Cover
By Peter Gospodinov

Drawing on the cover sheet page after an
Original drawing by Rudolf Steiner

Cover image of Textile Art
"Dreamscape"
by Martha Liddle-Lameti
https://www.facebook.com/Marteldesigns/

.

Bibliography No. 329

The e.Lib, Inc.
Visit the website at https://www.elib.com/

Printed in the United States of America

First Printing: July 2023
Anthroposophical Publications
https://AnthroposophicalPublications.org/

ISBN: 978-1-948302-53-1 Paperback
978-1-948302-54-8 eBook

Table of Contents

Concerning the publication of the lectures given by Rudolf Steiner

The basis of anthroposophically oriented spiritual science are the works written and published by Rudolf Steiner (1861-1925). In addition, he gave numerous lectures and courses in the years 1900 to 1924, both in public and for the members of the Theosophical, later Anthroposophical Society. He initially did not want his lectures to be written down, as they were intended as "oral communications not intended for printing." However, after increasingly incomplete and erroneous transcripts were being made and distributed, he felt compelled to control the transcriptions. He entrusted this task to Marie Steiner-von Sivers. She was responsible for appointing the stenographers, the administration of the transcripts and the texts had to be reviewed before they could be published. Since Rudolf Steiner was only able to correct the transcripts himself in a very few cases, his reservations must be considered regarding all lectures: "It will just have to be accepted that there are errors in the originals that I have not looked at." «Es wird eben nur hingenommen werden müssen, daß in den von mir nicht nachgesehenen Vorlagen sich Fehlerhaftes findet.»

After Marie Steiner's death (1867-1948) the publication of a Rudolf Steiner Complete Edition started, following her guidelines. The present volume forms a component of this complete edition. Where necessary, more detailed information can be found in the text documents at the beginning of the notes.

The Liberation of the Human Being

Summaries of Lectures

The Real Foundation of a League of Nations in the Economic, Legal, and Spiritual Forces of the Nations

First lecture, Bern, 11 March 1919

Critical comments on statements made by leading politicians before the outbreak of the First World War and the social relations between nations at that time. The League of Nations Idea in Wilson's Senate Speech of 1-22-1917. The necessity of taking the capital and labour question into account to establish a League of Nations. Two aspects of the capital problem: the relationship between the use of human skills and capital, furthermore the distinction between possession and management of capital. On the commodity character of labour when considering the Marxist view. On the necessity of a threefold structure of the social organism. Characterisation of the individual social spheres, especially economic life, with the focus on the property question. Time-critical reflections concerning militarism by Herman Grimm.

Discussion

Critical consideration of basic socialist views: On dictatorship of the proletariat; on the problem: "Each according to his abilities, each according to his needs"; criticism of (party) programmes. The present and future aspects of "Threefolding." On the question of militarism considering Clausewitz's formula. About J. G. Fichte's "Bolshevism."

What Is the Significance of the Work of the Modern Proletarian?

Second lecture, Bern, 17 March 1919

On the contrast between the bourgeois doctrine of the world's moral order and the proletariat's reality. The proletariat as a living critique of modern civilisation, illustrated by the effects the materialist conception of history, the theory of surplus-value, according to Marx, of the commodity character of labour and the class struggle. Viewpoints that emerge behind the external demands as new streams become apparent: Firstly, the longing for a spiritual life enabling a dignified existence; secondly, the demand for a legal order in which labour-force is freed from its commodity character. Thirdly, the overcoming of the class struggle through new legal relations. About what is to be done or what is to be refrained from by the State. The idea of the threefold social order and aspects that describe areas in more detail.

Proletarian Demands and Their Future Practical Realisation I

Third lecture, Winterthur, 19 March 1919

The proletarian movement as a living critique of modern civilisation. Discussion of three concepts that live in the proletariat: the materialistic conception of history, Marx's theory of surplus-value, the class struggle theory. On the nature and meaning of a free spiritual life and the need to replace the ruling entitlement to privileges with legal rights. From the unitary State to the threefold social state organism. The two limits of economic life. The labour force as the main factor in price formation. About the sum of the means of production as the realistic countervalue of money. On the relation of the means of production to the rights sphere and spiritual sphere. The consequences of a transfer of the means of production into common ownership.

Concluding remarks on the discussion

The idea of threefolding as the opposite of a Utopia and in contrast to the old order of class status. The human being as the focal point of the three members of the social organism. On the difference between ownership of property and administration. The overcoming of thinking in programmes and overcoming habits. Proletarian demands and their future practical realisation.

Achievement

Fourth lecture, Basel, 2 April 1919

Class struggle. The tendency of recent times to weld together economic, spiritual, and State life is illustrated by Austria's. Points of view on the independence of spiritual, legal, and economic life. On the problem of economic associations. The regulation of labour relations, currency, ownership of property, and the property cycle in the threefold social organism. Democracy in the Rights State. The elimination of contemporary capitalism in connection with the liberation of spiritual life. Freedom, equality, fraternity. The vocation of the proletariat to liberate humanity.

Concluding remarks on the discussion

The free-land and free-money idea and the currency question. The social function of capital. On the necessity of acquiring social awareness in the schools. The threefold structure of the human organism as an image for the threefold social organism. Justice in social life and problems of the rule of law.

Social Will and Proletarian Demands
Fifth lecture, Basel, 9 April 1919

On the Communist Manifesto and the Marxist conception of history. On the question of ideology and the theory of class struggle. The dissolution of the old relations of production by the productive powers. The scientific way of thinking infused Marxism way of thinking and its consequences for social life. Tendencies towards unification. The proletarian world view and its connection with the bourgeois world. The world war because of State structures. The sterility of a spiritual life dependant on the State, illustrated by the Goethe Society example. The recovery of the social organism by dividing it into three separate limbs. Labour law and its significance for determining prices. On the problem of the socialisation of private property. The division of labour and egoism. The importance of a free spiritual life for the circulation of capital. Spirit or matter? The social organism's threefold structure as the revelation of a primarily higher truth and the difference from the earlier social class divisions. The individual person and his relationship to the three members of the social organism. The courage for a new social will.

Concluding remarks on the discussion

The human being as the victim of ossified concepts. The circulation of the means of production in place of nationalisation. Brotherhood and the present Christian assertion. – the Threefoldness of the Human organism and its starting point in the book "Riddles of the Soul."

The Humanistic Basis of The Social Question
Sixth lecture, Bern, 14 October 1919

Personal preliminary remarks. One-sidedness in the Marxist way of thinking. The desolation of the soul of the proletarian because of the materialist worldview. The commodity character of labour. The dictatorship of the Proletariat and the Communist Manifesto. On the socialisation of the means of production and the problem of surplus-value. The task of anthroposophical oriented spiritual science. The alienation from life of previous social views. On the independence of economic life from the legal sphere. Danger of political revolutions and of so-called spiritual revolutions. Lenin and Trotsky as the gravediggers of civilisation. The liberation of education as an urgent task. The protest of future generations because of the socialisation of the means of production. On the possibilities of realising Threefolding in Switzerland. The interaction of liberalism, democracy, and socialism.

Concluding remarks on the discussion
The difference between the threefold idea and the old-fashioned social classes. Parliamentarism and State. The worthlessness of social programmes. The laws of the social organism. Threefolding as a time challenge.

Spiritual Science (Anthroposophy) and the Conditions of Culture in the Present and Future

Seventh lecture, Basel, 20 October 1919
The Dornach building as an expression of a spiritual movement. About eurythmy and the character of the "philosophy of freedom." Woodrow Wilson's understanding of freedom. The consistency of his critique with Lenin's and Trotsky's views. The question of freedom and its foundation in the "Philosophy of Freedom." The transition from the philosophy of freedom to Anthroposophy. Overcoming the profound damage to humanity because it is cut off from the cosmos. Pathways to higher knowledge. Three types of revolutions: the spiritual, the political and the economic. About the shortcomings in the views of Saint-Simon, Fourier, and Blanc. Rabindranath Tagore's critique of the times. Tasks of anthroposophical oriented spiritual science.

The Spirit as a Guide Through the Sensible and Into the Supersensible World I

Eighth lecture, Bern, 6 November 1919
Goethe's idea of the primordial plant. The relationship of Anthroposophy to natural science and religion. The ideological *monopoly* of religious confessions. Natural science in the Goethean sense as a starting point for religious knowledge and spiritual knowledge. On the loneliness of the modern human being. The idea of repeated earth lives in Lessing's "Education of the Human Race." Dreamlife and the subhuman. About hypnosis. The human being and human development. Spiritual knowledge as the basis for future social coexistence.

The Spirit as a Guide Through the Sensible and Into the Supersensible World II

Ninth lecture, Basel, 10 November 1919
Anthroposophical oriented spiritual science as a continuation of the scientific way of thinking. Goethe's idea of the original plant. The power of the religious denominations as instruments for preventing the exploration of soul and spirit. On the importance of the inner soul work in the form of

concentration and meditation exercises. On the essence of memory. On the conscious handling of the power of memory. The significance of the conscious will. The soul-spiritual relationship with the others. The realisation of repeated earth lives and its significance for the social coexistence of people. Will and desire. Mediumship, hypnosis, and spiritualism. Fearlessness and the ability to suffer in connection with the inner path of development. On Schelling's methodology. Intellectual modesty as a prerequisite for spiritual research. Supersensible vision and its importance for the social coexistence of people.

Appendix
   From a questionnaire, Münchenstein, 10 April 1919

Notes

The Future and Anthroposophical Publications

About the Author

About the Translator

About the Artist

The Liberation of the Human Being

THE REAL FOUNDATION OF A LEAGUE OF NATIONS

In The Economic, Legal and Spiritual Forces of The Nations

Bern, 11 March 1919

First Lecture

Over the last four years, we have often heard that, as far as historical memory stretches, things have never been as appalling as were the recent terrible events. One does not usually come across the idea, that at least an attempt must emerge from recent catastrophic happenings that struck humanity, to reshape the social organisation. Or that we should think differently from the way we are used to, seeing how the frightening events of recent years differ from previous human experiences.

Yes, if one attempts to reflect thoughts that contrast the ingrained thinking habits, one usually encounters the accusation: Well, again a Utopia! — When one looks at the fundamental attitude of such an allegation, one realises that precisely the people who think like those who call out "utopia" now, were the ones who would have held what happened afterwards for a fantastic dream. That is if someone could have described the catastrophic events that affected us later, in the spring of 1914. They call themselves practical, these people. How did they speak before the world-shattering disaster struck? Let us look at some of them.

We need only look at some of Europe's leaders, at that time, in the spring of 1914. Practical people, scorners of what they call Utopia, almost literally spoke something like this: The affiliation between the European superpowers, thanks to the cabinets' efforts, offers a firm guarantee that for the foreseeable time, nothing will shake world peace. — These are not fictional statements; you can read it in the parliamentary reports; it is depicted there in various ways.

Someone who did not depend on such people's mindset in the inner condition of his soul, who tried to gain an unbiased view of events, spoke perhaps as he did in April 1914 before a meeting in Vienna, says again to you today: It was my intellectual conscience at that time, and my ability to observe, that forces me to say: We are, in as far as our social and international relations have advanced, in a condition that I can only describe as a carcinoma, cancer in the lives of nations — that will soon have to erupt dreadfully. Maybe the violence of events will force people to consider those who speak from out of this soul constitution less as Utopians than those who talk about events as I have just indicated to you.

Today, on the other hand, one hears the practical people who are so superior to those they call Utopians, say: We can at present, not reach the highest pinnacles of reorganisation towards a new social order, we must move forward step by step. Indeed, some thoughts are — say such people — beautiful, and you may accomplish such things after centuries, but today it is up to us to take the next steps. It is relatively easy to realise that you must first take the next steps, of course, but it will be a poor mountaineer, who has no idea when he takes the following step, which way he should go, and no idea which direction to go to reach the summit.

Those who do not think in the sense of these scorners of Utopia, but perhaps just realistically, may need another comparison still, to show what is lurking in the shadows. He may not have to start from the disastrous war that has erupted like carcinoma in recent years. But he will have to point out that many people now think like someone who inhabits a house with cracks and fissures that threaten to cause the house to collapse, but who cannot decide to do anything about it or build the place anew. Instead, they devise all sorts of deliberations about connecting the individual rooms by doors, so it will be easier to help one another. The doors will not be of much help if the fissures have become too wide! This way of thinking is possibly due to certain developments, which speak a louder and clearer language than people are often inclined to take heed of today.

This catastrophic war and the horrific experiences brought a feeling of detachment, which has gradually crystallised into the views at the heart of the noteworthy assembly, held here in Bern as a Conference of a League of Nations. The call for a League of Nations has evolved from the terrible events of recent years. We will have to admit that it might seem justified, this call for the League of Nations. There might even be more reasons to explain the need for uniting the nations, called for by so many people currently. Perhaps it is more important not only to ask: How can we establish this League of Nations? What measures can we best take — how to envision this — to ensure that it comes about? Perhaps we can raise the question: What are the grounds for establishing such a league of nations? Only when one looks at the forces that live within different countries, can one perhaps recognise, to what extent one can achieve something fruitful with such a League of Nations? And does it not seem necessary, to modify the question a little, because this illuminating conception of a League of Nations, which is particularly apparent to the world, was conceived out of a probable situation that has not occurred?

In 1917, Wilson spoke to the American Senate. There a thought arose in connection to another idea, that went something like this: There is a precondition for this League of Nations. It is that no-one must gain what can be called victory or defeat decisively in the war. Wilson looked to an outcome that did not lead to victory or defeat of one party. And from this direction of thought, he now derives the urge to set up this League of Nations. Indeed, the idea was realistic; but the probable situation from which this idea was born at the time, is no longer valid; today, the case is such that there was a decisive victory on the one hand and a decisive defeat on the other. Yes, perhaps it is precisely for this reason that, for example, we must look at the question of the League of Nations in a completely different way.

When discussing the League of Nations' question publicly today, I am particularly aware that I must be careful in approaching this question. As a member of the defeated nation, it is impossible to ask the question without people assuming the answer comes from someone who feels part of a country that perhaps wanted to belong to such a league of nations, for this, after all, was undoubtedly the mood of the people of Central Europe. The Paris events exclude the German from asking such a question today, and one should not be under any illusions about this. But that is not the question I want to ask. For me, it is about asking a question and formulating an appropriate response, in which also those can participate, for whom it may be impossible to participate in this League of Nations for the coming years. In other words, this is the way to ask the question: Whatever current agreements are reached, what can every single nation, whether it has suffered victory or defeat, contribute out of its own strength to an actual League of Nations that can bring humanity what it longs?

But there one must, since a League of Nations must undoubtedly have to be involved in international affairs, focus on the most critical global matters, which, regarding all situations, will soon concern all nations. If one studies the current conventional approach of circumstances, then one must view it from two directions. One looks at the State on the one hand and economic life on the other. Those who presently seek to work towards cooperation between the nations, look firstly at the State regarding the guidelines, asking: what should the State do in this or that matter, where things are ripe for change? — Or, to come to an explanation, people today look, I might say, as if hypnotised, towards the economic life; because the economic conditions seem to be the only ones, which cause today's conflicts, the most significant disputes at least of the present. In these considerations, taken from these two perspectives, one aspect is usually not considered.

Even when assured that the present relationships and the people are considered, this is rarely the case. Here I will try to be bold enough to explore what one discovers when one looks at the State on the one

4

hand and economic life on the other. Above all, I will not shun to empathically ask, from the people's viewpoint: What must the States do to unite into a league of nations? What needs to be done first — and do not think I want to criticise or condemn — to implement vital matters for the future? When one raises this question considering the States' structures, the standards of the different States, and try to find something that includes all the nations in a world federation or a world parliament, I would like to ask the question today: what should the member States do? Another question: what should the States do for the well-being of the people? In many respects, we have come to know through the past few years' terrible events, what the States have achieved with their actions; they have just led humanity into this dreadful catastrophe. We cannot deny it; the States led society into this terrible catastrophe!

If it is not evident that a person should think twice when he realises that his actions resulted in all manner of evil, he must ask himself: how do I do things differently? Could it not be more useful to say: maybe I will leave what I have poorly accomplished, to someone who can do better? — Then, you see, perhaps the question will lead onto a completely different track. Maybe we need to address the most critical international questions to find fruitful ground to assess what caused the cracks and fissures in the house wherein humanity currently lives; this house consisting of the different States. One may have to ask: whence did these cracks and crevices come? How did it happen that the States have driven people into this terrible, disastrous war? Apart from many others, two issues have come to be internationally important in recent times. These are capitalism and human labour. Undoubtedly, we had a "League of Nations" or something in that line: The Confederation based on international capital. Another "League of Nations" was also in the making and is asserting itself today: it is what lies at the basis of the introduction of an international labour force. You need to consider these two aspects if you want to come to the fruitful ground for establishing a league of nations, built on human concerns.

As far as capital is concerned, we see that, for many people, the management of money — and what has led to so-called capitalism, — is contra the interests of a large part of the population. Due to what lives in it, people feel it has led to these terrible events. And from many sides, they express — in opposition to capitalism — the radical demand, that all that had grown out of capitalism as social structures have to be changed today, that private enterprise must give way to what we have been used to call socialism. This objection, combined with feelings about the exploitation of human labour, colours international life. One needs to mention repeatedly: Even though the proletarian world population does not clearly articulate or consciously express this, in the subconscious of millions of people's lives, during capitalist development especially the human labour force acquired a character that must not continue.

Let us start by looking at these two aspects. Capital, the management of money in economic life, must be entirely separated from that with which it is connected today if you look at it properly. Two structures are presently linked with capitalism: one refers to something inseparable from capitalism; the other is something that should distance itself from it. Today the necessity for capital and the private ownership of capital is intertwined in the economic life. The question must be asked, however: Can one separate these two aspects from the organisation? For private financial organisations to function, human labour, based on the greater or lesser input of individual human capacities, is needed. One cannot separate it from its funding, the capital. Whoever tries to ask unbiasedly under what conditions the social organism is viable, will always come to the answer: When one takes its most important source away, namely that which flows into it through the individual capacities of the workforce, this social organism is not viable. What provides the capital is linked to what is provided by the skills of the individual human labourer. This indicates that in no way can the necessary personal human aptitudes be separated from its means: capital — in the State of the future.

But the private ownership of capital is something else. This ownership of private capital has a different social function than the management of the holdings, for which resources — provided by individual human abilities — is necessary. When someone, by whatever means, acquires or attained private capital, this gives that person power over other people. This power, which will mostly be economical, cannot be regulated in any other way than linked to the social organism's legal dealings. What generates productivity within the social organism is the labour that increases capital by utilising individual skills. What damages the social organism is when those who do not have the particular skills to perform such work somehow own the assets. However, they have economic power. What does it mean: to have capital? — to have several people working according to someone else's wishes, to have control over many people's labor. The only remedy can be not to separate people's labour and abilities and the generating of the social organism's capital. However, the possible fruitful effect of capital for the social organism is severed time and again precisely through the possession of wealth on the part of people who cannot perform the skills for utilising such wealth. That is something that can have very, very damaging consequences for the social organisation. In other words, humanity is at this historical moment in time, in dire need of severing capital ownership, from capital management. That is one question. Let us leave it at that for the time being. We will soon see how we can attempt to solve this problem.

The second is the question of the social significance of human labour. One can discern this social significance of human toil if you trace what has passed through the proletarian population's souls in the last decades. One realises then, how deeply what Karl Marx (and those who have worked accordingly) has said about this human labour force. What Karl Marx noted in his theory of surplus-value, struck into the proletarian souls! Why? Because they sensed the value of human labour force as a commodity, concerns the most profound questions about human dignity and a humane existence in general. Marx had to

7

formulate what he had to say about human labour's social importance by stipulating clearly that human work was not yet free from being a commodity in the modern capitalist economic order.

Goods circulate in the economic process; but in the current economic cycle, not only goods circulate. The commodity market does not only supply and demand goods. In the case of the furnishing of human labour, we must call it the labour market, as the labourer is paid for his work similarly to the way people pay for goods. Despite the standard employment contract, the person who offers his labour to the market must bear the burden of being deprived of his value as a human being when labour becomes a commodity. The terms of the current employment contract stipulate that the manager — in this case, the entrepreneur — compensates the worker for his labour, as a necessary part of the economic market. In short, the labour force becomes a commodity. To resolve this question, one must not stop at what Karl Marx said. Today it becomes a question of survival — be it on the part of the proletarian population, be it on the part of the bourgeois leading circles — to achieve liberation precisely on this point. We must go beyond that, which Karl Marx has been able to teach the proletarian population in this field.

Even people who believe they are socially aware and want the best for the proletariat, are inwardly convinced that whosoever has no property, only his ability to work to offer, must earn their living through wages. That is: they must turn their labour into a commodity. What is the best way to turn labour into a commodity? — for example, the question is formulated: how can labour as commodity be made most bearable? — We will never resolve this question so that it does not cause new social shocks. Can one not demand the opposite: How can human labour even be made into goods? How is a social organisation possible, in which human labour-power is not a commodity anymore? The factual situation concerning the work — let us call it labour for now — is that both the craftsman's and the entrepreneur's spiritual input create the product. The question is, how can this joint manufacturing of a product be introduced satisfactorily into the market, regarding what is now called the employer and the employee?

These are the two most important questions, which can and must be raised today throughout global, national life: What is involved in using capital in social life? On the other hand, what does it mean when one incorporates human labour into social life? Let us consider the situation of the worker at present. He can feel, even if he does not articulate it, even if Marx was not able to discover this by thinking it through: Together with the entrepreneur, I make my product. The product that we generate at the workplace, we produce together. Therefore, it must be a question of sharing between what is now called the entrepreneur and the craftsman. And a division must occur, which can satisfy both sides directly and concretely. What is the current relationship between the employer and the employee? I do not want to fall into agitator like phrases. However, let us look at this entire relationship, as it stands. Today's proletariat senses this soberly and intensively, even if they do not formulate it in clear terms. It lives in them subconsciously. The entrepreneur's monetary authority does not allow the worker to decide what the commodity they produce together is worth or what the joint product is. He has no control over how much falls to one or the other or to come to any agreement on the above issues. He can only sign an employment contract. But the worker senses in his soul that no-one can compare any kind of labour with a commodity.

Today we are talking about exchanging goods for goods or their representative — money — in the economic process. Moreover, goods or their representative — money —, is exchanged for human labour-power. The employee today feels that he helps the trader in the production of the goods, but the trader is over-privileged, in that the worker does not receive the portion to which he is entitled. That already indicates an imbalance, for individual human abilities generate the capital needed for production. To enable production, money is needed to utilize spiritual as well as physical activity. But a large part of humanity feels the wealth is managed unfairly, in a dishonest way.

Whether this is justified or not, we will not go into now; but this is how many people feel about it. This feeling unmistakably lies at the base of the present situation. Individual abilities are entrenched in a distorted way in the social organism, or at least it can be. The modern capitalist economy connects the exploitation of people's individual skills with the appropriation of the means of production. Thus, it facilitates economic power appropriation and economic supremacy. But this so-called power, this apparent supremacy of one person over another, constitutes nothing less than a legal relationship.

When someone indicates that the utilisation of human skills somehow intertwines with legal rights (as the one who speaks does), he should point out something innate in the whole nature of the social organism, something of more significance than things people tend to pursue today. The obvious question arising from such presuppositions: How is the sphere of Rights, how is the application of individual human abilities explained? Goods must always be produced anew, must come forth again and again from the labourer's activity, how is the utilisation of these abilities in the social organism justified?

Anyone who preserves an unbiased view of human life will gradually conclude that one can distinguish three hugely different fundamental sources of human life the social organism. These three primary aspects of human life flow together naturally in the social organism; they operate together. But how they work together can only be ascertained if one can look at the human being's actual situation. We must see humanity as a unity, a unified entity within the social trinity. In the social organism, in the first place, there are individual human abilities. We can trace this field from man's highest spiritual achievements in art, science, and religious life to applying unique human abilities, some grounded more in the mental, some more in the physical sphere. Capitalism bases itself on utilising these capabilities for the most mundane, physical activities, up to the economic process, usually designated as the material realm. Thus far, one can trace the coherent current of all the mental achievements. Within this region, everything is based on the appropriate, fruitful application of what must always be raised anew from the primordial sources of human nature, to flow into the healthy social organism in the right way.

In a healthy social organism, everything based on the realm of rights occurs in an absolutely distinctive way. This life of Rights transpires between person and person simply because it is a general human issue. We must have the opportunity to shape our particular abilities in the social sphere. The better we design them, the better for the prevalent social organism. The more freedom we have in getting out and using our abilities, the better for the social organism. Schroff stands in contrast to real life for everyone who does not proceed from theories, from dogmas, who can observe real life, for everything that applies to the rights sphere between people.

And a third aspect plays out in human social coexistence. It is altogether different from the other two, the individual human faculties, which come from inequalities of human nature and the law that comes from legal consciousness. That is the human need that originates in the natural foundation of physical and soul life and must find its satisfaction in economic life cycle through production, circulation, and consumption. This threefolding of the social organism does not originate in abstract thinking; this threefolding is a fact. And the question can only be: How can this threefold structure be regulated appropriately so that not a sick, but a healthy social organism emerges? Here is where — of course, I can only indicate with these hints — there is much to be gained. An unbiased view of the social organism leads us to say: it is precisely the ignorance regarding this radical difference between the three fundamental characteristics of social life in recent historical development, which has led to the dispute we are engaged in today. It is something in which we will become more and more entangled. Where did it start?

In recent times everyone's attention focused as if hypnotised, on the economic life. They claimed that for humanity's progress, economic life should merge, with the purely political State. The State where everyone is equal, as it is the domain of Rights. Firstly, specific industry sectors, especially the telegraph system, the railway system and so on, those sectors that seemed to be the most suitable, must merge with the State. They looked towards the State in the same way as to economic life. And what does the socialist thinker of today do? He only inherits bourgeois thinking in this respect. He does not want only specific sectors of the economy that seem suitable to be nationalised or socialised. He wants to socialise, nationalise either the entire property or company. He only wants to draw the final consequences of what has gone before. Now one could cite many aspects. One need only mention what role, among the fatal causes of the war that was being prepared for years, was played in the outer political arena by the — I need to mention one word only "Baghdad railway." One could cite hundreds and hundreds of such examples.

What does this mean? It means a merging of economic interests with the interests that belong purely to the State. The result is that the State administrators, in rendering the services they are empowered to execute, must follow economic interests. And the political interests of the State are thus entangled in and come into conflict with economic interests. In recent times, the States' entire configuration has shown this mixing of economic life with political life.

Anyone who could look at Central European life from this point of view — like the one who speaks to you today could look at Austrian territory —, knows that much of what has wiped out the Austrian State was caused by something that people are not inclined to realise today. In the eighteen sixties in Austria, only economic life was at the base of the State's configuration when establishing a constitution. The Austrian Imperial Council offered four electoral constituencies: The large landowners, chambers of commerce, towns, markets and industrial zones, and rural communities. These all are economic communities. Whosoever was elected from within these economic communities, rendered the law in Austria. What emerged as the life of Rights out of such purely economic interests, of course, could not harmonise with something, that comes out of the spiritual-individual grounds of humanity, with the national affairs of the so-called Austrian State. And

12

so, matters got mixed up in such a way that laws were drawn up, by what the elected representatives of the four economic body of voters wanted to make into law out of their industrial interests, in a bogus state. That, in turn, embroiled itself into — what people currently gladly incline towards — it embroiled itself into the sphere of spiritual interests and aspirations, into all that entails the complexity of spiritual life.

On the one hand, economic life immersed itself in modern State affairs; on the other hand, the entire spiritual life was entangled in State affairs. After all, people regard this to be precisely in the spirit of modern human progress. To make all spiritual life gradually a part of the State's political life, became the ideal. How much has remained free today? There is no predisposition to keeping art and science independent from being incorporated into the State. No inclination to integrate spiritual life in the right way in its only authentic role within the social organism, to keep this spiritual life completely emancipated from all other aspects of life so that it can structure and administer itself.

In recent times, more and more people aspire to nationalise the entire school system. The developmental aim of modern humanity should be to accomplish a complete reversal in this area specifically. Just imagine: If the lowest teacher is not the servant of the State, knows how to place him or herself in a freely organised spiritual life, knows that he or she stands within a spiritual organism, how differently he will be able to act within the unity of the social organism, from when he must do what the State requires when teaching the developing child! Some may object out of some unfavourable experience. They may be afraid the science will be provided by biased scientists who will be employed because of their specific perspective. But science itself and its teachings are free. Such laws exist in many countries. Many people can assert this. Those who are aware of how things stand, know that these transgressions occur in employment, institutions' administration, and labour. Free spiritual life, powerfully integrated from out of its being into the healthy social organism, must be autonomous and distinct from State and the economic sphere to develop in its own right. I know the perceived objections: "If in turn the school is freed from the constraints of the State when everyone can send their children to school out of their enthusiasm for spiritual education, then we will return to illiteracy."

People who talk like that, hark back on past impressions under current conditions. And we will see in a moment, how these current conditions have a completely different effect than what these people who retain their past understanding, suspect. This, however, happens — it must be said in advance —, because the real truth can only live in the social organism if the necessary structure is present and includes the following: the spiritual organism, built on the individual physical and mental abilities of people — what we could also call the spiritual life in its full complexity; the legal body that covers the territory of the actual political State; and the cycle of economic processes in which only the production, circulation and consumption of goods are involved.

Do not think that this destroys the unity of life. On the contrary, precisely separating each of these limbs within the healthy social organization, will help the organism recover and regain its inner strength. Each member can allow the other its appropriate place. And suppose we aim at the recovery of our social conditions. In that case, we must demand the independence of these three limbs, i.e., the corresponding autonomy of intellectual life, legal life and the life that comprises the cycle of economic activities that, because of confused thinking and actions over the past centuries, has melted together.

The State cannot be an economist. We must adapt economic life to its specific circumstances, place it where it belongs. Economic life achieved this to a certain extent by developing cooperative, trade union life. But this collective, trade union life has repeatedly been improperly intertwined with legal relationships. What is necessary for economic life, is a system of association, bringing together definite groups of people according to consumer needs and the required production to meet these needs. People come together according to professional interests. Management of what circulates within these cooperative groups according to the corresponding human needs can only be the outcome of expert judgement from out of economic life itself. Now human labour and the role that capital plays come into effect. I can only indicate in a few lines how this works. Human labour in social the organism consists of the relationship between the work the craftsman renders, and some intellectual leader, who operates the capital by managing some economic activity or something beneficial to the social organism. This relationship can only be legal. The sphere of Rights must form the basis of the relationship the worker with the entrepreneur. It has to stand on a different ground than that of economic life itself. In this way, a radically different relationship is brought about, than what we have today. But today we must also make radical judgments about radical facts.

On the one hand, economic life today depends on what is inherently available. People must be able to make an expert judgement on this. In a certain way, a person takes over one or the other piece of land and through diligence and technology makes it fruitful, but only within certain limits. It is, to a large extent, dependent on his or her natural abilities.

Economic life, on the one hand, depends on what is intrinsically available. Still, it also depends on what has to be established based on the law, in the cooperation of all involved, no matter what kind of work they do. Whether they are intellectual or manual workers, they enter a relationship based on what is agreed upon by legal agreement with equality of all people as a basis. Note that this agreement does not belong in the association as part of the economic life but is purely democratic. All people are equal before the law within the political State. Here the exploitation of the labour force relating to the relationship between worker and manager is determined. It is only possible to set a maximum or minimum working day and what work a person can do. What they agree upon must be respected and as such will have an impact on national prosperity. When the employer demands too much or the impossible, or any branch of production does not flourish, other means to remedy the situation must be found. Economic life should stay within its limits regarding both elements: on the one hand, the limits owing to the natural resources, on the other side, the boundaries regarding the sphere of Rights. In short, we come from one limb of the social organism to the other limb, namely the political State. It must be possible to regulate all legal issues, and everything relating to the sphere of Rights to the greatest possible extend.

And then we come to the third limb, which in turn is regulated by its specific circumstances and needs and laws: that is the organisation of the spiritual sphere. On the one hand, the spiritual life must be based on the human being's free initiative, to offer their potential abilities to humanity within a free spiritual life. On the other hand, there is the free appreciation and free receiving of these spiritual powers. How can this be realised? When harnessing the spiritual life, free in education and all spiritual life branches- the funds implemented in the use of the capital — must be managed solely by the spiritual organisation. How can this be made possible? Only by implementing socialisation without turning human society into a unified cooperative, where perhaps only economic interests are involved, and everything is organised in favour of economic interests.

The healthy spiritual organism must be structured free from the other two branches — the State and the economic organism, as cited above. One must be able to make administrative decisions relating to capital and the whole financial life. The spiritual organisation must manage all required circumstances relating to the human being's economic affairs with his unique abilities — then alone can one achieve healthy, fruitful socialisation. It is the only way to separate the utilisation of capital from private ownership to benefit a healthy social organism.

What will happen there? Well, many things will happen. Let me give you a few examples. It is quite natural that people acquire private capital and property during economic activities. But one cannot separate the exploitation of private capital from the exploitation of the workers' skills. When the entrepreneur ceases to utilise these skills, he must relinquish this personal wealth. After all, all private property utilises social forces, and it must, in turn, flow back into the social organism, from which it comes. A law will be necessary within the legal system — because possession is a right, the right, to use any object or anything exclusively. A law must stipulate that what a person has acquired as private property out of economic life for their free usage, must flow back into the spiritual organism after a specified time. In turn, a different person must be found, who can appropriately reuse said capital.

Something similar is to be implemented for all property, analogous to that required for spiritual property and belongs to general humanity thirty years after death. One cannot assume that one has more right to possess something that is not spiritual property. It does not matter how long someone may hold on to private capital, — be it inherited or otherwise acquired — what they own through utilising labour force, will sooner or later have to be freely put at the disposal of the spiritual organism. It must, after all, flow back into the spiritual organism. Private property acquired from economic activities will develop alongside. It will be possible to freely choose who to employ and who is considered competent for the required work. But this must be subject to the rule of law. The political State must make it impossible that a significant proportion of capital is available for private use by someone who does not use his personal skills but can enter the economic life and utilise other people's labour and skills.

It is possible and is made possible through these three limbs of the social organism that human productivity always remains linked to individual human abilities. This tripartite structure of the social organism appears in our times to be a radical thought. And yet, those who are not comfortable with this thought, who do not take the first step to the summit that we need to climb to implement the proper social order, do not understand the most immediate everyday obvious direction that we need to take. They are not working in the true spirit for developing human needs but are working against the current social development direction. Today, we must face facts that stem from past influences. We must counter these with the inherent ideas of the human social order. And one such rudimentary idea is this threefold social order. This thought is now being put forward for people who do not consider it a pure Utopia, but who might see it as something efficient, related to the State's internal organisation.

And now the question will be asked: what does this have to do with the League of Nations? This threefold social order is, in fact, directly related to foreign policy! Because if we want to find the answer to the question: What should the State refrain from doing? The solution you will find to be: He should refrain from getting involved in the spiritual life's functioning and those belonging to the economic life. It should focus on the purely political sphere, which is strictly legal territory.

It also ensures that in non-political life, the necessary consequences will result. Over the whole world, one area's economic interests will be accessible to negotiating the exchange and transport of goods with the commercial interests from another region. The same goes for the relationships within the sphere of rights and the spiritual sphere. When the spiritual sphere is free from the other two spheres, tensions will never need to be relieved through aggressive actions. You can experience this in the smallest way. Spiritual interests can only be implicated in warlike conflicts when affairs that relate to the State interfere. Here, too, one can only judge from experience; but even small experiences can express reality. You could observe it in Hungary, for example, if you had an eye for such things. In the times, in which state life in Hungary had not yet blended into everything in the German-speaking parts, the people in the numerous German regions, who had German children, sent their children to German-speaking schools. The children of Magyar parents who lived in the German areas went to the Magyar schools, and vice versa: the Germans who lived in areas with Magyar schools, sent their children to areas where there were German schools. This exchange of the pupils was free. It was a free interchanging of the spiritual heritage of language, just as one can furnish other spiritual goods in free trade, from country to country, from city to city. This free exchange of the spiritual heritage of language produced a profound peace for Hungary in all areas where it has been fostered. It recognised the imprinting of the inner folk spirit.

When the State interferes, things change. What happens in inner political life, in time always happens in external political life. Someone who has an eye for such things could see how deeply peaceful the German intellectuals in reality were. From the mood of these German intellectuals, the spirit of war would never have awakened! But due to the situation regarding their relation to the State, the wrong impression arose. I do not mean merely to contradict or do anything other than summoning an understanding of the facts. The economic sphere of a tripartite social organism will live out its full potential in international economic life when the people who work in and grow out of the commercial fields institute the economic relations and not the State. In the threefold social order, there will not be only one parliament, but three parliaments. A spiritual, economical and a Rights parliament, for which there will not be only one administration, but three administrations working together. Only from such areas will people emerge who can play a significant role in an intergovernmental organisation. People need to consider the human being as a whole and not only the State or the economy.

The role of the spiritual leaders will be different when it grows out of an emancipated spiritual organisation. It will be a different scenario from that, for example, between the Central States and America in the exchange of professors, something that could only emerge out of spiritually inappropriate links to the State. Everything stands on a sound basis in the international arena when there is a healthy foundation for the three separate social spheres. The human beings who can contribute appropriately to global life will then emerge from these individual social spheres. This seems to be the answer that validates the coordination of the different nations and ensures that each country can contribute to the league of nations' proper future ideals.

A German can also agree to this even when they exclude the Central European countries or Germany from the League of Nations. They can work in such a way that, by healing their own area, they work towards a healthy union of the future nations; they can contribute their bit. This answer, everyone can find for themselves. Each State can also respond by developing its specific policy towards other countries. For example, the States who participate in a peace negotiation with the German Empire elect their chosen peace delegates. When the chaotic former German empire implements the three limbs: — the economic organism, the state organism, and the spiritual organism, the only possible result when it elects individual delegates for each area, will be representatives who work appropriately within the healthy social organism.

It is indeed possible; this is practical politics. In recent years I have often presented these thoughts to people. As perhaps some of you have seen, I offered summaries of these ideas to the newspapers. A very satisfying number of people signed it, among which are those who do not doubt that they have the right to share these matters. I have often had to listen to people saying: a large part of modern humanity perceives such a structure as bringing the old back to life, people currently resist such ideas, thinking society will be divided again into the traditional three classes: the food providing class, the military class, and the academic class. The very opposite is the case! Nothing is as far removed from these old structures of farmers, soldiers, and academics as what I mean here; for not people are divided into classes, into professions, as in earlier times, but a splitting of the social structures must follow. The social organism is re-structured. Through this, the human being will function, as a complete, self-enclosed being within the established system. Only this liberated human being will be able to lay the basis for the ideas, the impressions and the actions that must play a part in such a modern league of nations.

One does not want to become one-sided when thinking about these things. And you can easily do that if you only incorporate your personal impressions. Therefore, in conclusion, I would like to refer to someone else now, after having brought forward what I consider necessary for the recovery of the social organism, something radically different from what has developed thus far, and what led to this terrible disaster. I want to refer to someone else, a person I often refer to when I look for a superior spiritual observer of what reveals itself in humanity's development up to present times: Herman Grimm. He once said, when expressing his thoughts on the modern social evolution of humankind: Looking at today's Europe you see on one side, how people have come into contact with each other, in a manner which former times could not dream of; but at the same time, you can see intruding into what you call modern civilisation, that which our confrontational armament expresses- so he says as a German — in our militarism and in the armament of other States, which can only lead to an invasion, one fine day. And when you look at what happened — the words sound genuinely prophetic. In the nineties Herman Grimm wrote these words: — he died in 1901 — When you see this, says Herman Grimm, it is as if a future human conflict may result, for which one would instead like to set a day for the universal suicide of humanity, so it does not have to live through the terrible experiences, which would follow from these circumstances. Since then, people have witnessed many things because of these conditions. What people saw could easily arouse thoughts that no longer consider the proposed ideas to lead to a Utopia, especially if they have noticed what in truth arose. You might want to justify some practical people who have recently been accused of believing in something impossible that will lead to Utopia.

The above will help people think differently and change not only their actions but also their thinking. We will need other structures in the future, but we ultimately need people with new ideas, which can only grow out of a new division of the social organism. International alliances, we have thoroughly experienced! Whether what is striven for offers firmer ground than the old associations can only be decided if you go back to the ground rules of past human social coexistence.

Did we not also in the past see something like an international life develop through marriages between members of the most diverse royal houses? After all, there would be no objection if the royal houses manifested in a more promising way! Something could have been possible in the sense of this "international alliance," which would have been particularly useful even under the monarchical principle! — We have experienced other international alliances—for example, the efficient international social democracy. We have shared a global social democracy. We have experienced various international situations. What was based on instinctive international family relationships has fallen apart. Unbiased observation shows that what is built on the economic violence of unspiritual capitalism will decay.

But what international socialism is indeed aiming at, is fundamentally the longing for power. In the future, this dominance will have to give way to the sphere of rights. Because what man can usurp through his striving for power in social life can only liberate humanity if incorporated into the legal life — if the life of rights illuminates it. And so perhaps the impression may be allowed to arise in present society regarding globalisation, that something other than these old conditions must form the basis of a genuinely fruitful League of Nations. It must be based on entirely new human ideas, utterly new human impulses and not on princely blood, nor the power of capital or labour.

Rights must provide the basis for the truly liberated complete person. For solely, this truly liberated, whole human being, alert to international sensitivities, will have the right understanding of what is then to light up as the light of international law.

Discussion

1st speaker: stated that the solution proposed by Dr Steiner was not clear to him. Nor was it possible to take down socialism as a great spiritual concept in the way Dr Steiner had done, since a new Rights sphere will not ensue by wiping away the healthy core of socialism. The idea of a three-fold division seems to be a solution, but it is an arbitrary solution. The Land reform, according to this speaker, is characteristic of the times. Finally, socialism's progressive spread is a testimony that socialism is not an imaginary system but a reality.

Rudolf Steiner: It is, of course, difficult to discuss whether that which I indicated, is seen as being possible or not in all its facets by each person; after all, this is an individual matter, and each listener will, of course, have his or her own opinion. So, I do not want to answer this specific question.

I want to make a few very brief comments on the other speaker's other ideas regarding the principle. The views I expressed may have been radical and therefore, may seem invalid. Whoever has followed my thoughts today though, has perhaps noticed, from the description of these ideas, that what I said was by no means the result of a sudden idea that occurred one fine morning or mere assumptions on my part. I built them upon what was proved somewhere else. It is unnecessary to prove to you once again, what socialism, for example, has already established!

I have expressed the thought that the theory of surplus-value and its relation to human labour is particularly plausible to the proletarian souls. I then described how to take this one step further. I have also shown that I do not want to wipe away what the previous speaker has just pointed to, namely modern socialism. Those who have listened to me more closely can probably also confirm that I have made enough suggestions in my lecture concerning the importance of contemporary socialism. What I said, could not be understood otherwise, but in the sense of the example mentioned.

23

I meant that if you do not embrace modern socialism, you live like the inhabitants of a house that is threatened with collapse, who do not decide to build a new home, but recommend that all the rooms be connected by doors so that they can help each other. So, it is possible, with some goodwill, to see that I am in fact, attaching importance to modern socialism. And it should not be difficult to deduce from this, that what is already in place under modern socialism is not enough; I could, of course, further elaborate in forty or fifty lectures.

I want to point out one more thing. Of course, I again must be as short as possible under the given circumstances, so that whoever wants to, can say that I have given nothing to the honoured listeners to take home. I want to state that I have the utmost respect for modern proletarian thinking, Marxism, and everything built on Marxism. I was a teacher for many years at a school for workers' education founded by Wilhelm Liebknecht, and I was involved with helping, so to speak, with the integration of the socialist thoughts within the labour force. And may I point out that it would not be incorrect to say: I believe that several older editors of German socialist newspapers, even speakers who after all make not unimportant statements in Germany today, are perhaps my pupils. So, I know not only modern socialism as such — from the way I have put forward my points of view, it would have been possible to see that — I also know the significance which this socialism has in the life of the modern proletariat. If you were involved in this for years, I might say decades, then you do not need to wait for a great, unique idea to form a system just because it would be nice to have one as well, but you continue to build on what is there. And if you look at things in detail, you can see from the further construction of the ideas, that I respect what is already there. But now we must not lose sight of one thing. Indeed, when kept within the field of theoretics, ideas in themselves are nothing more than expressions of symptoms of what is happening in real life.

Do not assume that I am trying to suggest that the modern labour movement's driving force or anything else is merely abstract. On the contrary, I am trying to say that the thoughts — I do not only think of economic forces-, symptomatically express deeper-lying inner forces. I believe that in the future, we will not have such a causal view of history as presently prevalent, but we will look at it from a more symptomatologic perspective. But now we must find out how specific thoughts, which we all can regard as symptoms of specific underlying facts, present themselves. Today many very radical forms of socialism are known. Do you not think some people can be subconsciously aware of this and misinterpret what is said? Perhaps the previous speaker did not mean it that way either — do not believe that I am so critical of what is emerging at present — even though I must consider it with the weight of what I said in my speech — as some people in leading circles do. For example, it is already possible for me to react with absolute objectivity to the consequences of social thinking and social development today.

I want to point out something that might seem significant to you. You see, Lenin and Trotsky are also socialists. Anyone who will not be intimidated by what people allege about Eastern Europe, who ascribe everything to the "wicked Bolshevists," will perhaps look more objectively at what is happening. They will realise that everything that people currently blame on to the Russian socialists is still attributed mainly to Tsarism and what preceded it. And those who look objectively will then have to say to themselves above all: From a specific point of view, Lenin particularly, is a kind of last consequence of Marx, it is also how he sees himself. And Lenin draws attention to two things in Marx. Firstly, he points out that the modern social movement must strive to proletarianize the State itself through the proletariat's dictatorship. However, the State is only — I must briefly hint at this — taken over by the proletariat's tyranny because it is the final consequence of its existence. That which is predisposed to germinate in the State is the culminating result of social democracy: namely, the State kills itself, it dissolves.

Well, the various dark sides of this socialist State must come to the fore. Lenin, for example, is not deluded about this. That is also better than indulging in illusions, as so many people do. But he works at forming a kind of State, which carries death within itself, which dissolves. Then comes the genuinely new stage, where one does not reward work equally, but the motto is: each according to his abilities, each according to his needs. — And at that moment: to each according to his abilities, to each according to his needs — which ought not to be only a socialist, but a very general ideal — at that moment, Lenin, like Marx, makes a strange remark, which allows us to look much more in-depth than usually. He remarks: This social order, where each person has a place in the social order according to his possibilities and needs, is of course not possible with the people of today; for this, a completely new breed of people must first come into being. Yes, you see, some might not want to and cannot wait for a "new breed of human." Because otherwise, the time might come when it would be better to launch the general suicide of which I have spoken. Instead, they will turn their thoughts on contemporary life and endeavour to understand their mistakes from the present state of things. And in this respect, I believe that by pointing out the question: What should the State do and what should it not do, things already become clarified from my, albeit brief and sketchy, train of thought.

I have tried to indicate how the entanglement of economic life with the State, the entanglement of spiritual life with the State, has caused damage to the social order; it is possible to multiply the examples I have given a hundredfold. Does it not stand to reason that we should think about how we can remedy this damage? A cure is possible by not continuing merging with what has arisen, but by reversing it. Of course, you could call it naïve, but I believe it was clear from my lecture today how deeply what I have explained reaches into the underbelly of modern life. How far this is the case, however, must be left to the judgement of each individual. The thoughts currently realised and recognised are indeed not new, and nothing new will come about with these ideas. I have presented the concept of threefolding to many people, especially during the difficult war years, who could have realised it. I have also found understanding in some circles. It has not led to a bridge from understanding through the head to courageous will to do something. This bridge was not built.

I have had a strange experience in recent days, which could perhaps point out that what I have said is deeply rooted in reality. It is not a wiping away, but rather a taking up or a continuation of socialist thinking: I spoke — which is not precisely easy today — to a workers' assembly invited from the street. Then — as I experienced many times during my work in Berlin — the socialist leaders objected to my statements manifoldly. And after plenty objections raised, a Russian woman appeared who — I am just telling you! — said, among other things, that perhaps one had heard many things to which one could object this or that, but it would be impossible today to stand by the old ideas or even the old socialist thoughts, that it was necessary to move forward to new ideas. We will not come to a real, thorough rebuilding of the house, but only to new doors, which cannot help once the whole thing collapses if we do not engage in genuinely new thoughts. And that is why I told many a person during the difficult times, that people could have avoided a lot of the misfortune of the last few years if more people thought like the Russian woman I mentioned.

I am convinced that, if the Central European negotiators of that time had made the ideas that I put forward here — one of which they were very well acquainted with — the foreign policy's contents, the content of the peace treaty of Brest-Litovsk. The world would have grasped these thoughts if they re-explained them. Of course, one cannot possibly explain these ideas in all its details in one lecture; but one has the feeling that it must currently be living in the human soul, as it is rooted in reality. I do not think that I am so brilliant that I know better than others what must happen in every detail! I am not a person who presents programs, and I do not provide programmes and utopias, but I want people to grasp reality. I have no interest in having all my suggestions carried out in detail. If at any point, one begins to work in the spirit of what I have said today, then let not one stone of the content I have conveyed remain upon another. Something quite different will perhaps result, but it will nevertheless be justifiable in practical life. With programmes, whether socialist or other programmes, one always wants to see that what people have thought out is realised in programme form; it is a question of tapping into reality at one point. Then what comes out of it may become something considerably different!

I have said it only appears to be incomprehensible because one cannot understand it in the same way as other programmes. It is possible to state that it is easy to introduce any programme with a few thoughts and prove it. But it is not easy to appeal to human souls, to appeal as I have wanted to do, namely, to turn these souls back on themselves, to give them suggestions. Then perhaps they will think out something quite different. But basically, the most necessary thing today is for people to know that they must start from reality and then the rest will come about. Therefore, we need not despise something, as the Land Reformers aspire to do. I had a conversation with Damaschke many years ago in Berlin; I pointed out that his thoughts certainly had excellent capacity. However, they could not possibly enter powerfully into real life and could not fully understand real life because the ground is not elastic. Therefore, I told him that it is not possible to translate his ideas directly into reality. There is no other way to go forward than to keep in mind the tendency of the times, which results from the fact that people have come to an impasse, through the entanglement of legal life, economic life and spiritual life. Then something becomes apparent that it is not difficult to prove, namely that one should not continue to use them in combination with one another, but to start reversing the situation!

What I have said, is intended to foster further thoughts on how to accomplish socialisation and how one can utilise human labour appropriately without anyone gaining undue control over the labourer. And as I have said: imperfect as it must remain, because it is not possible to deal with it exhaustively in one lecture, I still think it is necessary today to approach things with a little goodwill; for the facts speak too loudly! And even in the face of what might well seem different in the socialist field to four years ago, the facts speak too strongly today. I will soon elaborate on all this thoroughly and in detail in a brochure because I consider it extraordinarily necessary for the present to give detailed proof of what I have now only indicated.

I think there is one thing we must not lose sight of today. I had a memorable experience yesterday. When I was a little boy, I used to learn the following from my religion books: I learned that one must realise that Christ is either a fool or a hypocrite. Christ must be either a fool or a hypocrite, or else he must be what he had made himself out to be. And thus, it was written in the religion books: Since it is not possible to consider him a fool or a hypocrite, he must be the Son of the living God. — I also heard this as an answer to the social question here in Bern yesterday! I read it in my schoolbooks more than fifty years ago, and I listen to it repeated today — as the right solution to the social question. Between reading this in my religion books at school and this almost word-for-word repetition, which one could hear again and again almost ad verbatim during the difficult times, however, lies the experience humanity should have undergone because of the great catastrophe it lived through. We should learn something from this immense catastrophe! Above all, we should have become more willing to accept the thoughts that may have seemed somewhat sketchy today, but which perhaps, by how they point to the subject matter, show that they are at least trying to delve into the depths of the issue.

2nd speaker (Baron von Wrangeil): Sees the right solution in the threefold structure of the social organism proposed by Dr Steiner. How to realise the idea seems to him to be another question. The fundamental error of socialism is that it leads to an overvaluation of the State.

3rd and 4th speakers: Essentially objected that a realisation of the idea of threefolding would unnecessarily complicate conditions, which speaks against this solution. The threefold structure would lead to fragmentation, whereas human life should form a unity.

Rudolf Steiner: Well, I think that perhaps I do have to say something very briefly. I can quite well understand what the honourable previous speaker wants, but I have the feeling that he does not understand himself very well! I think he should judge the whole situation we are in from a somewhat broader point of view. We human beings do not just have the task of making our lives comfortable. There are many other considerations in life than making ourselves comfortable! And I believe that a large part of the damage we suffer today comes precisely from the fact that a considerable number of humans strive only to arrange life comfortably, just for themselves. But what is important seems to me to be something else. You see, I would not bother you with any ideas about a threefold division if these three sections were not the social organism's inherent reality. That this threefolding wants to come about does not depend on us; we cannot change it; it occurs as of itself. During these difficult times, and I must return to this, I had the opportunity to speak to many people I believed could do something from positions of authority. Two and a half years ago, there would still have been the possibility of doing something — I said: What you put forward here is not simplistic. It has come about through decades of observation of what wants to happen across Europe during the next ten, twenty, thirty years.

If you look at the course of events, you will see that this threefold structure is happening whether we like it or not. There is no other possible way to arrive at an understanding of the social threefoldness than to recognise from the totality of the present, the possibilities of development for the future — you will see that, whether we like it or not, this threefold social structure is taking place. In earlier times it arose instinctively; more and more in more recent times a merging, a unifying of the three parts has occurred. These three parts seek to separate again to correspond to their typical characteristics and become independent again. — And I drastically mentioned to some: The person at the helm at present, could still with rationality do much in this direction; people have the choice — regarding revolution, Goethe also said: Either evolution or revolution — people have the option to act rationally now, or they will experience revolutions and cataclysms.

Not only people up to now at the helm will experience catastrophes, but also those merely clinging to the socialistic dogmas will. Threefolding of the social organism is vital. And you can also see: That which must come about naturally always appears under certain extraordinary conditions in a specific one-sided development; these three members want to become more independent. And they become unnaturally separated if they do not get their natural sovereignty. When the spheres are confused and thrown together; they develop in a way that holds humanity back. The spiritual power, the spiritual organisation, be it a church-state or a state church or whatever, becomes autonomous. Even if it cannot encompass the whole of spiritual life, it nevertheless seeks to incorporate as much as possible.

When the State takes up the sphere of the legal life, it, in turn, makes that which seeks to become independent subservient to the State. What wants to realise itself in an unnatural way in political life comprises everything that is today the much frowned upon

31

militarism. For you see, many a healthy opinion has been expressed about militarism and its one-sided relationship to State life, especially during the war. But suppose one dive to the bottom of these opinions with common sense. In that case, one also realises that militarism is nothing other than the one-sided outcome when one does not give political life its natural independence. And Clausewitz said: War is the continuation of politics by other means. Clausewitz says this within a particular context; one can still go more in-depth into these things, as in the last few years, one has heard many such one-sided statements. It is also possible to state that a marital dispute and the divorce is the continuation of the marriage by other means! Such one-sidedness has been voiced very often in recent years; one throws everything together.

But what everything rests on, if one wishes to develop fruitful views in life, which will then also pass into realistic facilities, is that one recognises these relations as healthy. And so, these spheres want to become independent and develop independently. In recent times, the economic organism has greatly engulfed the whole of public life, so much so that today many people see nothing at all but an economic organism. And apart from that, only the administration of the economic organism. That is what can lead you to the proof. But if I have achieved nothing more than to stimulate some of you, that is quite enough for me. That is all I want! I do not believe that it is possible to give only one right answer to what should happen socially.

I would still like to add the following: You know, there are two Bolshevists at present: one is Lenin, the other Trotsky, I know a third, who, however, does not live in the present, whom few people think of when they talk about the Bolshevists, that is Johann Gottlieb Fichte! Read his "Closed Trading State," and you will have, theoretically speaking, precisely what you can read in Lenin and Trotsky! Why? Because Fichte spins a state system out of his own soul! From the forces with which you can reach the highest heights in philosophy, he develops a state system, a political, social order. Why did this happen? Because a single human personality can generate nothing socially fruitful! It is possible only from person to person. Just as language cannot develop if a man lives alone on an island, but is only possible as a social phenomenon, where people live together. That which is social, cannot be achieved by a single individual! It is not possible to draw up a programme on one's own. But it is possible to think about the social order in which people must naturally relate to each other and find their place within the correct social order.

The social question will not disappear from the agenda! It is there and must continue to be solved ever more and more. But the task before us now, is to answer the question: How should people relate to each other in the tripartite social organism? Then you will always more or less find the solution. In the social organism, people must encounter each other so that solutions arise from living together. Genuine social thinking is the preparatory work which reveals how people can solve social questions in concrete social life.

I already told you I do not imagine I could be competent enough to set up a social programme. I pointed out that living in this natural threefold social order, and letting institutions come into being in the world which corresponds to the impulses that live in this natural threefold social order, then, out of this interaction between people the healthy social order will come into being through the people, appropriately! Then people will be able to work together. It is impossible to do it the way the modern Marxists say: first, we create chaos, then the proletariat's dictatorship comes to rectify things.

No, at least it is necessary that this preparatory work first is done. We must ask ourselves: How must people stand within the social organism, so that through cooperation, what is demanded of us today by clearly speaking facts, can emerge?

The Liberation of the Human Being

WHAT IS THE SIGNIFICANCE OF THE WORK OF THE MODERN PROLETARIAN?

Bern, 17 March 1919

Second lecture

Do not assume that my purpose is to speak to you about understanding and reconciliation between the various classes of the population tonight, as particularly the ruling, hitherto dominant classes so often do these days. At present, there is so much talk of reconciliation and understanding. I want to come to you tonight from an entirely different standpoint. I want to speak to you this evening of an altogether different awareness, of recognising the challenges expressed loudly today by the social realities and of the great historical forces that are currently entering the field of human development. I want to speak of what seems to me to be demanded by the proletarian movement, particularly, of today's historical forces that are, one could say, revolutionising the world.

To speak of a different approach to the world is almost forbidden by modern civilisation. What did we hear during the last decades concerning this modern civilisation! Let us remember for a moment how the hitherto ruling classes have felt about this modern civilisation, one might say, right up to the terrible catastrophe of the horrific war which has descended upon humanity in recent years. How often has it been said how far we human beings have come in creating, in producing! How we have made it possible for thoughts to be sent far across the world quickly, how connections are possible between the most distant countries, and how spiritual life in all its forms has spread enormously.

Well, I could sing these praises at length. Not that I want to sing them, but the ruling classes do! But now, let us look at it from the other side. What made this modern civilisation, to which they sing so *many hymns of praise, actually possible? To a certain extent, this was only made possible by those who, out of humanity's innermost essence, could not agree with what the bearers of this modern civilisation were doing. It was possible to hear voices coming from the other side of this luxury culture, which, in essence, uttered the words: It cannot go on like this! As wonderful as your civilisation may be for you, it cannot be otherwise that the vast majority of the earth's population cannot have any direct share in this civilisation. They must feel excluded from this civilisation. They must, as it were, look on from the outside, but on the other hand, they must work for this civilisation! Did there arise awareness in the last decades for the background and reasons for this call? It is impossible to confirm that there has been. In general, some people are speaking an extraordinary language today. In the last few days, I have witnessed some of what has taken place here in Bern at the League of Nations Conference. It was possible to hear all kinds of beautiful speeches, at least the gentlemen thought them excellent. But anyone who looks a little deeper into what the world-changing activities throughout Europe today mean, would realise above all that no-one talked about or expressed thoughts about the most crucial current question, which moves a large part of humanity to an ever-increasing degree.*

The open nerve of the social question was missed and ignored. This conference showed extraordinarily little understanding of this question, and it reminded one of something else, namely of the weeks of the spring and early summer of 1914. It was possible to hear many a peculiar speech from the ruling circles and their leaders. One can cite numerous comparable addresses, such as the one made by a leading statesman in a Central European State before a parliament in 1914. He said: Thanks to the European cabinets' energetic efforts, we may hope to assure peace among the great powers of Europe for the foreseeable future. — This is what they said in all possible variations in May and June 1914. And then? Then came that which killed millions of people, which crippled millions of people. That is how well they foresaw what has been asserting itself along with such a praiseworthy modern civilisation!

If I may make this personal remark, I had to speak differently from these statesmen. Before a meeting in Vienna in the spring of 1914, I had to say: Whoever looks at the life of present-day European, he sees in him something like creeping cancer, which must break out. — Just as the gentlemen of that time talked past what was a black cloud in the political sky of Europe, so today certain people are talking past what is most important: the social powers and forces entering the lives of the peoples of the earth. Since this is how things are, there is a genuinely minimal prospect of reaching an understanding through reason.

But an approach from another side, as I have already said, is possible. And this perception seems to me to appear if one takes the following starting point. Up to our time, the proletarian population was basically in a completely different situation than it will be from now on. When one does not merely look at the proletarian movement theoretically but have practically experienced it, one realises there was boundless, penetrating criticism. Criticism of the harm the structures and basic rules of the hitherto leading circles have wrought through centuries, through three to four centuries. For everything, they believed they had to impose on humanity, the modern proletarian experienced as world-historical judgment. And basically, what was going on within the proletariat was an immense, powerful reproach. Simultaneously, the hitherto leading circles remained within their bourgeois culture and sang praises to it. In their lecture halls, they listened to what suited them best, enjoying in their theatres the make-believe world of their affairs, which they perceived as such a salutary modern civilisation. Simultaneously, the proletarian masses found themselves, in the hours they could spare from the day's heavy, arduous work, discussing the profound questions of human development and world history's serious problems.

Modern technical development and the capitalistic development connected with it took the contemporary proletarian away from all other human connections involved in producing the old crafts. It placed the labourer at the machine, harnessed to the capitalist world order and thus excluded from the immediate perception of what incited the leading circles. Then the proletarian, out of general interest, and from a certain point of view, the highest human interest, turned his soul gaze toward the upper classes. And the proletarian assemblies called out repeatedly: "It cannot go on like this!"

A new stage has now begun. Following this emerging new stage with serious attention seems to be one of the most necessary social tasks today. How did the modern proletarian experience social order development over the last three to four centuries since modern capitalism and modern technology entered human history? How did the contemporary proletarian feel about that which he had to observe as an outsider? In how far could it be of use to him? Was it possible for him to have a part in this so that he might have something worthwhile for his soul?

The traditional leading circles spoke to him of various powers and forces active in humanity's historical development; they talked to him of different moral world orders and the like. But the modern proletarian, turning his gaze upwards to these ruling classes' activities, perceived little of the power, of the inner originality of such moral world orders. He perceived that the actions, the thinking, the conceptions of the leading, guiding circles essentially exist because of their ability to live under their economic structures and economic order. Thus, they can establish their civilisation as a superstructure on the misery and oppression of larger masses of humanity who must work for them. The modern proletariat sensed that contrary to the contemporary situation, these newer thoughts on human development, were fundamentally true. The proletarian felt the truth in contrast to what the others fantasised about misleadingly; they spoke of a moral, divine world order where people live in mutual social relations with each other on earth. The proletarian felt that this was a profound lie. And he thought that the real truth was that people could live as they do because it is possible to exploit economic activities for their personal convenience, to their own advantage. And thus arose — and one must now say, as the correct heritage of that which was bourgeois science — the materialist conception of history, that conception which did not allow the compelling forces behind the historical development of humanity to be anything other than economic forces. And this resulted in the belief that everything that belongs to religion, human science, human spirituality, rises like a kind of "superstructure" above the economic forces. Below this, as the only reality on which, at most, the superstructure acts back, the economic forces prevail. The modern proletariat was right in the face of what the bourgeois world order has made of social life — a mere economy.

A second aspect, which emanated from Karl Marx's ideas as a thinker and spread into the proletarian assemblies, into the proletarian

38

souls, is not the spiritual question, as I have just characterised the materialistic conception of history but the legal problem. It culminates in the one word you all know, but which had an electrifying effect on the modern proletarian movement. This word evoked understanding in the contemporary proletarian's innermost perceptions when put before their souls by Marx and his successors: it is the word surplus-value.

And behind much of what has been said around the word surplus-value, what the modern proletarian actually feels to be his most crucial human challenge, hides the question, whether more or less conscious or not, more or less merely felt or intellectually posed, but which was felt deeply: "What is the meaning of my work within the within the modern social order?" And it must be said: what Karl Marx gave as an answer in various ways is brilliant. — But today we live in a time in which we must go further than even Marx went, especially if one understands Marx in the right way, not in the way the opportunistic politicians suppose, but from an entirely different point of view, as we shall see in a moment. When the modern proletarian raised the question of the meaning of his labour, it became a question of his position within contemporary society, of his human dignity. He was confronted again and again with the problem that the capitalist economic process absorbs his labour. He experienced that his work had become something that can only be an illusion, namely: a commodity. The modern proletarian can merely sell his work-power as his only "possession." He experienced that he must carry his ability to work to the market, must have his labour treated according to the rules of supply and demand, as an objective commodity on the commodity market separated from his being. The peculiar thing about human life is that something can be accepted and applied, which is not in reality, true but false. And one such a falsehood is that human labour-power can ever become a commodity at all. Because human labour-power can never be compared to ware or priced in the way items are priced, in any way. It is something fundamentally different from commodities.

Therefore, it is a fundamental lie when that which can never become a commodity nevertheless becomes just that. Even if people do not express it in such an exact way, it is nonetheless how the labourer experiences it, and I would like to say, the centre of the proletarian question of modern times. Because human labour-power has become a commodity, what should have been a legal relationship between the entrepreneur and the worker concerning labour has become a relationship of purchase. And modern bourgeois national economists do indeed talk as if it were possible within economic life to exchange goods for goods on the one hand, and goods for labour on the other hand. A so-called contract of employment in the modern sense of the word does not make the matter any different; a legal agreement can only determine the relationship between the entrepreneur and the worker, which we shall see look at later. Human labour-power could only become free from its commodity character — and it must become free — if the only contract between the worker and the employer were not about work delivered, but rather about the distribution of the jointly produced commodities or services. This way, it would serve the healthy organism in a valid sense. Here the demand that hides behind the Marxist theory of surplus-value shows itself. At the same time, it clarifies why one must go beyond the merely Marxist ideas.

And now we must ask the question: How does one alter the wage relationship? How does a commodity distribution contract take the place of the labour contract? Here we touch on the second factor that has continually passed through the modern proletarian's soul and was hurled at the leading circles as criticism. And the third was the conviction that everything that takes place in contemporary society, and which has led to the conditions into which we have gotten, is not in harmony with modern society. It is a struggle between groups of people, in which one group has the advantage over the other; this is the class struggle of the modern proletariat with the leading classes. Indeed, these three points: the materialist conception of history, the doctrine of surplus-value and labour-power, and the theory of class struggle have been studied with more contemporary vigour than anything that has been written within bourgeois society in more recent times. People recognised that what human development has come to in recent centuries merely resulted from economic structures. Any other interpretation regarding human nature is basically a great lie. The whole of spiritual life which had become a kind of cultural luxury for the ruling class became an "ideology" for the modern proletariat. This word was heard again and again. It became a mere web of ideas and sensations and feelings, which poured out like smoke over the actual reality of economic matters.

But one does not fully understand the matter if one only understands it in this way. One only understands the point if one knows that in the face of this desolating situation, which is a legacy of the hitherto ruling class's ideas, the modern proletarian soul has had time to reflect on human dignity, on how to become truly human while working on the machine. Within the enclosures of capitalist economic activities, awakened a real longing — not for spiritual luxury nor abundance — but an authentic spiritual life.

Today, it is still possible to hear in bourgeois circles how the modern proletarian question, seen from this or that side, is actually a bread question. Indeed, it is a bread-and-butter question; but the fact that it is a bread-and-butter question need not be discussed in an assembly where proletarian understanding prevails. It is not a question of thinking like a certain bourgeois sociologist and educationalist who now travels around a lot in various regions. Among other things, he recently coined the words: One only must know present poverty once, then one will immediately come to long for the humanisation of human society. — Behind such remarks, there is usually nothing else than the question: How can we continue in the delusion of the old life of the ruling circles, by losing a few chunks in the easiest way possible, to those who do not participate in the life of the ruling classes? How is it possible to get to grips with the labour question while maintaining the existing social order? — It is not the question of bread, that is the issue. It is above all a question out of which soul-impulses people must fight for their bread. It has to do with much deeper historical forces than those who often talk about history this way even suspect.

And today the three questions I have just described have entered a new stage. Much is not yet expressed clearly, but someone sensitive to historical forces' workings can discern it. Then one can sense the trends which herald great world-historical upheavals. Today the proletarian movement is no longer a mere critical movement, today it is a call by the world-historical powers themselves to go over to action, that is, to raise the great question: What is to be done? — And here it seems to me that what I have just described must be transformed — transformed so that, in contrast to the purely material life hitherto characterised, we can consider another aspect. We must allow the

41

oppressed part of humanity a genuinely human existence and nourishment for the soul.

That is the first question, the question of the spiritual life: How can the ideology of luxury, the abundant spiritual life be transformed, into something that the innermost nature of the human being needs for a dignified existence? Apart from the spiritual issue, the other factor that established itself is that labour became a commodity in the Rights sphere. This was only possible because, in the social order that emerged under capitalism and modern technology, Rights became an entitlement in many respects. How can we replace privilege with laws that protect proletarian labour from being exploited as a mere commodity? And the third is: How can we possibly develop other forms than those that resulted in the class struggle? To the proletarian, it was evident that, what has thus far been established, can only result in a mutual battle. But he holds the consistent impression that the struggles that have taken place in recent history must be overcome. Whether the class struggle is necessary, will at the present stage of development, turn into the question: How do we overcome the class struggle? — The question of surplus-value, which has shifted into the realm of prerogatives within the social order in recent centuries, is the basis of another question: How does one establish within human society, in the real sense of the word, a state of law that satisfies all human beings?

Regarding the first question, the spiritual side of the social problem, one only must realise how deep the abyss is between the hitherto ruling classes and those who, on the other side, are striving for a new world and social order. We must admit that what imbues the modern proletarian as spiritual life has in essence been inherited from the bourgeois class, which was able to cultivate science, art and so on. — But this spiritual life had a different effect within the proletariat. The proletarian was in another position regarding his inheritance of science etc. than what emerged as modern spiritual life among those who belonged in the bourgeois, leading circles. One could be a very committed follower of current intellectual life. One could consider oneself very enlightened, yet within such a social order, one is a member of a ruling class that is not ordered according to authentic, current spiritual life. To be a naturalist like Vogt, a scientific populariser like Büchner, one could believe oneself to be a totally enlightened person — this perhaps suits the head and allows intellectual conviction. Still, it is not appropriate for a genuine understanding of the human being's position in life. How these people stood in life could only be justified because the social order derived from quite different powers. It was inherited from obsolete religious and moral world views or forces presented by these ruling classes as scientifically substantiated powers. Therefore, the modern proletarian simply became part of the contemporary scientific spirit because it was the culture of modern times. It had, however, quite a different effect on the proletarian soul. I want to remind you of a small scene that made particularly clear the effect of modern spiritual life on the proletarian. He was compelled to grasp this contemporary spiritual life not only out of the head forces but out of the complete human being, from out of his full position within humanity.

I stood on the same podium in Spandau with Rosa Luxemburg whose life has now ended so tragically, many years ago. She spoke about science and the workers, and I, as a teacher at the Workers Education School, had a few things to add to what she said on the same subject. The theme: "Science and the Workers" gave her cause to express precisely that which is so characteristic of the modern proletariat's intellectual life. She said: "Despite the contemporary viewpoints about the origin of the human being, the attitude of the leading classes is still rooted in the notion that the human being came from angelic beings who were initially good. From this foundation, the differences in rank and class have developed historically and were justified emotionally and perceptively by these ruling classes. However, the modern proletarian is driven to take bourgeois science seriously in a completely different way. He must accept when he learns that the human being was not originally an angelic being but climbed trees like an animal and behaved most indecently. To look back to man's origin in the sense of the modern worldview does not justify class differences; on the contrary, it justifies all human beings' equality."

You see, that is the difference! The proletarian was forced to accept that which the others asserted intellectually — which was not very deeply rooted, even if they were so enlightened — he was compelled to take the matter up with his whole being, with the bitterest seriousness. But it entered his soul in a completely different

43

way. One must simply become attentive to such things. In this sense, one will realise the modern social question is first and foremost a question of the spiritual life and strive to develop a spiritual life that fulfils all human beings. Then, if one engages in trying to understand the causes of all that I have been able to describe today, I must admit, falteringly, because if I wanted to describe it in detail, it will require too much time. If you look for the causes and then ask yourself: at what must progress aim? — it is possible to say the following: today it is not a question of whether the materialistic culture is the real substructure of spiritual life, but how we can arrive at a spiritual life that can satisfy the human soul, the soul of all human beings.

Today, it can no longer be a question of critically interpreting what surplus-value is, what human labour-power represents within the capitalist world order. Today, we need to find the answer to how we free human labour from the commodity character and how we achieve that "surplus-value" does not remain a prerogative but becomes a right. And if there must be a struggle within the social order, then may it be the class struggle which has gradually emerged in the last centuries? Today we are at a stage of development where criticism alone is no longer decisive. The question is: What is to be done? — For those concerned with the fundamentals of life, the answer is, I would say, very radical. For some, it may look less extreme than it is, but it is quite radical because proletarian thought is in many respects only the inheritance of bourgeois thought. After all, proletarian habits of thought are the inheritance of bourgeois habits of thinking. The first questions to be considered are: How can capitalism's damage be eliminated? What can we do to stop the oppressive character when human labour is regarded as a commodity? How can we overcome class struggle humanely? We must ask the question from a much deeper point of view today. And great demands regarding historical facts are being made today on the proletarian ideas and habits of thought.

For it is up to him to be equal to the times, to ask himself: How do we get beyond the devastation that the cycle of surplus-value production has wrought in life, has wrought in legal life? How do we move beyond the destruction of present class struggles? The three most important current social questions need to change from the negative to the positive.

If one looks at the causes of the present living conditions, one finds that there is, in reality, a tendency to continue what the bourgeois world order has brought about. Many are asking themselves: How can we overcome capitalism? How can we overcome private ownership of the means of production? They then come to the antiquated order of human social institutions, of the cooperative and the like, that is, they come to the ideal of shared ownership of the means of production. That is understandable, and honestly, it is not out of any bourgeois prejudice that I speak of these things here. It is solely from the perspective: Is it possible to achieve what the modern proletarian wants by the means some socialist thinkers today believe they can achieve it? Is it possible, by resorting to the framework of the old State and inserting the economic order into this old State, only in a different form? Is it possible to achieve redemption from the oppressiveness of the past thereby?

Let us look at the modern State. It came into being because at a time — in the 16th and 17th centuries — when modern technology and present capitalism were developing, the leading circles had to call the proletariat more and more to the machine. They found that their interests were best satisfied within the framework of the State. And so, they began to let economic life flow into the State in those branches where it was convenient for them. And especially when the modern achievements came along, large parts of economic life, such as the postal, telegraph and railway systems, were taken up into the economy of the State, as it has been handed down from time immemorial. At that time, spiritual life was also allowed to enter the modern state structure! And more and more this fusion of economic life, legal life of the State and spiritual life took place. This fusion not only led to all the unnatural conditions related to the oppressiveness of modern times, but it also led to the devastating effects of the catastrophe of the world war.

Anyone who studies the historical facts today will not ask: What should the States do? — on the contrary, he may be forced to ask: What should the States refrain from doing? What they thereby brought about, what happened, we experienced in the killing of ten million people and the crippling of eighteen million people. And so perhaps the question does force itself into the soul: What should the States refrain from doing? — This is what I can only hint at here, but what is genuinely possible to ask at present from the deep foundations of genuine social science.

If you look at certain political-social conditions, as they have developed, but also how they have typically led to their well-deserved end, then you only have to look at Austria, as an example. What had evolved then — I spent three decades of my life in Austria and got to know the conditions thoroughly. During that time, I experienced what developed due to the constitutional structure of the Austrian State. — which could only be as calamitous to the mixture of the different nations like a fist to the eye. In the sixties, Austria changed to a common constitutional system. And for those who can follow historical facts, precisely what was founded at that time in Austrian constitutional life, what Austria's politics had already become in the sixties and seventies, led to the current situation. Why? Well, at that time an Austrian Imperial Council was founded. Firstly, the purely economic administrations of the large landowners, the administrations of the markets, the cities and industrial towns, and the rural communities' administrations were elected to this Austrian Imperial Council. They had to represent their economic interests in the State parliament. And they did, they made laws that fitted their economic situation. They only made laws that served commercial interests. However, concerning the law, one does not deal with the same issues that one has to deal with in economic life. On the ground of economic life, one has to do with human needs, with the production of goods, the circulation of goods, the consumption of goods.

In the field of legal life, however, one has to do with that which, apart from all other interests, concerns the human being, in so far as he is purely human, in so far, as a human being, he is equal to all other human beings. Judgments must be made from entirely different backgrounds when one asks what Human Rights are. It must differ from trying to find out how we can introduce some product into the economic cycle. The unnatural coupling of the financial districts with legal life is what ate away at the so-called Austrian State like cancer.

There are many examples of this problem throughout the modern States. It is not a question of merely studying these matters, but to find the right point of view from which one can gain insight into actual reality, into that which lives and weaves in society, not that which people imagine is politically or economically right. And again, look at the German Reichstag, what a happy memory of this democratic parliament with equal voting Rights! Here, the Farmers' Union interests could be represented but at the same time a purely spiritual community, such as the Centre, as well! We see welded into, melted into purely political life, something that belongs only to spiritual life. And this led to unnatural conditions! Again, one could cite many examples in addition to this one. If one wants to understand modern humanity, one must approach it from a radical perspective. One must have the courage to look such things in the face; then one will come to something that modern people do not yet want to admit, I would even go so far as to include all parties. But the only impetus for a healthy social organism is the recognition that henceforth there must no longer be welding together, a coupling together of the three spheres of life — spiritual life, legal life, and economic life — but that each of these spheres have their own particular laws, and therefore must also create its specific social structure from its specific foundation. In economic life, only commodity production, commodity consumption and commodity circulation belong. The laws appropriate to economic life must be applied for administration and legislation. In the field of legal life, that which springs directly from human legal consciousness must prevail, that in which all people are equal as human beings.

In the field of spiritual life, that which can freely flow out of natural human talent must prevail. Modern Social Democracy has made inroads from an entirely different perspective — we cannot spend time on this aspect today — in one area. It has established that religion must be a private matter. — This acknowledgement must be extended to all branches of spiritual life. All spiritual life must be a private matter regarding the constitutional state and the cycle of economic life. Spiritual life must be directed from out of its own forces, must continuously establish its reality out of its own impulse. It will not be spiritual luxury or spiritual abundance, but it will be a spiritual life that must be longed for in the same way by all human beings.

In looking at the spiritual life of the Middle Ages, concerning science, religion, and theology, it was often said: Philosophy, the wisdom of the world, follows theology. — Well, this had changed in recent times. It has changed, but how has it changed? The worldly sciences have become servants of the States' earthly powers, of the economic cycles. And they have truly not become better as a result. And why have they not become better? When one sees that fundamentally there is a trend towards uniformity, a uniform force, starting from the highest branches of spiritual life down to the utilisation of the individual abilities of the human being, carried by capital and capitalism, then one gets to the bottom of the question that arises here. Whoever does not separate the functions and the operations of capital from the rest of spiritual life in the modern social order, does not penetrate to the bottom of the matter. Working from the basic principles of capital is only possible in a society where there is a healthy, emancipated spiritual life, from which the development of such possibilities emerges.

Things need not always be as grotesque as when an important modern researcher, a physiologist, wanted to characterise what the learned gentlemen of the Berlin Academy of Sciences, were: He called them, these learned gentlemen, "the scientific protection force of the Hohenzollerns." You see, the matter had become something entirely different science was no longer the servant of theology. Still, whether it has risen to a higher dignity by becoming the servant of the State, that is another matter. I would have to speak a great deal if I were to present the well-founded, well-argued truth in all detail that only reversing the current tendencies and freeing the spiritual life from the State, can lead to the recovery of our social organism.

How different will the lowest teacher feel if, in all that he must present, he knows himself to be dependent only on administration and legislation based on spiritual life itself than if he must carry out the maxims, the impulses of political life! Apprenticeship should also have sprouted out of this sphere. Exactly here, servitude has developed. This status as a servant to economic life, indeed corresponds to what has developed there. In antiquity, it was called the food-providing class. Exploiting class and exploited class has developed in modern times. However, things developed quite parallel with each other. One is not possible without the other. All that has to do with the relationship between people — and this counts for the agreement between employees and employers — can only be administered by the social organism's spiritual sphere. Everything connected with Rights, and above all, with labour relations, must remain in the *political, constitutional domain of the State. But commodity production, commodity circulation, and consumption must be a separate member of the social order, where only the essential laws of the organism's financial part are active.*

Thus, by getting to grips with the fundamental issues, one comes to the radical view which may prove uncomfortable for some, that, for the recovery of our social life, three independent social organisations must develop side by side which will work together in the right way precisely because they are not uniformly centralised, but are centralised in themselves: a parliament which administers spiritual affairs, an administration which serves only these spiritual affairs; a parliament and an administration of the constitutional State, the political State in the narrow sense; a parliament and an independent administration of the economic cycle for itself; as it were like sovereign States side by side. Standing side by side, they will realise what the modern proletarian soul wants. A mere centralist nationalisation of the social order will not suffice.

Just take economic life, for example. On the one hand, it is connected to the natural environment. It is possible to improve the biological bases by improving the soil and the like. It is possible to improve the working conditions by improving the primary requirements, but there is a limit beyond which one cannot go. One needs to view it from another side when one encounters these limitations. Just as the external natural constraints limit economic life on the one side, the boundary on another side should be the constitutional State. By the constitutional State, rights and laws are determined separately from economic life. Just like the judge, separated from his family or human relations, judges according to the law. He lets his human will function from a different source than everyday life. So, even if the same people determine the issue — for through all three areas of the social organisation the same people will be in control — they will, when they assess from the side of the constitutional State, judge from quite different principles.

To cite just one example, stipulating the type of and the amount of work expected humanely, as well as the time necessary to perform such work. All this must be independent of price formation prevailing in economic life. And just as nature, on the one hand, imposes price setting on economic life, so on the other hand free, independent humanity, out of a consciousness of Rights, must always first determine the character and conditions of the labour needed. And the political State, which remains outside economic life, must assess the value of work within economic life. Then labour itself will establish the price; the commodity character will not be imposed on labour; labour will partake of price-formation. The value of the work will not define price formation. Just as nature acts from without on economic life, must the law act from without when incorporated in labour-power.

It may be objected that the prosperity of a social organism depends on labour first asserting its Rights. But this dependence is healthy, and it will lead to a sound improvement in the same way as, for example, soil improvement by technical means when necessary or expedient. But assessing the value of labour will never be compatible with human dignity if economic life functions within the State framework, operating as a gigantic cooperative. Economic life must be taken out of State issues and be allowed to work out of its own forces. The life of Rights, political life and stability issues must operate out of its own elements.

People must speak from the truly democratic basis about that which touches all people. That will have the right effect on economic life and on what must come of it. Never will a justifiable economic life develop from a type of cooperative or a cooperative instituted by the State. It will become clear that if things stay as they have historically developed, new oppressors will advance likewise to the present ones unless real democratic foundations are created outside of economic life. Just as the State's legal life must stand outside economic life, so must the entire spiritual sphere from the earliest schooling up to the university. Then that which develops out of this spiritual life will provide a genuinely spiritual structure for the other two branches of social life. Then it will be possible for that which emerges as profit in economic life to be returned to the general public from which it was taken. Then it will be possible for something similar to take hold for material goods as it does today only for the more exclusive spiritual goods. For, of course, the spiritual assets of modern society are the most cherished of all. As far as intellectual property is concerned, produce must become available to the public no later than thirty years after death, becoming free property, so that anyone can administer it.

That is what people today cannot accept concerning material goods. Possession is not what social economists often make it out to be in their weird dreams. Possession is an exclusive right to enable the management of one thing only: — the means for production; possession of soil and land is a right. And this right is not a prerogative. It can only be a right if it corresponds to all men's legal consciousness and when judgment is determined solely on the grounds of Rights. It must become possible by the rule of law that profit is transferred back to the spiritual organisation. Profit must be at the spiritual organisation's disposal to find the right individual with the right abilities to continue producing goods in service to society, not for mere profit. By this means, it will be possible to supply humanity with ever new individual abilities. There should be an authority leading it correctly, not into bureaucratism. The State must supervise the administration of the worker's spiritual skills, and it does not become the property owner. The right of ownership should be freely handed over to a spiritual circle that can administer it best.

You will see from this that it is from such backgrounds that one comes to radical views which will surprise even you; but I, for my part, am convinced that the facts of world history demand such things of men today. I am convinced that what the modern proletarian wants cannot be achieved in any other way than by working towards the separation of powers. That is the only possible "foreign policy" today. And strangely enough, every single territory can do this for itself. If Germany were to respond to this today, as I recently asked in an "Appeal to the Germans and the Cultural World," signed by many people, the Germans could respond to this threefold division today. They would perhaps be able to negotiate with the other States differently than currently possible, from the position of a wholly defeated state, completely overcome precisely by its former centralisation, and basically unable to do anything at all.

I do not want to take sides, but only want to state that what I am saying can become the basis of all domestic policy and a valid foreign policy. Each country, each nation can implement it and carry it out on its own. Today, when one considers the enormously revealing facts, one is convinced that it is no longer merely a question of changing certain conditions according to the old ideas. It is necessary to take new concepts and new facts as a basis. In recent years we have repeatedly heard people say that there have never been such tremendously horrible events in human history, as those in the last four and a half years. But after this statement, you do not often hear what should resound, namely: Never was it so necessary to rethink what the social question points to as most needed, but which nobody thinks about or mentions. Today it is clear that it is the people who must act. It is not necessary to come with ready-made programmes! What I have developed here is not a programme, not a social theory.

What I have developed here is a theory of humanity that is in line with reality. I do not presume to be able to draw up a programme for all the conditions that are to arise. No person can do that on his own. Just as little as someone can learn a language — which is a social phenomenon that develops out of human beings living together — on their own, so all social life must evolve in the living together of human beings. For this to happen, however, people must first understand the proper relationships within the three structures of the social organism. The same person can be in the economic parliament, in the democratic parliament, in the spiritual parliament simultaneously; he will only have to judge objectively from the right perspective belonging to a specific sphere. How must the legal, economic, and spiritual life be administered when they are in the right relationship to each other? What must be done to implement the social structures, is what we should try to find out; not an abstract, theoretical programme of what is right in all cases! I especially believe that the modern proletariat would know how to bring people into the right relationship when working together. Simple because the contemporary proletariat has experienced how the various interests, the legal, the economic and the spiritual interests, work against each other.

In this way, the three different spheres are brought into mutual engagement, so that, out of their own powers, there ensues an existence that guarantees a dignified life for each human being, and a viable organism for the whole. Even if it is radical, I believe goodwill and insight can achieve this social programme, which is not a programme in the usual sense — we must call it so because for once we have no other words — to bring this social programme to life. The social question will undoubtedly come to light. Certain people believe that we will solve the social problem that has arisen by doing this or that. [...] No, the social question has arisen because human beings have reached a particular stage of development. And now it is there and will always be there and will still have to be solved anew. And suppose the people do not get involved in every new solution. In that case, forces will finally come into disharmony. It will increasingly lead to a revolutionary shaking of the social order. Revolutions must be defeated step by step on a small scale; then they will not appear on a large scale. If, however, one does not defeat what enters life day by day as justified revolutionary forces, then, yes, one need not be surprised if that to which one does not want to pay attention discharges itself in great shocks. Then one must instead regard this in a certain sense as something comprehensible.

Thus, I believe that it is precisely in the proletariat that an understanding could develop for a far-reaching overview of the social question within the threefold division of the social organism. And I am convinced only when such an understanding develops will the proletarian understand himself as a modern human being in the real sense of the word. He was torn out of the old social laws, placed on the desolate machine, harnessed into the soulless inhumane economic activities. Thereby he had the possibility of reflecting on what is worthy of the human being and what makes human life genuinely worthwhile; he could reflect on the fundamental basis of what is genuinely human.

Therefore, one may also believe that, if out of the modern proletarian class consciousness will develop that which is still hidden, what stands behind it: the consciousness of human dignity — an existence worthy of human beings must be granted to all human beings — then, with the solution of the proletarian question, with the liberation of the proletariat, the resolution of a vast world-historical problem of humanity will take place. Then the proletarian will not only redeem himself, but he will also become the redeemer of all humanity. Then, with the proletarian liberation, the whole of humanity, that which is worth liberating in this humanity, will be liberated.

The Liberation of the Human Being

PROLETARIAN DEMANDS AND THEIR FUTURE PRACTICAL REALISATION I

Winterthur, 19 March 1919

Third Lecture

Please do not assume that I wish to take the floor today to speak to you of understanding between the different classes of the present day. It happens so often in certain quarters that people want to talk about it. I want to speak of an entirely different kind of understanding, as we shall see in a moment. Lecturing about comprehension is out of the question when one looks at how life has changed in the last decades, perhaps even longer ago, and into our times. The results are plain to see from the loudly speaking facts. These facts are rather frightening for some people who would not have dreamed of these circumstances occurring a short time ago. What does it help to talk about understanding when listening to those who long so profoundly to be understood?

A few days ago, one could again hear all sorts of things in Bern, at the so-called League of Nations Conference. They spoke about the desirable and, as people believe, possible international life in the future. Indeed, it reminded one of certain statesmen's speeches that always went out from the same assumption in the spring and early summer of 1914. Let us cite a few words from one such speech by a former statesman of the afterwards warring powers. It went something like this — he spoke to his Reichstag —: Thanks to the efforts of the governments of the great European powers, we may assume that European peace will be secure for a long time to come. — In May 1914! The peace they spoke of caused at least ten million dead and crippled eighteen million! That is how well people understood that which lay dormant at that time.

If I may make this personal remark, in the spring of 1914, in the face of what one could see approaching if one were not blind and deaf to the realities, I said the following in a meeting I held in Vienna. In the present social organism, we suffer from creeping cancer, which must break out as a potent ulcer in a noticeably short time. — One could talk like that back then. Well, I think the facts have shown who was right — someone who spoke of the creeping cancerous disease in the social order of the present time, or those who spoke as the statesmen of that time did to stupefy the people, to anaesthetise the people, to create illusions. Again, very many people are talking about the international organisational structure that is to come about between nations. And they talk past and think past what is and will be most important, which is already the most important and essential thing, which announces the social demands of the present. How did certain groups interpret, up to the terrible years that began in 1914, the life of our so-called modern civilisation?

One heard it said time and again how enormously humanity had progressed, how it was now possible to travel quickly over long stretches of the earth to do business. They marvelled how thoughts flew across the earth at lightning speed, how science and art — what in certain circles is called science and art — spread and so on. Praise upon praise was sung for this modern civilisation. And the last four and a half years? What has become of this modern civilisation of Europe? What happened could only have come about because this modern civilisation, to which they sang such praise, rested on hollowed-out ground. However, it was hollowed out not by anything hostile to humanity but by the justified demands of a large part of the earth's present population. They did not feel that what this civilisation has brought them was worthy of the human being. But this civilisation was only possible because it rose on the substructure of countless people whose existence was unworthy. And what is worst, a deep gulf had opened up in terms of understanding between those who, on the one hand, sang the praises to modern society and on the other hand those who after a hard day's work, assembled in their halls and shouted: "It cannot go on like this!" There was little inclination in the leading, executive circles for an accurate understanding, as they should have sought decades ago, perhaps more than half a century ago.

For half a century, the proletarian movement has been growing increasingly. And it is growing in such a way that one can say: Until now, the life of the proletarian population stood as a powerful world-historical critique of what the hitherto ruling and leading classes generated in the development of civilisation. Today the facts speak a clear critical language. The previously ruling classes have very often rejected what they have heard as the cry: it cannot go on like this — How did they take it? One need not seek so far — I would like to cite a distinct personality belonging to the past ruling classes, such as the German Kaiser. Referring to the proletarian masses, insofar as they were socialists, he said: "These animals who are undermining the soil of the German Empire must be exterminated." — Or another time he said — these are his own words: "These people are the enemies of the divine world order." — Not the enemies of the people, but the enemies of the divine world order. — As I said, it was not necessary to explore that far, to find people with various strange ideas.

For example, in the German Empire, for specific reasons, which I do not wish to criticise here, the Social Democrats voted in favour of war credits, at least the majority did. They had done their soldierly duty, had behaved in the required way regarding the so-called world war. Indeed, it was not surprising that the bourgeois intellectual circles seriously believed — and this is a fact — that the future soldiers would obediently allow themselves to be used. They saw the patriotic behaviour of Social Democracy. Indeed, in the former empire, they would have quite gladly been used. If things had turned out significantly different, they would again very gladly have been used to approve taxes in the Reichstag. Such a blessed memory!

Well, even on many a socialist side, they could not have imagined the loudly speaking facts that have now come to pass. The socialists have often emphasised: After this world war, the government will not be able to deal with the proletarian population in the same way as before — it will have to consider their will. Well, the facts have changed quite a bit, haven't they? This government, or at least a large part of it, does have much regard for the proletarian populations will. On the one hand, you can see what the Austrian socialist Pernerstorfer says of the attitude of certain bourgeois circles during the world war, namely that millions, in so far as they belonged to the warring nations, gladly made their peace with Social Democracy; but they would like to make peace on the condition that the other, to whom one offers lifelong friendship, hangs himself afterwards. — But if we look at the other side, there was no suggestion of much understanding either.

I speak from personal experience here because I worked for many years as a teacher at Liebknecht's workers educational school and observed what had developed as a world view in proletarian souls. When one knows what was living in the proletarian soul, one knows what, when attending those assemblies after their working hours, was wrested from them, even from their physical health. What resounded in their souls were three demands. Some did not clearly verbalise the three aspects. But there was a deep feeling in the proletarian's souls of what these three demands stood for. The first was about the materialistic conception of history; the second was about surplus-value, which is especially important for the proletarian. The third was concerned with the class struggle — even if clothed in different concepts. It clearly indicated that he has become what one can call a class-conscious proletarian.

What is, in reality, contained in these three demands? At first, it looks totally theoretical, quite school-like, when one says: one professes to the materialist science of history. But today, we want to speak in practical terms and not theoretically. What did the proletarian wish to express concerning his worldview when he speaks of a materialist conception of history? Modern history reveals how modern capitalism developed simultaneously as modern technology; he had heard an old song from the leading circles. But the proletarian noticed extraordinarily little of what they claimed to be stimulated in the human soul by this old song. The leading and governing circles proclaimed: The human being lives in a specific social order from generation to generation. Humanity lives according to what develops historically. Humanity lives according to laws, which correspond to the divine world order. They termed it the moral world order; if one wished to be one of the enlightened, one described society's dominant ideas as the historical life of humanity.

The proletarian heard those who spoke about their lives conditioned by spiritual and moral forces which move and weave through the world. But for his part, the proletarian saw little of these moral powers; People spoke of a divine world order, but one did not notice it. He saw how people acted, their behaviour towards each other. After all, he had been harnessed to the capitalist economic order, the soulless, desolate capitalist economic order that evolved simultaneously as modern technology. Technology has called many people away from the old handicrafts, which people used to say provided a golden basis. — it had a golden foundation in a certain way —, but what the modern proletarian experienced on the factory machine had no golden footing. This social order revealed how the labourer was caught up in the capitalist economic order while standing at the machine. With the advent of this new technical and capitalist life, he saw how the leading circles, traditionally belonging to a specific social domain, arranged things according to their own interests in the emerging modern State. He saw, above all, how the predominant circles from what they had gained through the current economic order, through the current State, set about it. He saw their so-called spiritual leaders, teachers, jurists, doctors, lawyers, physicians, etc. And he noticed, as mentioned before, that in this spiritual leadership, no divine moral world order prevailed. Instead, he saw how these leading circles were also dependent on the economic order because he was trained in observing human beings' dependence on the economic order.

Capitalism, modern technology, the exploitative system placed the spiritual leaders in their respective positions within society. In certain circles of this spiritual life: one often heard the following: Those faraway Middle Ages, philosophy, worldly wisdom — and by that one meant science in general — was in a certain sense the handmaiden of theology. But less emphasis was placed from their side on the fact that in more recent times, science had not become free but was now a faithful servant of the modern State system. Again, one does not need to go as far as a famous modern physiologist who once said of a learned body, the Berlin Academy of Sciences: those scholars who belong to this Berlin academy of sciences are the intellectual protectors of the Hohenzollerns. As I said, there was no need to go that far straight away; one could see, for example — and it all came to a certain height during the World War — one could see some strange things during this world war. Indeed, the mathematicians, the chemists, although one cannot directly prove that they obeyed orders from above, their science is less dazzlingly, less openly connected with that which pulsates through life. History is more correlated to what pulses through life. Whoever follows what has been presented as history precisely by those who worked and acted as civil servants in this area can form a more unbiased judgement than many others. For *example, look at everything that was said during this world war and even long before about the Hohenzollerns' historical significance. Indeed, history will present the Hohenzollerns differently in the future! It is fair to assert that what these gentlemen produced was a faithful reflection of what those in power wanted to show. It was in no way a free spiritual life. It was a spiritual superstructure constructed on the superstructure of the last few centuries economic order, especially in more recent times. No wonder that the proletarian, under these conditions, said to himself: All these ideas about a moral world order, all the statements concerning history! Does the divine world order come into play here? Every human being is dependent on the economic ground structure. Depending on the economic bedrock, he forms his thoughts and acquires his feelings and, in the end, determines his religious ideas. All else are only ideological superstructures! What is truly real is the economic world order!*

As I have said, one can understand the impression that arose in the soul of the proletarian. The ruling class required the proletarian to obtain a certain amount of education; it could not use the old illiteracy in its economic order —, he was thus compelled to receive the education he longed. Education of the labourer corresponded to the scientific ideas about the world in modern times. The ruling circles embraced this newer science, which emerged simultaneously with modern technology and capitalism. — But this proletarian was also compelled to something else apart from taking up science.

I want to cite again an example that I gave the other day to illustrate this question. One could be such a daredevil natural scientist as Karl Vogt, the chubby Vogt, or a scientific populariser like Büchner. One could be quite a freethinker, enlightened like both these gentlemen; one could say to oneself: I do not want all the old prejudices. Still, whatever this modern scientific attitude had produced in the upper classes, something quite different awakened in the contemporary proletarian soul. The leading circles spoke of the human being's descent from the animal. I do not want to talk about whether this teaching is nonsensical or somehow justified in any way, but it is the contemporary opinion. This doctrine was planted in people's heads by the ruling classes. The head reigned supreme. But in the social order to which one belonged, laws prevailed that were actually not derived from the basic idea that all human beings

60

descended from some animal or other. The learned classes found it more comfortable not to set up the social order according to this modern scientific view.

I once stood — I mention this again here in this city —, on a joint podium with Rosa Luxemburg, who recently met such a tragic end. She and I spoke before a largely working-class audience near Berlin about science and labour. In her compelling, calm, and serene manner, talking to modern proletarians, she talked above all about the spirit of modern science. She spoke to these modern proletarians something like this: Look at science today. It says said that man does not have a spiritual origin. She said — and I quote her words almost verbatim — people believe that man was originally a rather naughty creature that climbed trees, that we all descend from such beings. Of course, she then said — there is then, no reason to make distinctions of rank among people, as the current social order does. — Yes, you see, one could be an enlightened person and belong to the top class, one could convince people via the head, but when Rosa Luxemburg spoke in this way, it had a different effect on the modern proletarian.

The modern proletarian had great, gigantic confidence in this bourgeois science — it must be said — because he believed it contained the absolute truth. He was compelled to ask himself: what is this science? Apparently, it applies to all human beings. Called away to the machine, to the factory, into the capitalist economic order, torn away from everything that had gone before with no traditions to rely on, he had to find an entirely new relationship to life. He asked himself if this was what the world was in the eyes of modern science. On this, he focussed, it compelled him in the depths of his soul. He felt that things could not go on like this. He demanded change.

There was a second demand one could repeatedly hear if one did not belong to the leading circles and thus, had certain preconceived notions about the proletariat, but if you lived among them, knew their thoughts, and spoke to them. Time and again could feel and sense it. Anyone who has lived within these circles knows that with the concept of "surplus value" and everything connected with it, Karl Marx and his successors have thrown something into the working class in a theoretical way, which had an igniting effect. Out of their living conditions, this modern working-class profoundly and painfully understood what surplus value is. Here is the point where one must say: Today, we stand at a turning point in historical development. The upper classes brought about the criticism that lived in the modern proletariat. It caused a turning point for humanity. Today the working-classis called upon to act. Action will only be possible if, precisely regarding surplus-value, people dare to go beyond what Karl Marx meant when he spoke of surplus-value and what is related to it.

What was it that evoked such a profound reaction in the modern proletarian soul related to this added–value? It was because it touched the fundamental nerve of the whole current economic system! On what is the economy on which we all live materially based? What is commodity, production, circulation, consumption? In this cycle of economic life that existed since ancient times, only goods should circulate. It has peeled itself off from older forms. The modern proletarians labour-power has become a commodity within the contemporary capitalist economic life. Labour is bought; it is exchanged like a commodity for other commodities. — This was the perception of the modern-day proletarian. Changes took place in small chunks to divert his attention, so to speak, still fundamentally working-class labour has become nothing but a commodity. Here the modern proletarian feels more profoundly than has hitherto been expressed in theoretical terms, even in socialist science, that this way of life is unworthy of human existence.

He sees in his existence only the continuation of the old slave existence of the medieval system of serfdom. The slave is sold; the proletarian owns nothing. He has to carry his labour-power to the market to sell. But can one take working-class to the labour market without bringing oneself along? Is one not so bound up with oneself that one suffers the same fate as one's labour-power? That is what matters: Not just finding another form of compensation for the purchase of labour-power as a commodity but striving towards finding a way to strip labour of its commodity character altogether. The problem of work as a commodity is precisely the more or less clearly expressed enigma of the modern proletariat: how can he be given a dignified existence even though he has nothing to contribute to the social organism other than his labour-power? What does it mean when labour-power, which one cannot compare in any way with any other commodity, is utilised as a commodity? What is the reality of the *situation? It is the exceptional lie: that which can never, in fact, become a commodity, labour-power, is made into a commodity in modern life. It is an enormous lie. An untruth bequeathed existence; the lie must be transformed into truth. One can thus radically formulate this dilemma.*

And the third aspect is what the modern proletarian sees as a battle. He looks at modern economic life; he has a feeling in the depths of his soul that economic life can only blossom out of public spirit. How would one articulate this? One could say: the entrepreneur — the employer, and the worker — the employee, produce something together. Within the social organism the product is of mutual interest to all. But the entrepreneur buys the workers labour-power as if it is a commodity even though they manufacture the product together. The employer gives the employee no part of the product other than the purchase price for his labour. A legal contract cannot compensate for this State of affairs. As long as this contract is based on the proletarians work, it transforms labour-power into a commodity. Only when the agreement between what is today called the entrepreneur, or the manager and the employee is about the proper division of the product between them will it be a fair social community. But what does the modern proletarian experience instead of such a public spirit? Well, he sees the class struggle. He perceives the production of goods with physical labour-power by his class as a class battle. He observes the surplus-value flowing to the entrepreneurial class, with no sharing within the social organism of what has been produced. The proletarian is genuinely not so stupid that he believes that surplus-value need not be returned. If one were to eat everything produced by manual labour, there would be no schools, no intellectual culture at all, there could be no State, no taxes and so on. Even the proletarian knows that what is necessary for the advancement of humanity flows from the surplus-value. But the working-class wants something else.

And those who only see the modern proletarian question as a question of bread suppress the actual facts. Indeed, it is a question of bread, but what matters is how people feel about this question. The proletarian views the present social situation from quite different grounds because he leads a degraded existence. That is what matters. And instead of a sense of community, he feels the class struggle between himself and those with whom he mutually produces the surplus-value. What, then, is the life–experience of this modern proletarian? To answer this question, one arrives at the practical measures by which the working-class demands can be satisfied in the future. One can say: Yes, in the most recent centuries, spiritual life has become a superstructure, emerging from the ideology of the economic system as a smoky haze. But deep inside, the proletarian feels the longing for true spiritual life, for a spiritual life that can satisfy human existence. Even if he believes that all spiritual life comes out of the economic order, he will rather have a different spiritual life. He wants an independent spiritual life, one that is free and self–reliant, an authentic spiritual life. That is one aspect.

The second is: He looks at the modern State. What does he see? He sees the class struggle, and he has the feeling that where the class struggle reigns, a prerequisite that belongs to all of humanity is missing. In a social order in which there is class struggle, privilege prevails; for from where would the battle of the ruling circles against the propertyless classes come from if not from prerogative? But it is not privilege that must prevail — so says the soul — it is rights that must last. That is the second demand. It is the one that can be expressed like this: The modern proletarian sees in the current State the embodiment of the class struggle. But he sees himself supplying his labour-power as a commodity, unavoidably caught up within the current economic order. Indeed, theoretically, the proletariat has hitherto acknowledged as a science that everything is dependent on the national economy. But in the depths of the soul, he wants to become independent of the economic life that now rules. He wants an entirely different life that is not dependent on this economy. From this point of view, let us look at the incredible, far-reaching facts of the present day, which disturb Europe, which will disrupt Europe more and more. The leading circles purely material interests have given rise to a specific spiritual life that does not provide all citizens with a dignified existence. Through technology and capitalism, the top classes have turned the modern State into a privileged community with unequal Rights for the lower classes; The life of Rights must eradicate class differences through laws.

Economics harnessed labour-power to the circulation of commodities; it entrenched human labour-power in the commodity market. It must be removed from the economic cycle. This is what the *present world-historical facts express. How did all this come about? One must consider a few facts, which could be multiplied a hundredfold. You will perhaps be surprised to hear the viewpoint I will now indicate. We stand at a decisive turning point of the social movement. In recent times, one has often listened to the intelligent statement — and this is not just a phrase — that something like this world war catastrophe has never before occurred in historical memory. But less often do we hear people ask what we can do to prevent this from ever happening again. In a comparatively short time, people have come to slay ten million people and cripple eighteen million. If this is so unique, must we not acquire different habits of thought? You must excuse me if I seem somewhat radical. Let us look at individual facts which, as I said, could be multiplied a hundredfold.*

A rather characteristic example of how a State can emerge from the past epochs conditions is Austria. I am allowed to speak about it because I spent three decades, half of my life so far, in Austria. One can study what happened to the Austrian State to see how a social organism must inevitably come to ruin. In the sixties, a so-called bourgeois state was created out of the old Austrian patriarchalism and despotism, namely the Reichsrat (Austrian Imperial Council). The deputies were elected according to four voting districts:

1. *The voting district of the large landowners*
2. *The voting district of the chamber of commerce*
3. *The voting district of towns, markets, and industries*
4. *The curia of rural communities*

The latter was not even elected directly but indirectly because the rural communities were not considered entirely secure. The representatives of these four voting districts were now in the Austrian Imperial Council and made the laws. They were in charge of the sphere of Rights. But what does that mean? It means that they were economic representatives. Representatives of pure economic life in the parliament made the laws. What must inevitably be the result? Economic interests must transform laws and rights relating to labour-power and property. Strange as it may seem, many a bourgeois national speech mentioned property: Possession is a privilege, possession of the means of production, possession of land is a legal right. Nothing not related to property has any meaning in the national economic process. Only establishing possession is of significance — that is, the right to solely use something, excluding others.

The right to determine how to use or distribute possessions is what ought to comprise the economic basis. In the State, we are dealing with prerogatives instead of Rights. Here we have an example that we could multiply infinitely. In the old order, these rights were not determined by electoral law, and that is how it could develop the way it has. The federation, which called itself the Farmers' Union (Bund der Landwirte), was, for example, a purely economic interest group in the farmers' association. In the German Reichstag, there was the Centre (Zentrum) which was a purely religious community. A spiritual group was thus incorporated into the sphere of Rights. All this ties in with the hitherto leading circles interests and what they have gradually made of the modern State. The State developed out of the middle ages' framework into the current technological State with its capitalism. The educated — theologians, jurists, physicians and especially schoolmen were already included in the State. All of intellectual life was harnessed to the State. The thought hypnotised them: The State accommodates our interests, so let it also administer the spiritual sphere in a way that suits our interests. And they believed to serve progress, in the spirit of the modern age, if they channelled specific branches of the economy, the postal system, the telegraph system, the railways into this modern State.

That is the tendency: to melt everything together in the modern State. It is a bourgeois tendency. Socialism, too, is fundamentally nothing other than the inheritance of the

bourgeoisie. Incorporating the old co-operative ideas again, they consolidated the capitalist economic order, which they should defeat, as they justly demand. Using the State as the framework, he wants to turn the social organism into a large co-operative. This is a bourgeois heritage. A cure, a natural recovery of the social organism, can only result if one recognises why the damage to society came about. The damage arose because three fields that have nothing to do with each other became intertwined in the modern State. More and more people were asking: What is the task of the State? — What it has, in fact, done resulted in the devastation in Europe in the last four and a half years! Today it is much more appropriate to ask: what should the State refrain from doing? — This is the question we should be asking today. Look at the whole series of disputes so far. You will not be surprised if I tell you that it is the most necessary practical demand today based on the most conscientious consideration of social life and equally good science. I cannot present this in all its details in a single lecture. What is needed to fulfil the proletarian needs is to retract the intertwining and nationalisation of the three quite diverse spheres.

So that we understand each other better, let me remind you of those three basic ideas of the modern era, which at the end of the 18th century, out of the innermost needs of humanity, sounded as a motto during the French Revolution not so long ago: Liberty, Equality and Fraternity. — the people of the 19th century were by no means stupid when they stated again and again that these three ideas are incompatible with each other, that freedom is incompatible with equality and so on. Nevertheless, one can perceive these ideas as healthy fields of the social organism even if they contradict each other. And why do they contradict each other? They only contradict each other because they should not be jumbled together. They should be divided into three independent limbs, side by side. The three spheres must operate separately in the future social organism if it is to function healthily.

First of all, into a spiritual organism, where all spiritual life has its own legislation and its own administration, where the most unimportant teacher does not have to follow what the State dictates. The influence of economic life will not constrain him. He may work in an organisation based on spiritual laws; he knows he works purely in a spiritual domain. We should not become more and more tied up in a bureaucratic organism, for spiritual life can only develop when heart and mind can act out of individual initiative, from out of each human beings' personal abilities. If we cultivate a free spiritual life, then life can offer every human being a dignified existence. For then, that which develops as spiritual life will not be based on economic or State coercion. It will arise solely out of the impulses that lie at the basis of a free humanity. The person who works within the spiritual sphere will do something that is of interest to all society. The only role of the organisation will be the nurturing of spiritually free individuals. The individual human capacities in schools, secondary schools, universities, art, and science form a unity. These purely intellectual branches, in turn, work together with the specific facilities that are involved in the distribution of capital within the social organism. Capitalism can stand on the right footing if it becomes the bearer of a free spiritual life. This alone would fulfil the present demand to incorporate the means of production in the social order. For only a free spiritual life can give rise to social understanding. Only in a free spiritual life is it possible to continually transfer that which comes into being through the productive property from the land and natural resources — this concerning the free spiritual life.

In a healthy social organism, the independent organisation of the constitutional State, the actual political State, manages relations concerning regulation and administration. But above all, it has to regulate the human labour force. It must be lifted out of the economic process, not through abstract laws, but by the people themselves. How must the economic process be conducted? The commercial process depends on circumstantial boundaries, namely the available natural resources in a region, the soils yield, etc. Technology can improve the result to a certain extent, but there is a limit; on all this, the pricing will depend. That is the one limit. In a healthy social organism, there must be a second limit. This second limit is the legal system of Rights which exists independently alongside the economic organism. In the political organism, human beings are equal. It embodies that which concerns every person democratically; here, people must communicate with each other. Here decisions in the interest of humanity are made, where the degree and nature of the human labour are determined. Only a decision made on legal grounds, independent of the economic aspect, can allow labour to flow healthily into the economic process. Then the labour-power of the human being is not part of pricing. The price is determined in the same way that the soils value with its yields and the available resources are evaluated. This will be the great economic law of the future. Economics will operate between two borders so that economic forces do not determine the measure and price of human labour.

And the third independent area will be economic life itself. For the sake of brevity, I can only hint at the importance of this transformation of economic life. I will give you a concrete example to see that I am not presenting theories, but one can apply this to practical life. One need only name the word "money," and then every person will immediately be thinking about economics. But you see, money is known to most people; some understand it out of the abundant quantity they have at their disposal, others out of the little they have; everyone thinks they know what money is. But what money actually is within the social organism, most people have no real idea. Our learned teachers of economics today have little idea of what money is in reality. Some believe that the value of money is based on the value of the gold or silver it represents; others think it is a mere token, according to what the State prints on the bill or stamps on the coins. Some speak of the metaphysical process of money and so forth; after all, science always needs to choose rather erudite words. But what is relevant is that most learned gentlemen today agree that there must be something concrete for money to be a medium of exchange. And that is the gold treasure, on which one must always be able to rely so that the money has a specific value. Since England is a world power and insists on the gold standard, this one cannot change from one day to the next. But what is it that money in reality represents? The national economists believe that money represents its value in gold. Here a tremendous scientific step forward is necessary. People will not accept the answer to this question yet. I will go into more detail in my forthcoming booklet on social problems.

But anyone who takes an unbiased look at the economy will find the answer if he asks: What is the tangible equivalent for the money in circulation? — he will realise, as strange as it may sound to people today: gold is only of illusory value, wherever it may be. The real value is the sum of everything needed to produce the goods in a social region, including land and soil. This is what the money represents; it is everything that the money should express. All the beautiful qualities which the national economists ascribe to gold are, in truth, attributed to the capital goods. Therefore, precisely from the distribution of commodities with the help of money, the question must arise: How can something in ever continuing transformation, constantly adjusting, but established as the best value, underlie all national economy? How can money be a consistent basis of economic life, representing the actual value? Everything within the means of production must be shared, just as money, by its nature, is shared. No one can work with the productive property unless the whole social organism participates

— two things we have to consider. Firstly, the social organism would not survive if it did not include individual skills. The human being should work for the social organism employing his abilities as long as he has them and as long as he wants to use them. But when he no longer works for the social organism, the means of production he administers must be transferred by law (sphere of Rights) to the general social organism. I need only point to one branch of our modern life, where this already happens. The contemporary person regards it as the lowliest, the most insignificant because of how capitalism treats it: spiritual life. What one produces mentally is undoubtedly connected with the individual's ability, but thirty years after death, it passes into collective possession and no longer belongs to the creator. — This most insignificant commodity is treated thus today. One must find a way to transfer what the individual produces back to society. This transition is what it is all about. It is also quite just in the spiritual sphere. For what one has based on one's abilities, one owes to the social organism. One must return to the social organism what one has gained based on one's personal skills.

In the future, through the law, prerequisites for production must be transferred back to the public domain. As done in the previous social order, the bureaucratical socialising of the means of production is not the correct answer now. Out of capitalism, the present oppressor evolved. Similarly, the oppressor of the future will emerge out of the bureaucracy if one were to work towards a co-operative socialising of the means of production. A just development would come about when what the individual produces with his skills is transformed into society. That is what we must strive to accomplish. Then, when one thinks this through, one will understand the saying what sounded forth from the old economic State and spiritual realms: if we want to keep humanity together, we need the mutual support of throne and altar. In more recent times, the throne is often a presidential chair, and the altar is a Wertheim Cash register. The attitude of both is often quite similar. Whether it would get significantly better if throne and altar would merely turn into office or machine and factory, and if management would become mere bookkeeping, is the question. The current social demand is deeply justified; However, we are living during a historical turning point. We need thoughts that thoroughly transform the old. The working-class needs to understand that spiritual, economic, and political State life under the influence of the bourgeois of modern times must be reversed.

Does this modern proletarian understand the social structure by studying how the individual economy and society must interact? Has he studied the class struggle? Has he come to know their relationship to one another? He must grasp that what I suggest does not disturb the unity of the social organism. On the contrary, mere centralisation jumbles everything together and paradoxically disturbs harmony.

The three branches, spiritual organisation, legal or state organisation, the economic organisation, should be separated from one another, each operating their own administration, working with their own laws. Do not tell me it is too complicated for sovereign states to interact if this is implemented! It will all work out in a much more harmonious way than now because everything is confused and chaotic. When the modern proletarian perceives the answer to his demands for practical solutions to his questions, for the fulfilment of his hopes, then he will be able to adapt himself to this structure, which may still sound strange today. And I do not think that there could ever be so much understanding for the recent historical signs in other circles as there is in working-class circles. I have seen it in the last four and a half years and have often spoken out: What is demanded by the threefold organism is not an abstract programme, not a figment of the imagination that arose in one night. It is born out of the reality of life itself; it is what will take shape in the next ten, twenty or thirty years., especially in Europe. It will come to pass whether you want it to or not; you have the choice to accomplish some things out of free choice now, or you will face revolutions of the most monstrous kind. — Well, the revolutions have come!

I believe that someone placed by the external conditions of life at the inhuman, lifeless machine, harnessed to desolate capitalism, must understand these ideas, which differ from the old and are intimately related to the new, the emerging, the becoming. And I am convinced and believe that of the modern proletarian in particular, if he understands these demands and the possibility of their solution in the proper sense, he will become a class-conscious proletarian working for the liberation of his class. Still, at the same time, he will liberate the human being. Then he will put something else in the place of the class structure: the threefold social order. He will not only liberate his class but all humankind, that is to say, the whole of humanity, everything that genuinely deserves liberation and should be free.

Discussion

The organiser expresses in heartfelt words his astonishment that the workers movement is being met with understanding from a hitherto unknown side. He expresses his gratitude not only for the lecture but also for the spiritual work that preceded it.

1st Speaker (Dr Schmidt): Agrees with Steiner's objectives, asks for the way to realisation. Up to now, the socialist movement worked towards: Party, trade union, co-operative movement. The three spheres of life will remain interconnected, as they are today, but the movement will fashion them. The first aim must be to change the economic order in the sense of equality.

2nd Speaker: It will be easy to agree on the content of the goal. Threefolding is a utopia (with reference to Fourier). The path to this goal is predetermined by the development of the time: the class struggle.

3rd speaker: The spiritual movement must also be considered. Ideas have preceded every revolution.

4th Speaker: War experience has confirmed the materialist conception of history. Contradicts the statement that socialism has adopted the bourgeois belief in the State. The dictatorship of the proletariat has no other purpose than to prepare for the abolition of the State. Spiritual freedom will only be possible in a free producing community. Only the proletarian mass movement has a chance of success.

Rudolf Steiner. What the honourable speakers have stated does not offer much opportunity to elaborate — these objections based on standard views are to be expected. I want to mention that I have considered every detail in what I presented to you today. I want to take a little more of your time concerning a few points that seem important to me.

First of all, I would like to draw your attention to the following: when something like what I have said this evening is said, there is always the objection: I cannot imagine how things will be in reality. And on the other hand, it is demanded that one should not present any utopia. I believe that it will take some time for people to realise that what I have said this evening is just as far removed from utopia as black from white: It is the opposite of utopia. Things belong somewhat together. What I wanted to say can be characterised in no other way than as I have stated many times: This is the trend of the next ten, twenty or thirty years. Whether we like it or not, we will have to carry it out, either through reason or by revolution. There is no choice but to carry it out because time itself wills it.

Humanity has, at times, reversed the direction which it has taken. It is not, of course, a question of an actual return to earlier states, but the way back is a way to an entirely new form of organisation. Of course, we know that trade unions, co-operatives and political parties have all achieved tremendous things in recent times, and we owe a great deal to them. But on the other hand, it must be said that there is something unsatisfactory despite everything that has been achieved, something not yet finished. Today we are not facing new facts. But there is something that finally demands a different orientation contrasted to what we have had up to now! — I was not offering ideas at all! It is just the opposite of what might be called the thrust of a concept. What did I really put forward? I put forward a possible social organisation. I have pointed out how people should relate to one another to find suitable approaches.

A utopian always presupposes that the social order should be shaped in a specific manner. He thinks he is wiser than all the other people; one has to wait for him to speak, and afterwards, there is nothing more to be said. Then, if he cannot make contact, he sits down in his attic and waits. It does not occur to me, not in the least, either to wait for a millionaire nor do I believe in any way that I know about these issues better than other people. You see, there is a social phenomenon that the human being as an individual cannot attain, and that is the human language itself. It is a well–known fact that when a person lives on a desert island, grows up alone, without hearing other people speak, he does not come to *speak. Language develops out of a social phenomenon in the human being, through other people. It is the same with all social impulses. We cannot arrive at anything social at all unless people interact in the right way. I had to develop a concept. It does not occur to me at all to think that one can reform anything with a theoretical idea. I sought to answer the question: How will people, when they live together in a fair society, manage economic life, on the one hand, legal life on the other, spiritual life on the other, how will the social order improve? Preferably, there will be associations in the economic State, composed of producers and consumers, etc. If they live in a democratic constitutional state, the ideals, the impulse for equality of all men will be realised. When they work within the spiritual organisation: How will they interact? You see, you only have to look at reality. A judge can have aunts, uncles, grandfathers, grandchildren, and so on. He can be quite fond of them, love them tenderly, and that is good. But if one of them steals, he will have to judge in exactly the same way as when he would have to judge a complete stranger.*

Professors have often told me that I want to divide humanity into three classes. That is the opposite of what I want! We used to divide society into the educated class, the farmers and artisans, and the military class. But the present learned class teaches nothing. The farmers and artisans cause only violence, and the defence force tells the dispossessed what the possessors want! Yes, you see, that is what we must defeat: the class system. We must overcome it precisely by dividing the organism so that the human being is the unifying factor. A person will be able to be active in the economic organism and, at the same time, represent the political State while also belonging to the spiritual life. Thus, it induces unity. I want precisely to liberate the human being by dividing the social organism into three parts. Just understand what this is all about: It is the opposite of a utopia; it is reality. It is a question of calling on people not to believe that they are inventing some dubious utopia, but to ask: How can people be organised so that, working together, they find the correct procedures by themselves? What I propose is the extreme opposite of all other social reform ideas. All the others start from a definite concept; here, we start from the true social structure. Here we propose a proper social division of human beings where all differences are wiped away because, as mere human beings, they establish the unanimity themselves. Therefore, I would be sorry when you got the wrong impression. Do not take precisely the opposite of all utopianism to be a utopia! It is actually the only objection that I regret because it means the nerve of my arguments did not strike home. It is the crucial thing that I would like you to heed particularly. So, it is also not a question of overestimating the strength of a concept. Here we do not aim at utopia, but we give the people power — what they say, think and feel, what they want to be placed humanely in the social organism. Precisely because we are thinking in real terms, it is not easy to point out details. One can do so, but anyone who is in the habit of thinking in a genuinely practical way understands that when people come to their own judgement, they may come to different conclusions, even while both suppositions can be correct.

I will give the following example: You see, in the future, too, of course, one will need the means of production when applying one's personal skills; the manager of any enterprise will not produce goods for his own sake; therefore, those who work for him will freely sign a contract with him because they will realise that their work will prosper better if it is professionally managed. This absolutely must be the foundation in the future. It will happen naturally. People will realise: Something new comes about under the given conditions; there is no longer any ownership, but only an administration. I have already mentioned that we can treat material property similar to what people regard as the most spiritual assets. After a specific time, it must pass to alternative management. Not as with copyright after death, but when the entrepreneur no longer works productively with the productive property. Such transfer details are complicated. Still, precisely because we think in terms of reality and not utopia, people will discover the correct relationships if they work together in the right way. That is what matters.

You see after such decisive facts have occurred as after the recent world war, one can believe that new ideas are needed, but you cannot keep insisting: You must meet our demands! That is what has been proclaimed for decades. We will not get anywhere by saying: we want a society that provides freedom for human beings — but how? I have said that up to now, it has been a kind of political demand. But now the matter is progressing to practical life. The previous speaker quite rightly referred to Russia. At the moment when such crucial facts occur, we can no longer grope in the dark. We can envision something quite definite. I believe that is what I have presented: it is not a programme, but a direction. You can start from present conditions if you want to.

Just make a reconstruction of the conditions in Russia. You can, at any time, in any sphere, see what happens when, for instance, schools become state-owned — observe how free spiritual life becomes impossible. Start by establishing free schools first, by establishing free co-operatives in economic life, and so on. You can work on any aspect, whatever the starting point may be. Do not restrict yourself to Swiss conditions. Life is becoming more and more international. In Germany, something quite different is needed today than, for example, a few years ago. One can continue to work from any starting point; it will only be a question of developing it further. I am sure, be it a co-operative, a trade union or any party, there is always the possibility of something coming into being. Whatever the starting point, one can organise things so that the three social spheres become evident in all fields of activity. Then we will arrive at a genuinely appropriate organisation demanded by a healthy social organism, not a utopia or utopian socialism.

To avoid any utopia, that is what we must strive for above all else. We must eradicate any belief that one can achieve anything with abstract ideas. In social life, one can only work with people who know what they have to do in any specific situation they find themselves in. It is not a question of a struggle between those still called dispossessed and those called possessors. When people work in the direction that I have put forward today, it will serve both haves and have-nots. If the haves resist, they will soon lose their possessions. But the masses must know what is to happen. In this respect, you see the situation around the social impulse is worse than that of the medical and technical fields. If someone knows nothing of bridge–building and yet proceeds to build a bridge, it will collapse. If someone cures someone, well, you usually cannot prove whether the patient died despite the cure or perhaps even as a result of the treatment. And in the case of the social organism, things get most annoying because it is usually not possible to prove what is a remedy and what is a mess up, which is why we typically keep talking in vague terms.

You see, I heard a speaker who also spoke about social issues; he mainly wanted to prove that you do not need anything but Christ, then everything in social life will be fine. We should not start a debate on this issue now, of course, but it reminded me of something I read in my schoolboy days almost forty-five years ago. It said: Christ was either a hypocrite and a fool, or otherwise he was what he called himself: The Son of the living God. — As I said, I am not criticising, I only want to mention this now: I was in when Bern a gentleman gave a speech at the end of the League of Nations Conference in which he said that the whole League of Nations was disorganised — I believe that as well —. He continued to say that it is inevitable that it should be disorganised if one does not consider that Christ was either a fool and hypocrite or otherwise, he indeed was the Son of the living God, as he called himself. — In short, precisely what was in my textbook forty-five years ago, that is what the Lord brought before His faithful assembly. And note: In between lies the World War! After having had two millennia to make their concepts known to the world, they could not prevent the world war. Is it not precisely through the world war that we must learn something? Is it not healing for the social organisation if we learn something new through the world war? Do we have to stick to old conservative ideas, which suffered shipwreck due to the world war in many respects?

I want to emphasise this in particular. It was foreseeable and especially valuable — I say this without any rebuff — that things were spoken as they have been today. I want to stress that staying rigidly with sentiments expressed during past centuries and conservatively holding on to concepts formulated for decades did much damage in the world! May socialism not, through this conservativism, injure itself! For this damage would be perhaps much more significant than what has already happened.

You may have heard what I said at the end of my lecture, that we could count on socialism and even more on the proletariat to bring about the liberation of humanity. Therefore, it is not a question of overestimating an idea. I have not said anything about socialism having to come to an agreement with the State; on the contrary, it is a question of the proletariat solving a human problem! I believe that it is not important what the individual demands for himself, but what he has in common with other people. One cannot but fail socialist demands if one wants to secure them individually. It must be part of the human community. So, what I am demanding is not just an idea, not just any utopia, but about how people can function inside the social organism.

PROLETARIAN DEMANDS AND THEIR FUTURE PRACTICAL REALISATION II

Basel, 2 April 1919

Fourth Lecture

Do not think that I want to take the floor here today to talk about that trivial kind of understanding of the social question that many people would like to talk about today and would love to hear. I want to talk about a completely different kind of comprehending, the kind of understanding that seems to me to be speaking loudly today, spreading across a large part of Europe. It derives from the appreciation of those historical forces that strongly and clearly determined the attitude towards and challenged the social question for more than half a century. How can one speak today of the superficial understanding mentioned at the beginning? Has not too much been lost? Have not many people been searching to grasp this issue for a long time already? Today, a deep abyss is opening up between the leading classes of humanity and the working classes who are pushing forward with new demands, justified demands that the times necessitate.

Let us take a look at more recent events to see how impossible it is to come quickly to understanding today. Much has been said over the decades about this modern civilisation. It is supposed to have generated such great things for humanity. How often have we heard, again and again, the adulation of contemporary technology, of modern transport! We all know the slogans about how much is possible today. — yes, possible for who! — how people can cover vast stretches of land in a relatively short time, how it has become possible for thoughts to cover almost any distance, how it has become possible to spread the so-called spiritual life! I do not need to elaborate on the whole hymn of praise that we hear so often. But how did all this become possible? It would not have been possible without the work of the greater part of humanity. The part of humanity that had no chance to enjoy all that has been so praised. The part that made physical, mental, and spiritual sacrifices to provide for those comforts of life without sharing in any way in all the achievements of modern civilisation.

Let us take a closer look at what has been happening for more than half a century, making it inevitable that we should still say that an abyss exists. And if there is much talk of understanding today, it is precisely because of fear, fear of the looming facts that are so threatening for some people. With what, for example — to take as a starting point a popular subject of the leading classes — with what do these upper classes particularly like to occupy themselves? The world view, the moral world view elaborated in endless speeches, in smug representations in words that seemed to be dripping with feelings, about how people must develop love for one another. People must spread brotherhood to regain spirituality. The hitherto leading intellectual circles of humankind gave speeches dripping with apparent deep feelings. Let us put ourselves in those mirrored halls or the like and let us think how they preached about love for your fellow human being, about love for one's neighbour. They preached over a stove heated by coals — I would like to characterise it by drawing your attention to this — coals extracted from those coal mines about which an English enquiry at the beginning of the new workers' movement brought to light some bizarre factors. Down there in the shafts of the earth, nine-, eleven-, thirteen-year-old children were working all day. These children who never saw the sunlight except on Sundays, for the simple reason that when it was still dark, they went down into the pits, and only when it was no longer light were they brought back up again. Men stood down there, completely naked, next to women, who were pregnant and half-naked while they had to work.

For the first time, a government enquiry drew attention to what was in truth going on among the people. No one felt inclined to clarify such experiences before, despite all preaching on humaneness, charity, and religiosity. However, that was at the beginning of the modern proletarian movement. But one cannot say that what has somewhat improved the situation of some people is due to understanding gained among the previously so thoughtless leading classes. A large part of these leading classes today is still just as uncomprehending of the actual demands of the times as they were fifty years or more ago. One does not have to go as far as a leading figure, at least an apparently leading personality, the former German Emperor, who called the socialist-minded people: Animals who gnawed at the substructure of the German empire and needed to be exterminated. These are his own words. As I said, one need not go that far. However, today's judgements in certain circles are not so different from the particularly characteristic judgment just mentioned. But today, facts speak an entirely different language than those expressed in recent decades. And the judgements that some people make, how do they compare to reality? The horrific catastrophe we have lived through in the last four to five years is a good lesson.

Allow me to make the following personal remark. The one judgement that I have had to form during the last decades on European political relationships, I have had to sum up in a lecture which I gave in the spring of 1914 to a small circle — a larger one would probably have laughed at me at that time —. I had to summarise what was wafting among the people of Europe at the time, among those people of whom one can say that they had something to do with the political destiny of Europe. At that time, one had to say, if one took an unbiased look at the times: We are suffering from a creeping ulcer, a cancerous disease, in our State and political relations which will break out soon. But what did the "practical people" say? What did the "statesmen" say? When one speaks of statesmen these days, one is tempted to put inverted commas around the word. What did they say? What the foreign secretary of the German Reichstag did say was the following. He said: Thanks to the efforts of the Cabinets, we can say that European peace will be secure for the foreseeable future. — This was said in May 1914 by a leading statesman. This peace caused twelve to fifteen million people to be shot dead, three times as many to be crippled. Just as these Statesmen once spoke about the political heaven, so many people these days talk about significant, dynamic facts happening throughout the cultivated world concerning the social question. People have no idea of what is coming, what is sure to come. However, many clever people give their opinion about the situation.

What I have to say on this matter is genuinely not spoken from any theoretical viewpoint. For years I was a teacher at the old workers' educational school founded in Berlin by Wilhelm Liebknecht, getting to know the diverse branches, and from there also active within the education system of the modern proletariat, in the trade unions, in the cooperatives and also within the political party. Exactly when one lived among and worked with the people who were striving out of authentic ideas and from spiritual depths to bring about the modern workers' movement, one can perhaps form a judgement, unlike those who only formulate thoughts about the proletariat. Such conclusions have no value today. Today, only the workers themselves can judge. In the hours that the workers wrested for themselves after the hard work of the day, other classes went to the theatre or played skat — I do not want to enumerate all the marvellous things they could enjoy. During such times, the working classes tried to enlighten themselves about their situation. One could learn how the modern proletarian question has become and will become something quite different from a mere question of wages or bread, as many still believe today, namely one of human dignity.

The question of a dignified existence lies behind all proletarian demands and has been present for a long time. Today's working-class demands rest on three foundations. The first rests on what the great teacher of the proletariat, Karl Marx, said about the so-called surplus value. Surplus value was always a word that penetrated deeply into the soul of the contemporary proletarian; it had an igniting effect. What word did the hitherto leading classes use to counter this surplus value? One may be surprised when I compare the following two things. The leading circles contrasted this surplus value with the outstanding, significant cultural achievements that civilisation has brought forth. What did the proletarian know of this cultural life? What was the most powerful human question for him? He knew that the surplus-value he produces makes this spiritual life possible, and it excludes him from it. For him, the surplus value was the conceptual foundation of spiritual life. What kind of spiritual life was that?

It was the intellectual life that emerged at the dawn of the modern bourgeois economic order. People often say, not altogether wrongly, that modern technology, modern industrialism, and capitalism created the contemporary proletariat. We will speak of these things in a moment. But at the same time as this modern technology, this capitalism emerged something else developed. Something that one can call the current scientific orientation. When the modern scientific orientation made its entry — it was quite a long time ago —, it was the last time the proletariat placed its trust in the bourgeoisie. The trust in the upper classes brought disillusionment of world-historical proportions this time. What was the factual situation? Well, out of the old worldview, whose justification we do not want to examine today, an enlightened, scientific worldview grew. The proletarian, who moved away from medieval craftsmanship to the soul-killing machine, was harnessed to modern capitalism. He could not acknowledge the intellectual life of the older classes. He could only accept the most modern outflow of life's circumstances. But for the working classes, this spiritual life became something quite other than for the leading classes. One must only look deep into the proletarian soul. One has to imagine how people from the hitherto leading classes, even if they were enlightened like the natural scientist Vogt or the scientific populariser Büchner, had only head-knowledge. They could be such enlightened people only because they lived inside a social order that stemmed from the old religious and other world views and in which the old concepts still lived. Their personal lives were different from the lives of others, which they had to acknowledge was only theoretically assumed. The modern proletarian was obliged to accept and take the

83

heritage of the bourgeoisie seriously. One only has to look at the significance of Lassalle's ideas about labour and wages for the contemporary proletarian.

Once, more than eighteen years ago, I stood — if I may make this personal remark — in Spandau near Berlin, on the same platform as Rosa Luxemburg, who had recently come to such a tragic end. We spoke before a proletarian assembly about science and the workers. Rosa Luxemburg used words that unmistakably had a powerful effect on the souls of these proletarian people. It was on a Sunday afternoon, and they brought their wives and children with them. It was a heart-warming gathering. She said that people, under the influence of modern science, can no longer imagine that they have come from angellike conditions, which could justify differences of rank and class. No, she said, more or less literally: the human being, the physical human being was once highly improper and climbed trees. If one considers this origin, there is genuinely no reason to justify the class differences of today. They understood this, but in a different way from the interpretation of the leading classes. They understood that the whole human being relates to this picture.

The proletarian languishing on the barren machine needed an answer to the question: What am I as a human being? What is a human being, after all? However, the modern proletarian could acquire nothing from science but a mirror image of what has emerged as the current capitalist economic order. He felt people speak the way they do according to their financial circumstances. His economic situation determined his position; he could only judge out of his personal standpoint within this economic order. The leading classes said: The way people live now is a result of the divine world order or a consequence of the moral world order, and it derives from historical ideas, and so on. The modern proletarian perceived all this. He said to himself: But you have placed me into this economic life, and what have you made of me? Please show me what this divine world order, this moral world order, these historical ideas made of me!

And the concept of surplus-value — this surplus value that he produced, and whereto he had no access — made possible the life the leading classes enjoyed. In him ignited the realisation that all that intellectual life provided only reflects the economic order of the higher classes. Ultimately, for the last few centuries, this viewpoint of the proletarian theorist was undoubtedly correct. These last years have amply demonstrated this in the most diverse fields. Can one say that the learned people — I do not mean the scientists or mathematicians, for they cannot influence the general world-view — but did the historians express something other than a reflection of the State-economic order? Look at the history of those States that entered the world war. The history of the Hohenzollern will look different in the future compared to what the German professors have written in recent years and the last decades. However, this history will be told by people of whom it has been said — in the words of the German Emperor — that they are not only enemies of the ruling class but enemies of the divine world order. Thus, what was intellectual life for the ruling classes became a boring ideology for the proletarian, something for which he could muster no understanding. Nevertheless, his deepest longing was to find a way to understand what human dignity, what human worth was. Therefore, the first proletarian demand is spiritual. Whatever one might say, the first working-class need is a spiritual question. A search to find what one is as a human being on the earth. This is the first need of the working classes.

The second proletarian demand arises in the field of legal life, of the actual political State. It is challenging to talk theoretically about what law in reality is. In any case, the law is something that concerns all people. One need only say the following about law: just as one cannot talk to someone who is blind about what the colour blue is and it is not helpful to theorise about the colour blue, so it is not possible to talk about rights with those who are blind to the law. The concept of law rests on a fundamental human consciousness of law. Behind the dictates of the political State — so exquisitely crafted by the ruling classes during the last few centuries — the proletarian has sought his *rights. Above all, the rights concerning his field of labour. What did he find? He found himself not entwined in the constitutional State but the economic State. And there he saw that despite all ideas about humanity and all theories about society, there remained for him a remnant of old inhumanity, a terrible remnant of ancient tyranny. This, in turn, is something Karl Marx brought home so strikingly to the souls of the proletariat. Slaves existed in ancient times. The whole human being was bought and sold like a commodity. They were serfs. Less of the human being was purchased and sold now than in the old slave days. Yet, part of the human being was even now still bought and sold like a commodity. The proletarian soul understood what Karl Marx and his successors have said, again and again. Human labour-power is sold. Labour-power becomes a commodity in the modern commodity market, where there should be only goods. This touches the worker's soul profoundly so that he says to himself — though often unconsciously: The time has come when my labour-power must no longer be a commodity.*

This is the second proletarian demand. It springs from the legal field. In drawing attention to this, Karl Marx once again addressed another issue sharply. But we must clarify this area even more radically than Karl Marx himself and work towards a world order, a social order, where the human being's labour-power is no longer a commodity, entirely divested of the character of goods. For if he must sell his labour-power, he may as well at the end of the day sell himself. How can I still retain my humanity if I have to sell my labour to someone? He becomes master of my whole being. With this, the last remnant of the old slavery, but not in a lesser form, is still here today in this "humane" age. By selling his labour, the proletarian found himself disconnected from legal life and ensnared into economic life.

When people argue that an employment contract exists between the entrepreneur and the worker, we must declare that it maintains the servitude of the labourer. Only an agreement between the entrepreneur and the worker from out of the legal sphere will establish a proper relationship. However, this can only happen when the agreement does not determine the earnings but only considers what is produced jointly through corporal work and intellectual work. Contracts can only exist about goods, not about fragments of people. Instead of having his labour relationships built on the grounds of law, what did the modern proletarian discover? Did he find justice? When he observed his situation, he indeed found no justice. Some people gradually got into the habit of seeing this modern State as a kind of deity, an idol. Certain people spoke about the current State almost as Faust spoke about God to Gretchen in the first part. One could well imagine a modern entrepreneur instructing his workers about the divinity of the current State and saying of this State: "Does not the All-sustaining, All-embracing State hold and sustain thee, myself, and Himself?" — One suspects he will probably always think 'especially me'. — Humanity expected its rights from the soil of the State. The modern proletarian witnessed privileges only for those who have acquired prerogatives from economic life, instead of it being available for everyone — the equality of all human beings.

If you look at what he found at the base of the constitutional State, you come to the third demand. Instead of finding his rights concerning his labour, he found the opposite. He found the rights of the so-called owner; he perceived the class struggle. The modern State is nothing but the class-struggle State. Thus, we designate the third proletarian demand aiming to overcome the class State and replace it with a State where judicial law determines the labourer's position. Labour and labour management are subject to regulation. What, after all, is property? Property will have to become obsolete over time; it is ready for the scrapyard; for what is it in reality? In the social organism, the only concept that is needed is the one that says: possession is the right of a person to use something for some specific purpose. Possession is always based on an acquired right. Only when rights are based on a proper democratic social order, will the so-called rights of ownership have an appropriate relationship to the workers' rights. Only then, however, is it possible to fulfil the proletarian's justified demands. When one looks at the facts that speak so loudly today, one sees that the gradually developing social organism is under the influence of modern technology and modern capitalism. One need only look at the three demands that I have just characterised to see what is necessary to heal the social organism. The spiritual, legal, and economic aspects are the three factors that we must consider. How were these three aspects of the modern historical order, so greatly influenced by technology and capitalism, treated?

Here we come to the critique of the emerging historical demand among the ruling classes. I can imagine that some will not fully agree with me in what I am about to say. But what has established itself shows that people's thoughts have lagged behind the facts in many cases. Therefore, it is perhaps justified to listen when someone says: We do not need to talk only of transforming conditions. No, today, we need to move forward to ultimately a new way of thinking. New thoughts must enter the human heads for the old ideas have uncovered what they have made of the human social order. Rethinking and re-learning, not just re-trying, is necessary today. What I have to say will deviate in some respects from customary ideas. Therefore, I ask you to consider the matter by observing the facts. It is just as sincerely meant as many other ideas as possible that are conscientiously brought forward to heal current social conditions.

I see, for example, how economic life, under the influence of the bourgeois social and economic order, has grown together more and more with legal life in recent times; how the political State and the economic State have become one. Let us take a truly characteristic example of the present. Let us take the example of Austria, which has just succumbed to fate. When, in the sixties of the 19th century, Austria finally decided to establish a so-called constitutional "State," it was not a country. The Reichsrat, that old, blessed Imperial Council — wanted a clear, short name for this Austrian State, separated from Hungary, the land of the so-called Holy St. Stephen's Crown, "the kingdoms and lands represented in the Imperial Council." How was the Imperial Council for Austria chosen? There were four voting districts established to vote for this Council.

Firstly, the large landowners; secondly, the chambers of commerce; thirdly, the towns, markets, and industrial towns; fourthly, the rural communities. The latter were allowed only indirectly. But what are all these voting districts (curia)? Economic curiae they were. Mere economic interests they represented, and they elected their deputies to the Austrian Imperial Council. What was to be done there? Rights were to be established, political rights. What were the ideas about political rights when establishing the Austrian Imperial Council on these four curiae? The idea was that in the Reichsrat, where laws are to be approved, economic interests must be converted into rights. And so, it came about, and it still is so, that basically, the State represents, openly or covertly, purely economic interests. Look at the League of Farmers in the German Reichstag. You need not ask me to give you any examples that are closer to home. We see how recent times have tended to merge the political life of the State proper with economic life. This was called progress. One began with those particularly convenient branches for the ruling classes, the postal services, telegraphic services, railways, and the like, and then expanded this. This was one factor that was fused.

The other features welded together were the intellectual/spiritual life and the political State. I know that I am treading on thin ice, so to speak, when I talk about this fusion of intellectual life with the political State as having led to the detriment of the social organism, damaging it and causing it to become ill. Indeed, for the ruling classes, this was necessary for the last centuries, especially the 19th century. But one must not assume that the administration of science or the other branches of intellectual life was corrupt; in fact, it is the content of science itself that was impaired. One need not go so far as the famous physiologist Du Bios-Reymond. In a beautiful speech — gentlemen always speak very beautifully when they talk of such things — he called the Berlin Academy of Sciences "the scientific protection force of the Hohenzollerns." During this enlightened age, they mocked how, in the Middle Ages, the sciences and the general worldview was the

89

handmaiden of theology. Indeed, one will never wish for those times to return.

Nonetheless, whoever looks at today's situation with unbiased judgement, knows that a later age will have a similar assessment of our times. The intellectuals and the theologians no longer wear robes, but short of declaring they clean the boots of the States in question, nowadays the learned men do in many respects wear the robes of these States. That is what you have to bear in mind, again and again, if we want to talk about what has indeed come about because, on the one hand, economic life has merged with the political life, and on the other hand, intellectual life fused with political life. Whoever looks into these things do not ask, as so many people ask: From what standpoint should the League of Nations, which will be founded soon, operate? I heard the other day in Berne how a gentleman who thought he was particularly clever said: "The League of Nations must establish a supra-State, it must call into being a supra-parliament. Yes, you see, whoever looks with an unbiased eye at what the States have achieved in these four terrible years, would genuinely not want to ask how the various procedures and institutions of the States can be applied to this League of Nations."

Will he ask how to make this League of Nations as similar as possible to the State? No, he will instead ask: What should this State refrain from doing? — For what it has done has not borne much fruit in the last four years. Suppose one honestly looks at the mechanisms of modern social life with a healthy sense of reality. In that case, one gradually articulates what the historical powers and forces indeed demand in modern times. While the world war was raging, I described to many a person what I am recounting here. I have been speaking to death ears. I have said to many a person: "You still have time now; While the cannons are thundering, the States that want to end this war sensibly must communicate what the times demand and what will necessarily come to pass in the next ten or twenty years. You have the choice today to either realise and accept reason or otherwise face cataclysms and revolutions." The warning evaporated into thin air. The times demand that we actually get down to creating independent social bodies: a free intellectual and spiritual life, a political State responsible only for legal life, and an economic life functioning independently. — How horrific this sounds to those who, in the sense of old habits of thought, consider themselves practical, that one should contrive this complicated threefold social organism with a specific spiritual organisation, a distinct legal organisation and a separate economic organisation standing side by side!

Let us look at what effect this will have on economic life, for example. On the one hand, economic life is limited to what nature provides, like climate and soil conditions. It is, of course, possible to deal with nature by making all kinds of technical improvements. But there is a limit beyond which it is not possible to go. The given natural situation is the one limit of economic life. We need only remind ourselves of extreme examples. Let us think of a country where many people can live on bananas. To transport bananas from their place of origin to the place where consumed is a hundred times less work than producing wheat from sowing to consumption in our regions. Well, such extreme examples clarify the matter. But even if things are not so explicitly defined, the fundamental natural basis is always a factor. This is one limit of economic life. There is another borderline. It is the one formed by the State, standing independently alongside the economic life.

The State must operate on a purely democratic basis because the sphere of law applies to all men equally. The consciousness that rights must be determined quite independently of economic life concerning human labour is rooted in the soul of every human being. Just as the seed with the forces under the earth is part of economic life, and these natural forces determine economic life itself, so must the independent State determine what laws economic life must comply with regarding labour rights. The commodity price must be determined by what the fundamental natural basis provides on the one hand and on the other hand by the labour laws, which is independent of economic life.

Labour laws must determine commodity prices. The price of goods should not define, as is the case today, what the labourer earns.

What, in the depths of his soul, every sincere worker secretly expects, is that the regulation of labour-power and also of so-called property — which will thereby, as a result, no longer be property —, will be separated from economic life. Then will no longer be a relationship of compulsion between employer and employee in the economic field, only a legal relationship. In economic life will only happen what belongs uniquely to economic life: the production of goods, the circulation of goods, the consumption of goods. It is possible to accomplish socialist ideas. Henceforth production should no longer be a means to make a profit from but to provide commodities needed. It is only possible if the rules are independent of labour and work performance, just like the natural limits of the economic order are independent of this economic order. Only then will the cooperative and associative systems develop in economic life; It must be administered appropriately and based on the economic life. According to the needs of consumers, production must be regulated in associations and cooperatives. Above all, the political State must not control the currency. Currency and money should no longer be subordinate to the political State but should belong to the economic sphere. What will money represent? It must no longer be represented by just another commodity, which is in reality only a luxury commodity, based on human fantasy, namely gold. — I can only hint at this; you will find it in my book on the social question, which will appear in a few days. — money will be represented by everything available in the form of the proper means of production. And the available means of production will be treated as it is supposed to be treated in agreement with modern social thought. It will be just as little worth as something else that is nowadays not worth much. What can that be? Of course, intellectual possession. Everyone knows this is something received from the social organisation. Yes, even the cleverest, most talented person capable of achieving ever so much and who produces beautiful *things, in so far as it is utilised in the social organism, one receives it from the social organism.*

In the same way that this most unworthy intellectual property is treated today, all so-called property will be treated in the future. But it will have to become common property so the person who uses this property can utilise it to benefit the social organism. Therefore, in the book to be published in a few days, I show how the means of production must remain under the management of one person only as long as his individual abilities justify this. If not put back into production, all profit based on the means of production must be transferred to the general public. Through the spiritual organism, it is possible to find the person capable of taking up this task for the social community again. It is not easy when you have come to know this social organism, to fulfil this modern demand that the means of production no longer be transferred to private ownership. But the manner must be found by which private property loses all meaning so that the so-called private owner is only the temporary manager because of his abilities to utilise the means of production for the good of the community.

Only when the workers' rights are regulated in the political sphere on the one hand, and on the other hand property in the truest sense of the word becomes part of a circulating system will a free contractual relationship of a joint production between the worker and the labour leader be possible. Workers and labour leaders will exist, entrepreneurs and labourers will no longer exist. I can only briefly outline these things. Therefore, allow me to point out that, in addition to the independent economic sector and the separate political sphere — the constitutional State — there stands the naturally sovereign sphere of the spiritual life. In the future this spiritual life can only develop according to its own proper, fundamental forces when it is placed on its own ground. When the least important teacher, up to the highest head of any branch of teaching or education, is no longer dependent on any capitalist group or the political State. All those involved in intellectual life will know that what they do depends on the spiritual organisation itself. Out of instinct, even if not strictly out of a particular appreciation of religion, modern social democracy has coined the phrase concerning religion: religion must be a private matter. In the same sense, as strange as it may sound to people today, all spiritual life must be a private matter and based on trust. People must have confidence in those who provide spiritual and intellectual content. Indeed, I know many people today fear that our descendants will become illiterate if we can choose our school. We will not become illiterate. Today, it is perhaps precisely the hitherto leading circles who have reason to think of education in this way; they remember how difficult it was for them to acquire that little bit of schooling which nowadays secures their social position.

Be assured what the social organism now demands of the people will never lead to illiteracy under the influence of the modern proletariat. I am entirely convinced that if one can actualise the fully democratic constitutional State, which safeguards workers' rights, every person will have a voice in the sphere where people are equal. Then especially the modern proletariat will not stoop to preaching illiteracy. It will of itself also demand a free intellectual life. People should not be led to the ballot box in the way that happened in some regions of a neighbouring State, where the monks and country priests have cleared out the asylums to allow people who did not even know their own names to the ballot box. Whoever wants to believe in these things and hope for their realisation must have faith in real human power and dignity. I have personally spent my whole life independent of any State order, never submitted to any dependence on any State order. I have therefore been able to retain impartiality and know how to build up a spiritual life independent of the State.

This spiritual life will not care for the individual human faculties in the same way the luxurious intellectual life of the past has done. The spiritual life that operates by itself will not be a philistine, bourgeois academic life. It will be a human spiritual life, stretching from the highest, most elevated spiritual creations down to the individual details of human labour and its management. The leaders of the individual economic areas will be followers of free intellectual life. Out of this free spiritual life will not emerge this contemporary spirit of enterprise, the spirit of capitalism. Employment contracts exist, but it is not really possible to determine a contract around labour. A current labour contract is a living lie because, in reality, labour is not comparable to any commodity. Therefore, one must say: If any contract is agreed upon in the future, it will be determined based on the jointly produced product, and then one will ask all the more: What was this previous contract of employment? On what was it based? — It was not based on any law but abuse of personal, individual abilities. It was an overextending of rights. But what is the origin of this overextending of rights? It arises from the cleverness which contemporary intellectual life has brought forth in abundance. The Spiritual life meant here will not produce this shrewdness when left to its own devices; it will not create these lies; it will bring forth the truths of life. There will be no more protection troops for thrones and altars. Still, the spirit itself will administer the individual faculties of persons right down to the individual abilities of human beings.

Capitalism is only possible if intellectual life is enslaved. If spiritual life is liberated, capitalism in its present form will disappear. I tried to discover how capitalism can disappear. You can read in my book on the social question how this capitalism will disappear when intellectual life is truly emancipated, and truths replace the lies. What I have set out for you today in a brief sketch has been ringing through humanity for a long time. At the end of the 18th century, the words "liberty, equality, fraternity" rang like a powerful slogan in France. — In the 19th century, very clever people have proved time and again that these three ideas contradict each other in the social organism. Freedom, on the one hand, demands that individuals can move freely. Equality excludes this freedom. Fraternity, on the other hand, contradicts the other two. As long as people were under the hypnosis of the dogma: The All-protecting, All-embracing, does he not embrace you and me? As long as people were under the hypnosis of this unified State idol, so long were these three ideas contradictory.

The Liberation of the Human Being

The three great ideas of liberty, equality, and fraternity will no longer contradict each other when the three areas, spiritual, legal and economic, have come into their own independent of one another. The spiritual, legal, and economic spheres will stand autonomously in the world. The moment that humanity finds itself understanding the threefold organism, these three ideas will no longer contradict each other. Then freedom will reign in the field of the independent sovereign spiritual organism, in the State — the organism of law which guards equality of all human beings. In the sphere of the economic organism, production and consumer cooperatives will form the basis of wide-ranging fraternity; there will be associations of the individual professions and adequately administered economic life in a fraternal manner.

It is something that can hardly be imagined today, but it is not a utopia. It is not something that has been concocted in some way. It has emerged from decades of observation of the current political, economic, and spiritual conditions that exist as a seed in the very bosom of human development and will be actualised in the near future. And in the loudly speaking facts of the present day, it is possible to perceive in the demands of the proletariat, even if many things are still expressed differently, that the longing for the realisation of these ideas is undoubtedly already present today. Many call what I am declaring to be utopia. It is reality, born out of a reality-compatible way of thinking. This idea of tripartition is not a utopia. It is possible. It can be tackled immediately from any social condition if there is goodwill, which is unfortunately often lacking today. If people believe that what I am saying is utopia, I want to remind them that the proposed social organism is viewed differently from how they are used to look at it. Usually, people who talk about social ideas set up programmes. I do not present a programme; I do not want to be cleverer than other people. I am thinking only of helping humanity — people should decide how best to apply the appropriate structures to realise the threefold organism. Secondly, if there is a free intellectual life, secondly, a free political and legal life, thirdly, an economic life *managed out of economic forces, people will find the best techniques to implement the three spheres out of themselves. I do not advocate legalising what is best for people. People must find the best solutions themselves.*

Nor do I think, as some suppose, of a rebirth of the Medieval social system and classes: Clergy (learned men), Soldiers (nobility), and farmers. No, the opposite is what I am talking about here. People should not be divided into classes. Class and status should disappear through the fact that outer objective social life is subdivided. The human being is the unifying factor that belongs to all three organisms. Within the spiritual organism, his talents and abilities are nurtured. In the State organism, his rights are secured, and in the economic organism, his needs are ensured. However, I believe that the modern proletarian will develop a profound consciousness of what it is to be human out of his class consciousness, that he will find more and more understanding for what has been pointed out here: for the true liberation of humanity. I hope it becomes clear to the soul of the modern proletarian that he is called to strive for the true goal of humanity. He must realise that he must become not only the liberator of the present proletariat — he must indeed become that — but also the redeemer of all that is human, of all that is genuinely worth liberating. That is what we hope; towards that, we want to work. People say: There have been enough words now, it is time to act — I indeed wished to speak in such a way today to make immediate action possible.

Discussion

1st speaker (Mr Handschin): Speaks very spiritedly of the oppression of the worker by the bourgeoisie. The bourgeoisie imposes violence on the proletariat. The toil of the workers has provided the private property of the propertied classes. Only communism will bring peace.

2nd speaker (Mr Studer): Points to the ideas of free money and free land to make the liberation of economic life possible.

3rd speaker (Mr Mühlestein): Shows how the old powers are rising again and nothing has changed in Germany. Criticism of Social Democracy and the Centre. Criticism of the threefold system:

Through it, the law is taken out of economic and intellectual life; But justice must prevail in all three areas, not only in the constitutional State.

4th speaker: Wants to report on a "Swiss Federation for Transitional Reforms"; but was interrupted, and the discussion closed.

Rudolf Steiner: You will have noticed that the two first speakers in the discussion did not put forward anything which I would have to discuss, since, at least in my feeling, what the two gentlemen have put forward essentially shows how necessary it is to take what I have tried to say in a perhaps feeble, but honest way, seriously. It is urgent to contribute, as far as is humanly possible, to the solution of the social question. And that we must take the time to do so, you will have gathered that from what the first speaker in this discussion has just said to you out of a deeply felt warmth of soul. Therefore, because it is already quite late, I would like to comment on just a few points. The second speaker mentioned the words "free land, free money." You see, something has been hinted at here about which one feels the same as with very many things in the present when one wants to approach the social question genuinely, as I have tried to do in my presentation. On such occasions, I have often been in the situation of having to say: I agree with you completely; the other person just very often does not say this to me! It is like this: If I thought that my ideas were simply plucked out of the air from somewhere, I would not bore you with them. I would know that they are far from mature. This is what I believe to be essential in the ideas presented to you today. You can find the material, the building blocks everywhere. I gave a similar lecture in Bern the other day. A gentleman came to me at that time, not only in the discussion, but the next day he came to me for a talk, and he also spoke about "free land, free money." However, we were able to agree after an hour that what is truly needed to regulate the value of money and the establishment of an absolute currency will only be achieved when the threefold division of the social organism, of which I have spoken to you today, is established. The administration of currency valuation must be taken away from the political State and placed in economic life.

As I have said, in my book "The Threefold Social Order," I will show that the basis of the currency will then be quite different from what it is today and will also be implemented internationally. As long, of course, as the leading State, England, holds to the gold standard. The gold currency will need to be maintained in foreign policy. But for internal affairs, there will no longer be any need for gold in the social organism as they will have the one actual currency, for the only real true currency consists in the means of production, which will then be the currency for money. Money is wholly misconstrued today. Money can only be understood if seen in contrast to the old natural economy. What is money in today's social organism? It is the means of conducting a shared economy — just picture for yourselves how money functions. I work to acquire something that someone else is labouring on, designing, or manufacturing. And as soon as money is something other than this, it is not permitted in the social organism. I could go on at length to confirm this statement, but I will only mention this briefly: this is what money must become! It will happen once all other machinations that play into the circulation of money ceased. For only money is the standard indicator, from which we can assess the mutual value of commodities. We can achieve this through the threefold organisation, and it is also partially striven for by the Free-land-free-money-Movement. That is why I have said: I am entirely in agreement with this movement — because I always try to acknowledge what is justified within the individual movements, to direct them into a broader common stream. I do not believe that one person, or even a group of people, can find the right solution because people must work together democratically to see what is right. This is what I have called reality; I do not regard it as an objective development. But I believe that the human being, out of his healthy experience in union with other human beings, will find what is effective in the social organism,

We have one thing in common that we all know to be a social phenomenon — today's egoists would probably like to possess that for themselves as well — namely language. Again, and again, this is preached in the schools: If the human being grows up alone on a desert island, he will not acquire language, for speech is only possible within social life. One must recognise [. . .] that everything hidden behind private capital and property, the hidden control of others — be it command of their labour or some other kind of mastery over them– that all these things, even human talents and individual gifts, just like language, belong to the social sphere. It belongs to social life and can only function within it. There must come a time when it is clear to people what they receive through the social organism they are consequently obliged to give back to the social organism. What I am counting on, then, is social understanding, which must come, just as the multiplication tables are an integral part of education in school. In this respect, too, we will have to be taught once again. There were times when schools taught something entirely different than they do today; one only has to think of the Roman schools. There will come a time when children will be taught social knowledge in school. Because this has been neglected under the influence of the new technology and capitalism, we have fallen into today's pathological conditions of the social organism.

As far as Mr Mühlestein is concerned, I have to say that I have nothing at all against what he has put forward. If his ideas continue to develop, they will then lead further to what I have said. For example, he did not consider at all that I do not — of course not!

— want to take the law out of economic and intellectual life. No, on the contrary, I want it to be an integral part. And because I want to have it integrated, I want an independent social science to develop, where it can actually become possible. Once it has been established, it will be possible for it to affect the other fields. Comprehensive thinking shows you that. For example, if you consider the following: Today, even scientific thinking does not yet think in a truly consistent and appropriate way concerning the natural human organism. Today people regard the lung to be — a piece of meat; the brain — also a bit of meat, etc. Science expresses it differently, but it comes down to be not that much else because, for it, these individual members of the human organism are parts of a greater unity. They do not see much else. The human being as a natural organism is threefold: we have a nervous-sensory organism. It is an autonomous organism that exists in itself, with the senses as channels to the outer environment. — We have an independent rhythmic organism, the lung-heart organism; it has its own outlets in the respiratory passages. — We have the metabolic organism, which in turn has its own outlets to the outer world. We are human beings precisely because we have these three members, these three self-sufficient members of the organism.

In my last book, "Riddles of the Soul, "I have stated that the proper scientific consideration should recognise these three members of the human organism. Now is it possible for someone to simply come and say that nature should not have developed these three members because all three contain air? — Of course, all three contain air! — The air is first inhaled through the lungs and is processed accordingly; in this way, the metabolic elements and the brain receive air, the air is sucked in and processed, and can therefore also provide what is necessary for separate parts of the human organism. I do not want to play this analogy game between physiological and social concepts like Schaffte, Meray, and others do; it does not even occur to me. I only want to draw attention to

101

the fact that thinking also fails to grasp the human being as a natural organism when one thinks that everything is centralised — but one understands the human being when one understands the three organic systems centralised in themselves. The human being is perfect precisely because he has these three organic systems manifested in him. It will be a significant advance for natural science when this is understood! And the kind of thinking that thinks healthily about the human being thinks healthily about the social organism as well. Spiritual life will be free and best organised when it emancipates itself. For in the field of emancipated spiritual life, we can already find people who will take care of this free spiritual life. There will be those who can truly guide this necessary realm of spiritual life. Those who will not want to take this up are subserviently dependent on capitalism or suffer some other bondage. Those who will be free stewards of the spirit will also bring the blessings of spiritual life to the other two members of the social organism.

And so, if the law is practised in a genuinely centralised State, the rights of the other two fields will be ensured of a constructive distribution; in all the things that Mr Mühlestein has touched on, justice must prevail. It will come once things are established. So that there will not only be justice in one organ and not in the other, I introduce these three fields. Precisely to have rights in all three, it is necessary first to establish the separate spheres. I would like to know if anyone can state: In a house, live father, mother, children, maids, and two cows that give milk. All need the milk, so must all of them produce milk, not just the two cows? No, I say: the cows have to produce the milk so that everyone in the house has an adequate milk supply. Otherwise, it is precisely then that they will be — forgive the somewhat trite comparison — milked by the State! That is what I would like to emphasise today; it is not essential to pursue favourite ideas, but rather to take what is pulsating in many hearts as a necessity, even if more or less unconsciously. Impulses that arise out of the forces of time, which want to realise themselves, and which we should now achieve through reason. But if we do not discover them through reason, this will not prevent them from becoming a reality. Dearly beloved present, we have the choice either to be reasonable or to wait in some other way for that which must occur because it wants to realise itself out of the forces of history. In this sense, I believe that proletarian consciousness can grasp these historical demands. As I said at the end, striving for and achieving, as far as possible, the liberation of all that is worth liberating in humanity.

The Liberation of the Human Being

SOCIAL WILL AND PROLETARIAN DEMANDS

Basel, 9 April 1919

Fifth Lecture

Out of the world war catastrophe, a powerful movement developed, carried by proletarian demands that speak to the people of today. Circumstances that have already taken hold of a large part of Europe speak of facts that will undoubtedly have to be overcome through a specific social reorganisation.

The question arises, especially when considering the initial direction of these loudly speaking facts: Does a more or less sufficient social will, emerging from a deeper understanding of our present historical world situation, already exist? For it seems that such a social will is what matters. Therefore, it filled me with great satisfaction that the students invited me today to speak from a particular perspective about the relationship of proletarian demands to the necessary social will. My ideas and suggestions are laid out in my soon to be published book "Basic Issues of the Social Question." With these ideas, I wish to serve the present times. We are dealing with a profound world-historical phenomenon in the case of the movement mentioned above. One can understand this in the light of what is happening today. There seems to be a renewed awareness of that programme that spread through the world seventy years ago, known as the Marxist Communist Manifesto.

Today it is not so important how one, according to one's situation in life, regards what is expressed by the statements of the Communist Manifesto of 1848 and by what is rolling over Europe this time. What matters is that we are confronted with facts that speak loudly, facts about which we have to take a clear standpoint. We will need to be

105

clear in the coming years and decades because of the necessary transforming of scientific and ideological ideas, among many other things. That is why I particularly like to speak about this question to students who want to participate in what can possibly evolve out of our present scientific and worldview, to think about and recognise what must come about in the future. Regarding what is usually called the social question, one can say that two significant demands occur. Both conditions are symptomatic of the phenomena of our economic life. Thus, one can state that one appeal culminates in the rejection of the management of the economic life of the civilised world, which has developed in the course of modern times by private capital. And secondly, it is possible to state that the proletariat demands a new attitude towards human labour-power. Now, even if these two significant economic phenomena occupied the social movement initially, this does not mean that the solution to the problem lies within the economic impulse. However, from the evolution of civilised humanity in modern times, it is evident how all human forces, all human aspirations, have been absorbed by that which has stemmed from economic development.

We may devote a few minutes of attention to Karl Marx. Not because I believe that the modern proletarian demands have arisen from what they learned from him. Because what lives in the innermost intuitions, in the basic impulses of the soul life of the modern proletariat was to this day most intensively expressed in the views of Karl Marx. At first, these ideas emerged slowly during recent centuries, then rapidly in the nineteenth century. And therefore, it is not surprising that the most influential thinker of the proletarian world — for that is what Karl Marx was, has above all turned his gaze to economic life. He was the interpreter of that which millions of people experience, more or less unconsciously, today. Well, precisely because the impulses that Karl Marx prophetically expressed in the first half of the 19th century and later on ripened in the last seventy years in the souls of millions of people, the leaders of the proletarian masses find his outlook to be so enlightened. Karl Marx intuitively felt what will emerge — and this is well known in the widest circles — from the development which economic life has undergone in the last few centuries, through the development of modern technology and industry, as well as through the management of these industrial and technical enterprises by private capital.

The whole course of human development seemed to him to exist in economic forms continually replaced by other economic forms through historical epochs. Karl Marx sees the modern economic structure based on capitalism as proceeding towards dissolution; this economic order, which has more and more need to proletarianize large masses of humanity, will turn against itself according to Marx. The constantly changing productive forces will inevitably dissolve the structures of economic life that emerge. The economic forms strive to remain conservative. The time will finally come when the productive forces can no longer fit into the old economic conditions. Marx believes that such a time is approaching, in that the proletariat, with its productive powers, will tear apart the economic order into which they have been harnessed.

The characteristic thing that lies at the root of this is that Karl Marx sees economic development as the driving force that compels the proletariat to generate a new economic order and world order. What Karl Marx imagines as the transformation of modern economic life is also connected with the transformation of everything that constitutes the complexity of state life and all cultural life. Karl Marx thinks about the development of humanity in the sense of modern scientific thinking. He has departed from the view of older socialist thinkers who believed that the most important thing is the human will, which intervenes in the structure of human social life. On the contrary, Karl Marx believes that the necessity of the economic order determines the human will. From the economic order itself, from how people produce and manage their products, the organism of the state is established. Thus, the laws are determined, the economy formed, and morality founded, and so on. What is called spiritual culture is a mere superstructure built on what is reflected by the economic life. And if

107

one knows what is going on in the souls of proletarian people, we can say that this view is widespread; the human being is caught up in economic life. How he feeds himself and leads the rest of his life determines how satisfied he is with the possible legal order. Economic life also defines how many think, feel what art they create, and what science they generate; spiritual life is considered an ideology in the broadest leading circles, particularly the proletariat. Again and again, one can hear the word ideology when the proletarian wants to designate spiritual life precisely. This is one aspect.

Another aspect comes to light when the proletarian turns his attention to state life. But in this state life, he finds what he calls — again in the manner of Karl Marx — the all-governing class struggle. And finally, he turns his attention to the economic life wherein he is directly involved. And since it is precisely this economic life that determines his life, he develops what he expresses in the words "Marxist conception of history." From this originates his conviction that basically, the whole historical course of humanity consists of economic struggles, is characterised by forms of economic life, and everything else depends on this material life. And this, in turn, is connected with the impression he has of the culture of the foremost circles, into which he cannot possibly penetrate with his soul.

On the contrary, seen with scientific rigour, he perceives it as luxury culture and ideology. Today, we are at a point in the development of European culture, where we must ask more profound questions than have been asked in socialist and non-socialist circles for seventy years: What underlies this view of the proletariat in reality, that all spiritual life is an ideology, that all state life proceeds in class struggles, that all history is only a result of material development? The thinking of modern humanity inclined towards materialism in its various forms led Karl Marx towards all his ideas and impulses. Now we may ask: Why, then, did the views of this critical, sharp thinker incline towards seeing only economic life as the decisive factor for all human development? Why has the thinking of the modern proletarian himself been forced onto the same path?

When viewed not from conventional history but according to a more profound historical viewpoint, we find a very, very strange phenomenon, which will bring us close to a possible answer to the question I have just raised. However, if one tries to look at it scientifically, one can understand the course that economic life has taken in more recent times. But, of course, one cannot deny that economic life was subject to an unavoidable scientific necessity; one cannot even say if one examines things properly: This economic life as such could be different. — But then, if one were to stop there, one would arrive at an extraordinarily pessimistic view of life. Another question arises. How one-sided, almost as if hypnotised, was the gaze and forces directed to economic life only? Other areas of life have advanced that today must be regarded as quite different from mere economic development. It lies in the whole approach of modern times to view the other two main branches of human social life: the life of the state and the spiritual or and cultural life, as having derived from the economic life. Thus, one could say, because of scientific prejudice, it became clear to Karl Marx and his followers: economic life is the causal factor of all social life. Out of it, political and legal life and spiritual life develops. But is that so? This is the big question.

Today we are at a turning point where it is necessary to realise that this fundamental view is radically wrong. It is impossible to see economic life as the causal ground of the other two branches of human life. It is just as impossible to understand the life of the state or rights as deriving from economic life as to understand cultural life as determined by economic life. That is precisely the peculiarity of the newer age; nothing in its world and life perspective made it possible to get beyond this prejudice: economic life underlies all other human fields. From a deeper insight, from a worldview more profoundly founded in human nature, three social areas clearly present themselves: cultural life, legal life, and economic life. They stand side by side. That is what we must endeavour to understand. Tidying up must be done — this, the proletarian will — the social will — demands. The error arises from natural scientific prejudices, assuming that the causal basis for the other two areas of social life, the legal sphere and the cultural sphere, lies in the economic order. Whoever wants to understand this must, above all, look at one thing. Look at how modern thinking, the current way of seeing the world, has developed. But more than one might think, this thinking, this view of the world, is connected with scientific rulings. If I believed that practical life was somehow dependent on theories, viewpoints, concepts and ideas, as can be understood from a one-sided philosophy, then I would not make the remark I have just made. But that is not how I see the course of history.

It appears to me that what expresses itself in social life, what provides the impulse and shapes it, is defined more or less symptomatically in the thinking of the time. I never want to deduce practical life from the way of thinking, but I would like to assert that how people look at things is a clear symptomatic expression of what is going on in the depths of the human soul. It shapes external life, practical life, and finally, economic life. Of course, this way of thinking in all spheres of life has been infused by what one could call scientific thinking. But to what alone does scientific thinking refer? There are still many prejudices concerning this question, and I believe those with this mindset will be surprised at the changes the present standpoint will still be undergoing. That which people consider axiomatic and valid today will most certainly be challenged; it will undergo significant, formidable metamorphoses. What do intelligent natural scientists believe? They deem that they do not yet understand life, nor do they yet understand the soul; they know only that which has no life and is temporal: what is dead. But the ideal is that comprehension of the living will develop out of the ever more advanced understanding of what is dead. But we must realise that the whole manner of looking at things over the last three or four centuries is at the nerve of scientific insights. Therefore, this entire approach is only suitable for understanding what is dead. This is precisely why natural science has become so great. This way of thinking is ideal for understanding the lifeless, all that undergoes death, in plants, animals, humans, and all *living things. Through natural science, we only know what is dead in everything. However, this thinking, which has made natural science so great, ruins science; it corrupts social thinking and what must be the basis of social will for the simple reason that we must direct social will towards the viable social organism. But if we do not even recognise the living in external nature, how is this thinking capable of somehow bringing about the viability of the social organism? It is connected with the innermost structure of modern thinking that the human being admits his powerlessness, his awkwardness in the face of social life. Above all, there must be a metamorphosis of the innermost human point of view, of the innermost human thinking, so that he will no longer be so helpless and clumsy in the face of things.*

Looking without prejudice at all that is new in social life, one feels that what Goethe brought forward in the second part of "Faust" in his homunculus scene as medieval superstition is coming to life in another field. In the Middle Ages, alchemists believed they could create a human organism by combining dead substances and dead forces; such ideas are born out of the human intellect that only has dominion over the dead. In modern times this idea has been abandoned as superstition. But it is as if this superstition transplanted itself from one region to another. The latest social ideas resemble a homunculus theorem. It seems people have no conception of how to shape a living social organism. It is as if people would like to organise the social organism out of the natural-scientific mindset that is only concerned with the dead in the same way that the medieval alchemist tried to assemble homunculus out of what was dead. That is, above all, what must be overcome. Alongside the economic development, there is the development of the state, which, among other things, consists of establishing the law, and then there is the cultural and cultural life. As I have said, it is possible to understand economic development in scientific terms. Is it possible concerning the other two branches of the human community — legal life and cultural life?

This question is answered when one looks at how these two branches developed in more recent times. Three to four centuries ago, at the same time as technical and capitalist development, the newer school of thought also came into being. More and more, the leading intellectual circles encouraged the inclusion of cultural life on the one hand, and economic life, on the other, into the life of the state. State life has already assimilated cultural life to a high degree. Thus, one can recognise the modern trend in that the spiritual and cultural branches of life, which formerly were more or less independent, have been incorporated into the legal directive of the state. In modern times, the gaze is hypnotically focused on economic life. The proletariat, embroiled in economic life, pursues their ideal by claiming the state just as formerly the leading circles claimed it. They aspire to use this state, which has developed out of all kinds of old forms. The modern state has to function as a framework integrating economic life like some giant corporation. One can virtually show how the current proletarian question slowly but surely fell victim to this economic hypnotism. Just look back to the eighties, to the seventies of the 19th century! What was the ideal among those who strove for social democracy in Germany? The two main points of this social-democratic ideal, until about the nineties, were the abolition of all social and political inequality; secondly, the termination of compensating labour with wages. These were two demands arising from the general predisposition of humanity. However, these demands were not yet entirely oriented towards economic life only. In the nineties, the two ideals I have just mentioned were replaced by two fundamentally different ones. First, the transference of all private property to the means of production and transformed into common property; secondly, the transformation of commodity production into social production directed by and for society.

The social-democratic demands were wholly phased out into a purely economic programme. Thus, I would like to say; it is precisely in its present economic programme that social democracy is the last executor of that which is, in essence, the bourgeois world view of the previous centuries. Only when one appreciates what the proletariat of today require does one realise this is nothing other than the final

112

consequence of the bourgeois economic world order. But it penetrated even further. What I have just characterised for you as the current world view, entirely permeated by natural science, has been developing within bourgeois circles over the last few centuries. It forms the basis of everything and provides the worldview and vision of life. From where did the leading proletarian spirits get their ideas? What inspires their social striving? It all derives from bourgeois scientific thinking. It is fair to say that up to this day, the final great confidence which the proletarian circles have placed in the bourgeoisie was the acceptance of their scientific orientation, for they have adopted the bourgeois world view. In accord with this bourgeois world view, they were placed at the machines. They were harnessed into the for them so desolate life of capitalism. Torn away from those professions that answer the question: What am I actually in the world? Standing next to the soulless machine as but a cog within this capitalist order, there is no answer to the question: what am I as a human being within human development? There arose for the proletarian above all the demand to answer this question from scientific orientation itself. The proletarian impressions of the new world order were very different from those of the bourgeois circles.

The bourgeoisie still lives in an economic order, in a lifestyle, which holds on to the old traditions. Although they are convinced of the validity of modern scientific ideas, it still has not taken hold wholly; they still retain what they have received as religious, cultural, artistic, or other impulses from elsewhere next to their scientific orientation. The proletarian expects this modern scientific orientation to answer the question: What am I as a human being? Oh, one has looked into the souls of numerous proletarians. One met with souls who have preserved their sense of humanity and their longing for human dignity. One knows how they long precisely from the modern scientific orientation side to get the question answered: What am I worth in the world as a human being? Then what is termed "ideology" is placed before these souls — a longing for a spiritual life that does not deny the human being his connection with the spiritual world. A cultural life that exists only in unreal ideas as an ideology cannot sustain souls. The

113

individual may not be conscious of this. The effect thereof nevertheless is felt in the soul! What brings desolation to the soul of the proletariat is this world view and way of thinking that they inherited from the bourgeoisie and the leading circles, which cannot bring fulfilment to the human being. The proletarian, who has been torn away from the old order of life, cannot believe in or feel connected to the ancient traditions to which the others still cling. And this scientific way of thinking, which can only grasp that which is dead, cannot give him an answer to the higher issues for which he more or less unconsciously longs, for the survival of his own soul within the world order. This rests at the bottom of every proletarian soul; no matter how wrong it manifests itself or what form it takes, it is the basis of what lives in the worker's soul. And even the rioting of the social movement was only caused by that soul wasteland that developed under the influence of what I just described. Let us look: How has the scientific world order changed lifestyles in recent times, bringing what we have just related to the proletarian? How did this develop?

Indeed, as it has developed in modern times, the belief in the state is firmly anchored in many souls. They do not want to change their faith in the state, which would best take everything under its wing, whether economic or spiritual and cultural life! Because this belief is so deeply rooted, little is learned from the facts. Do the last four and a half years not clearly tell what the states have achieved for a large part of the world? The time will have to come when people realise that what they have experienced as the most terrible world catastrophe is the consequence of the structure of the whole organisation of modern states. And suppose one examines what has led to this world catastrophe through the actions of the states themselves. In that case, one must ask: How did the states tried and been able to cope with this interconnectedness of the three spheres of life: cultural life, state-run or legal life, and economic life? Well, as states, they were driven into the world war! Anyone who observes the starting points of this world war will find solid arguments for discontinuing the entanglement of the inner structures that have occurred during the last three to four centuries of human development. From another viewpoint, however, it is obvious how cultural life has developed precisely in the period in which the state proudly claimed more and more power over spiritual and cultural matters. Thus, at the bottom, this is a chapter of historical development that we can only contemplate with intense pessimism!

Let us look at this cultural life of the last three or four centuries: Many songs of praise have been sung to it. But the characteristic qualities have been little emphasised. The voices of our time are compelled to speak out, to express something else about the spiritual life of the last three or four centuries, so praised by these hymns. Let me point out one characteristic feature of this cultural life. Do we not realise that great and influential people have appeared over the last three or four centuries if we genuinely look without bias? Have they not worked in the fields directly necessary for human life? It was precisely the most outstanding spirits who had a decisive effect. One should have no illusions about that. Let us direct our attention to a significant personality of recent times: Goethe. Do people genuinely know Goethe?

On the contrary! We don't know anything about this Goethe! Has that which lives as gigantic, significant, spiritual life in Goethe somehow penetrated people's souls? No, nowhere! After Goethe had been more or less a favourite of leading circles in Germany, a "Goethe Society" was founded in the eighties. Is this "Goethe Society" that would like to make it a matter of the nation necessary for Goethe's spiritual heritage? No, ladies and gentlemen! Someone who himself worked within this "Goethe Society" for a long time but was always in opposition precisely to the leaders of this society. May I tell you: this "Goethe Society" is a pedantic, scholarly elaboration of what has only externally, but not inherently, anything to do with Goethe!

The spiritual contributions of more recent times, of Goethe and all the other great souls, have not passed over into general human life.

115

On the contrary, it is a spirituality that, to a certain extent, modern humans could not accept. At most, if it was received, it was taken up as something extraordinary that one knew about and could chat about to show how informed one was in the salon. When, for example, the "Goethe Society" had experimented with its executive committee for a long time, it finally fell for the idea of appointing a former Prussian Minister of Finance, who had never had any inner relationship with Goethe, as chairman of the Goethe Society! This is only one of the characteristic phenomena; one could effortlessly increase it tenfold, multiply it a hundredfold, a thousandfold, even a millionfold if one were to penetrate deeper into this modern cultural life. Cultural life is characterised precisely by this. But, unfortunately, the broader circles of humanity have not been able to grasp these significant achievements. This tragically led to these accomplishments dwelling among people like parasites of human development. It belongs, in a more profound sense than usually thought to the development of social consciousness and social life as a whole in modern times.

And suppose one is not willing to see the significance for modern social development in such phenomena of spiritual life. In that case, we shall never find the transition to valid, substantial social will. In a certain sense, this modern spiritual life has become a sterile theory. Why? Whoever knows what the conditions of real spiritual life are, knows that spiritual life can never be harnessed to the sphere of power of any external force if it is to flourish. Natural science, which is directed only towards the dead, and all those branches of the intellectual, spiritual life that felt compelled to adhere to the scientific world outlook under the new conditions, could easily be harnessed to the structures of the states. But those branches of cultural life, based on the most individual abilities of the human being, which should develop spiritual will, were driven out of these state structures.

Modern cultural life lacks the thrust that the old religious ideas had because most people cannot absorb what should develop in humanity. These impulses, therefore, unfortunately, have to fall into a parasitic existence. There is an explanation for these phenomena. It is *because, in recent times, cultural life merged with the life of the state. Until people are made aware that a radical change is necessary for this field, recovery of social health will not be possible. Cultural life, education, and all the other branches of spiritual life must form a distinct, independent part of the healthy social organism; they must be detached from the state's political life, which is only supposed to take care of legal life. One could point to many different phenomena if one wanted to discuss how the administration of science and cultural life has become dependent on the power and constraints of the state, but also the inherent content of science itself.*

It becomes apparent how unsuitable a great scientist is, concerning social thinking and social will, in the following characteristic example: An unbiassed spirit, Oscar Hertwig, an important natural scientist in the field of biology, in his excellent book "Das Werden der Organismen — The Development of Organisms — a Refutation of the Darwinian Theory of Chance," has made an unspeakably significant contribution to the development of recent scientific thought. But unfortunately, the same Oscar Hertwig has made the regrettable attempt, in a small booklet, to apply his scientific way of thinking to the social and legal state. Thus, despite his outstanding work in natural science, it is impossible to find a more nonsensical and childish published work on social, legal and similar topics. This is proof that, under nationalisation, a way of thinking has developed that simply cannot penetrate what lies within the social demands. This cultural stream has become dependent on something else in a strange way; in the end, it is truly not at all rare what scholars such as the historian Heinrich Friedjung write. I am genuinely not speaking out of animosity towards Heinrich Friedjung; he was a dear childhood friend of mine, but today times are so acute that only objective interests can be considered. Heinrich Friedjung, the historian who, it is understood, wrote an epoch-making work on modern Austria. He used the historical method to examine historical documents. He placed himself in the service of the Austrian Foreign Minister, Baron Ahrenthal: he has proved, as he believes, by reliable historical method, that specific anti-Austrian machinations must have come from seven conspirators. There was a court hearing on the matter. Heinrich Friedjung could justifiably state that he is not a historian to take lightly, that the University of Heidelberg gave him an honorary doctorate. Even though he used a historical method to prove that the documents Baron Ahrenthal wanted to use to condemn the Serbs were genuine, the court nevertheless recognised them as clumsy forgeries. By this, the historical method itself was doomed.

Unfortunately, we live in a time in which such things are not taken seriously enough, above all not profoundly enough. Despite the seriousness with which it is pursued, spiritual life generally runs like a side stream beside the rest of life. I want to characterise this superficiality of modern cultural life with "the count with two trouser pockets." On one of my visits to the Nietzsche Archive, I met this count with the two pockets, a witty man. He was a familiar figure in the Nietzsche Archive. He had two trouser pockets, and he pulled a Bible for me out of one of them, a complete bible printed in pearl; it fitted in his pocket. He said: You see, I always carry it with me. I have another one, and he took out of the other pocket the "Zarathustra," also in pearl print, so that I could see it.

Thus, the count had carried with him or wanted to carry the two books most essential to him! This expresses symbolically how matters are for the modern human being, how it truly is, especially regarding the cultural sphere. The count with the two trouser pockets had the Bible in one pocket, Nietzsche's "Zarathustra" in the other. Despite all the hymns of praise, we can see how sterile and barren modern spiritual and cultural life has become. Thus, we realise that the state life, as it has developed in recent times up to the present day, has, as it were, led itself ad absurdum to the world catastrophe. Must not the question be raised: Is it not precisely the merging of the three most important branches of life, legal life, cultural or spiritual life, and economic life, which has driven us into the world catastrophe, making us incapable of coping socially? Whoever studies how the state gradually absorbed these three branches of human life cannot but *recognise that in the dissolution, in the separation of the three limbs mentioned lies the recovery of the social organism. It will no longer merely function in the manner of a homunculus. It will become alive, full of vitality once again only when one looks at the essential conditions of spiritual or cultural life on the one hand and legal or political life in the state on the other hand, and finally of economic life.*

But then one will discover that these three branches of life have quite different foundations, that they develop best when each of these branches of social life is strictly self-governing. The only reason why this was not possible in more recent times was that, as if hypnotised, people's gaze was directed only towards economic life. And so, one saw people with their labour power harnessed above all else into economic life. On the other hand, however, economics should only be concerned with commodities or commodity-like issues. This the modern proletarian feels also. It is what is expressed in his wishes, even if he formulates what he says differently. He senses that it is contrary to his human dignity to become a part of the economic process as if he is a commodity. Just as the price of goods is determined, human labour-power is also given a set price within this structure.

On the one hand, the most striking thing in the teaching of Karl Marx is that he brought to the people's attention the most profound impressions of the proletariat concerning labour-power: How commodities are brought to and offered on the commodity market. In the same way, the work of the labourer is bought and sold on the labour market. In this respect, one must become even more radical than Karl Marx himself if the social organism is to recover. On the other hand, we must be clear that human labour-power can in no way be compared to a commodity, which therefore cannot have a price like any commodity. The worker who has to carry his labour-power to the market feels that we have now arrived at that point in human development where a third aspect must follow the two other fields that have already become redundant over time.

The old slavery, when a human being could be bought and sold in person, has disappeared from human society. Serfdom, where already less of the person could be bought and sold, has been abandoned. The third issue is that the capitalist economic order has still been preserved and must also be discarded. This is that human labour can still be bought and sold on the labour market. To sell his labour-power, he must go along himself. He cannot separate himself from his labour. By having to be present himself, he is, in a sense, ultimately selling himself. That is what the labourer feels: We have reached the point in human development where only what has objective value as a commodity, detached from human beings, can be bought and sold. That is: economic life, the economic sphere, may in the future only be concerned with the production of goods and their movement and consumption.

Human labour has to be separated from economic life. There is no other way to create a healthy social organism but to manage economic life independently. Labour must become a legal concern, not an economic matter. Next to the economic organism, the constitutional state, the political state, must stand as a separate body. Brotherhood will reign in economic life on a grand scale, where an associative life regulates production according to consumption and so on. The political state, which is again entirely independent, like a sovereign state alongside another state, will function alongside economic life, in which democratic equality of all people will prevail. All institutions will have to facilitate the equality of all people in matters that concern society in general. Above all, that which relates to labour laws plus many other aspects will have to be defined.

Labour laws are, first and foremost, a question for the social movement in the present. In the independent constitutional state, economic equality will reign among people whether they work mentally or physically. Labour laws will control this. What will happen as a result? It will mean that economic life, as a self-contained sphere, will, on the one hand, be limited by the natural order, and on the other hand, through laws. Economic life depends on the natural order.
120

Whether the fields are fertile in any given year or not, what the earth provides at all, determines exploitation. It is possible to change soil fertility by technical means, but there is a limit to what one can achieve under the provided natural conditions. This will reflect in the pricing of economic goods in all the institutions of economic life. It will not occur to anyone to want to make nature dependent on the organisation of economic life. Just as autonomous as nature itself is, as independent as the germinating wheat that grows upward is from economic life, just as independent must labour rights be, regulated only by legalisation.

The worker enters the economic field with established rights outside the economic sphere, just as nature's possibilities lie outside the economic cycle. All price formation must be based on labour laws that arise outside economic life. Labour laws establish prices; the price of human labour-power is never decided within the economic cycle. This will be the only way towards a healthy relationship of the manual worker to the intellectual leader. Then the labourer will no longer need to enter into the present unreal contract regarding his labour-power; he will be able to sign a contract, where the product produced jointly is divided between the manual worker and the intellectual contribution of the director. In no other way than strictly separating the state's life from the economy can society achieve what is necessary for this field.

Equally necessary, on the other hand, is an independent, free spiritual life. The state is healthy is when it regulates only that which applies equally to all human beings. The spiritual life is simply killed if it is founded on the same basis as political life. Therefore, the administration of cultural life must be autonomous. It must look after and manage the individual skills of human beings. This will then be a cultural life emancipated from the state, which will support the human soul. This will not be an ideology; it will not be a cultural life that only delivers abstract concepts; it will be a cultural life that will prove it is practical and authentic. It will involve the human soul once again and place the human being within the spiritual order.

That is what today's proletarian still rejects. Yet, in the depths of his soul, he longs for such a cultural life because he feels that otherwise, the soul will become desolate. This call for a free organisation of cultural life is a terribly serious matter. The matter is so profound because all the impulses of men, all the standard views and thoughts of modern times, run counter to the health of the social organism. That is why it is vital to address those who represent the youth today about this demand for a free spiritual life that operates autonomously. If science and cultural life, in general, are to be sustainable into the future, we need a cultural sphere that is not integrated into the state. One should sense the difference when the teacher, on even the lowest level, knows that what he does is administered by an independent spiritual organism, and he is not dependent on the state. When the state no longer handles education, those who want to become theologians, lawyers, doctors will no longer be dependent on the state. Particularly when people sense that the spiritual needs of humanity develop out of cultural life itself, then cultural life will flourish, affecting the other branches of human life as a whole.

Having just discussed what form the proletarian demands for the termination of the wage relationship need to take, we can now point to the true nature of the question of capital. Many people today speak of the spirit, of that spirit which, in recent centuries, has become a shadow, an ideology. It is not possible to get anything out of this spirit that will sustain souls. This spirit, this cultural life, has also become, to a great extent, powerless to enter into immediate practical life. Therefore, Karl Marx found nothing other than economic life that still guaranteed him any realities. He said: Fundamentally, the human being can experience that his thinking certainly has meaning — that his thinking can really reach reality. But this was only applied to economic life. Cultural life must be based on facts and utilised in practical life. That is what makes these matters so tremendously serious. Then this cultural life will not be affected by those abstractions, which are today our greatest deep-rooted social evil. Cultural life will function on a concrete basis.

Let us look at this cultural life again from a specific point of view. We see how within cultural life, ethical obligations have been constructed based on specific philosophical ideas. Ethics of love for one's neighbour, of the divine or moral order of the world. About what are these ethics? They speak much of the necessary love of one's neighbour, of human benevolence, of human goodwill, of brotherhood. Their concepts, their ideas remain abstract, shadowy; they do not penetrate immediate everyday life. Philistine — that is the word, even if it radically expresses something that is not recognised — our cultural life has become philistine. It has become untrue. It moves in abstract heights and cannot submerge itself in the immediate, practical, everyday reality. But it must submerge itself in this reality. Anti-philistine it must become. When it immerses itself in the most mundane needs of life when the spirit confirms that it is possible to intervene in the most immediate, I would like to say, the most everyday actions of the human being. Only then will it be possible for the spirit's potency to show itself in social life. Then it will become apparent that resolving the problem of cultural life will simultaneously solve the question of capitalism.

Indeed, in abstract terms, there is much to be said for the fact that private capital has consigned modern human life to decay and economic war and that a change must take place. One can say nothing else at first but: private property must cease. One must be as honest as possible about this demand. It is necessary to state, precisely from a more profound social impulse, that nothing specific can be achieved by transforming private property into common property. On the contrary, barren bureaucratism would replace barren capitalism. The factory and the counting-house would replace the throne and the altar. Well, whether the conditions would be better is still doubtful. But, nevertheless, it is crucial that what truly lives in the subconscious of the proletariat should become apparent, namely that the management of capital, through the entanglement with the individual human abilities, intervenes in a particular way in the economic process. Not the egoism of the individual, but the general public should be served. In this field, the proletariat feels a fundamental national-economic principle, which, perhaps precisely because it is so significant and borrowed from practical life, has never been emphasised by the more recent national economists.

In ethics, altruism and egoism are regarded as opposites. Altruism is considered beautiful, egoism extraordinarily ugly. One does not consider the following: observing ordinary economic life within the modern social organisation, one notices the old primitive economy has been replaced by an economy based on the division of labour. The fact is that the more advanced the division of labour, the less the individual human being can work for himself within the national economy. In saying this, I am expressing an economic principle that I have been endeavouring to popularise since 1904. Unfortunately, humanity does not want to understand this economic principle. Whether we like it or not, in a social organism in which there is a division of labour — and this is the case with every social organism of the modern civilised world — in such an economic, social organism, it is not possible to work and act in an economically egoistic way. Everyone must share the work delivered by the individual. And all that which the individual accumulates comes to him from social capital. After replacing the natural economy with money and the further division of labour, a fundamental economic principle resulted inevitably. It obliges that a person should not work for himself, only for others.

The truth is that in a social organism, you can no more work for yourself than you can eat yourself. You will answer: If a man is a tailor and sews himself a suit, he works for himself. However, it is not valid in a social organism in which there is a division of labour. The relation he establishes within a social organism where there is a division of labour by making a shirt for himself is quite different from when he works in a primitive economy. It is impossible to present to you today, in these brief sentences, fully validated proof of my statements. It is

124

possible to produce such evidence, though, and I shall refer to these things in my book "Basic Issues of the Social Question." Thus, for example, one can provide proof that when a tailor sews a shirt today, he sews it for his fellow human beings. Today, the shirt is no longer sewn for the tailor's personal use and not produced in the egoistic sense. It is a means of production. A different characteristic arises simply because the tailor lives in a social organism based on the principle of division of labour. Underneath everything that happens, economic altruism is active.

One sins, that is to say, you put into the world what I would like to call: an actual lie when one lays a self-realising superstructure on top of this fundamental principle. Then one appropriates in a selfish way the fruits that are actually to flow to the general public in a wholesome social process. Thus, the egoism of today's economic order is nothing but a sum of lies, of sins against that which is, in reality, going on underneath the surface, namely the social law of economic altruism. And the reaction of the human proletarian soul — who feels that in the modern social organism, based on the division of labour, altruism reigns economically — to the unhealthy, mendacious egoism is expressed in the struggle against capitalism. What is today simply social ignorance in the widest circles of the leading classes of humanity must be replaced by social understanding. Then social awareness will see to it that management of capital is transferable. Care must be taken that the capital administration is always given to someone with the required individual abilities for such a task. When his abilities no longer justify that he maintains this responsibility, ways and means must be found to ensure that management of the capital flows over to another who, in turn, through his personal abilities, manages this capital profitably for the common good of humanity. This will be obtained through free cultivation of the individual human faculties in the spiritual organism: that there will be a circulation of capital. Today, there is a similar regulation for something regarded as the most wretched property of modern economy, namely intellectual property. Concerning intellectual property, people admit that one needs the social order; Even if it is based on individual abilities, spiritual achievement cannot be accomplished without the social order.

We always owe our achievements to social impulses. We are obliged to return the profit to the social sphere. Therefore, it is justified that what a person produces intellectually should become common property after his death. Similarly, even if the timespan must be different, ownership is only justifiable for the individual human being, as long as he can claim the right to exploit it through his abilities. When he can no longer actively engage his individual faculties, ways and means must be found to employ another person to administer the spiritual organisation, who is in turn at the service of the community. Circulation of ownership of the means of production will take the place of the present private property. This will be an excellent solution to the capital question. People stumble in this field when they talk about the socialisation of the means of production. This socialisation of the means of production would only create bureaucracy, and in turn, the same tyranny would arise from the ranks of those who today demand it. Therefore, it will never really establish a healthy social organism. To establish a healthy social organism, circulation of the capital between those capable of carrying out such a task is essential. The proper circulation of money or means of production means that it will be administered in the best interest of all over time.

I can only hint at this. It will be further elaborated in my book "Basic Issues of the Social Question." But you can see that cultural life and its diverse branches can function in its own right this way. An independent spiritual organism would be the correct course to take in the future for economic life as well since it depends on the spiritual abilities of people. Above all, it will bring not a mere shadowy thinking, a shadowy or luxurious cultural life, but a cultural life that generates consciousness of the spirit because it penetrates everywhere into earthly life. This is something that one becomes aware of when one observes the foundation of current human development. Therefore, the old slogan should be rejected today, asking which one is justified, spirit or matter. I speak to you from the standpoint of a spiritual science, but a spiritual science for which the old argument regarding spirit and matter has become nonsensical. Instead, there is a third member of which spirit and matter are the external expressions. Suppose one enters into this third aspect, where neither spirit nor matter, but the primaeval spirituality of the world itself is recognised. In that case, we arrive at the awareness that not only one member of human society is to be given the core role, but all three members, economic life, legal or political life and cultural life, each express their own primal characteristics.

Then the tremendous practical error today, that people base everything on economic life, will be overcome. Then an abstract unity will not be injected into the state organism. Instead, economic, state and legal spheres will form a unity. I am not thinking of reinstating antiquated social standings: The teaching class, the nurturing class, and the military class. On the contrary, everything class-like will be overcome by dividing the social organism into its three members. The human being himself stands as the unifying element within these three members. The human being is in some profession, in some position. He stands in a living relationship with the other members. Out of freedom and trust, he sends his children to the schools provided by the spiritual organisation. Everyone is bound to the economic life; the life of the state and law administers everything before which all men are equal. Weak-willed theorists presume that what I have just said endangers the unity of the state. Yet what has most threatened this unity of state life in recent centuries? Precisely the abstract merging of these three members of the social organism, which are supposed to develop independently, chaotically thrown together and fused. Exactly how cultural life would flourish under this unity, that is what I have tried to show you.

Economic life, however, has developed in such a way that despite the state's continuation, fierce opposition in numerous regions of the civilised world is growing against state life. Recovery will only happen when habitual thinking in this field transforms into a healthy social

127

organism filled with life. And this can be done in no other way than structuring side by side — as it were like sovereign states standing side by side, which manage mutual affairs through delegates — the economic organism, the legal or political organism, and the spiritual organism. Many still deny this today. Someone who, like the speaker, will soon reach the sixth decade of life and throughout his entire conscious life has always directed his gaze towards the development of the proletarian movement knows how many prejudices are still piling up today against the demands of our times. — not only thinking about the proletariat but always in touch through fate —, knows what fundamentally rests in the subconsciousness of the proletarian soul: the threefold structure of the social organism.

I have seen prejudices piled up decade after decade against what I believe is the only point of view that contributes to the health of the social organism. I am not pessimistic, and I am not shocked when events occur that might frighten many. I am not one of those who would say in old age: how much has been gone through in vain! — I would like to make one personal comment at the end of my discussion this evening so that you may understand the whole spirit out of which I speak. — No, I am one of those when they look back on their lives, would say: if you could be young again would you want to live life over again? I would never say: no — but I would always say: yes! Out of an affirmation of life, I feel far removed from many of my age who, as unfortunately has to be stated for many at present, could not come to terms with the loudly speaking facts of the present day. But, on the other hand, I feel close, even if I am three times as old, to those who are young today and, to my great satisfaction, I may address today. I believe they will face times in which, although at first much suffering, much pain, much tragedy will have to be endured, there will also be the possibility to rethink quite strongly, quite intensively, and to acquire new understanding.

Therefore, I do not fear that many in this very circle will call what I have discussed today a utopia. Something quite different could be called a utopia today, and it was also lately described as a utopia here in Basel by Kurt Eisner, who recently came to a tragic end. He said in his lecture: the world with its management and the social order in which we live could not have been imagined by the boldest utopians two thousand years ago. — The present reality is the most extraordinary utopia. How strange then, when one speaks of reality demanded of the human soul, of human reason, it is perceived as utopia. Those, however, who are young today, will emerge from today's practical utopia into reality. Strength and courage, and particular goodwill towards spirituality, will create a valid social will. And from this synthesis of true social life with proletarian demands will develop that which must come for the recovery of our environment. Thus, that spiritual path to knowledge that stands in flaming signs on the social horizon may be found through today's youth. That is why I gladly and with great affection answered the call that has come to me from the students.

Can one find among those who stand on the threshold of their life the strength and courage, the robust spiritual drive, the social will? Then will, despite all that is so oppressive and destructive today, the development of humanity continue. Then that for which we may again hope for will come. Then we can expect that someone will provide the proof that human life is always worth living when based on freedom of the spirit, that the equality of all human beings which can truly establish human dignity is possible, and an economic life which operates in brotherhood beside a free spiritual life and a democratic state where equality is the principle.

Discussion

Rudolf Steiner: I will take the liberty of responding to some remarks of the honourable speakers in the discussion.

First of all, I would like to point out that I understand that the things I have said concerning the social organism cannot convince anyone in the twinkling of an eye. I wanted to give some suggestions in this lecture, which has been long enough as it is, that people could follow up somehow. I understand how extraordinarily intensely what the first speaker said about private property and the demand for the socialisation of production gripped your minds.

I want to draw your attention to one thing: today, people submit to the idea that external facts are determined and fixed, but our habits of thought are far more firmly fixed. It is not easy to let go of what we, as a human society, have long become accustomed to in our thinking, not only for decades but even for centuries. Therefore, it will not be easy to notice that the demand for the transition of private property into common property is entirely justified. Still, it cannot be implemented without overcoming another element in the process first. Nevertheless, it is ultimately possible to overcome if you genuinely take what I have said today in the most profound earnestness. What socialists today do not surmount in their habits of thought, thus, neither in their will impulses, is the concept of private property. Still, because we have become so used to the idea of property, we cannot get beyond this concept of ownership. There must be property; therefore, since it cannot be private property, one demands common property, social property, nationalisation and so on.

If you think through what I have said today, the old concept of property disappears altogether. The objects which are property today — capital, means of production — must circulate. That means there is a living organism. It will happen more and more that the manager of some particular product will be the one most able for such a task. That this is no utopia, I have shown — even if not yet exhaustively — in my soon to be published book about the social question. But it is precisely a question of breaking out of certain habits of thought which are too much a part of life today.

I meant to point out that a person can only exploit the means of production as long as their ability justifies it. You see, all science, even those branches where one does not immediately notice it, are at present entirely under the influence of natural science concepts. All social and historical science, even national economies, are run with scientific perspectives. One thing, in particular, is never noticed. And in this circle, one may perhaps address just this one thing. Today, people suffer all too much from a disease that Marx rightly called "mors immortalis"; death cannot be killed. Everything is in motion in life; only the abstraction that the human being creates in his head remains and is immobile.

And therefore, people, in this time in which abstract faculties have developed in contrast to the previous conceptual disposition, especially since the middle of the 15th century, in this new age, which is fundamentally different from all earlier ones, people often fall victim to intellectual concepts. When we look into our most elementary sciences, we discover methodological, theoretical errors. It does not lead to sound living social impulses but instead develops into thoughts of hopelessness in the social field. That is why it is difficult to come to terms with the enlivening of concepts that I strive for in today's presentations. People tend to uphold the old idea of property. One must let go of the idea of property!

And the first speaker in the debate, if he thinks through what I have indicated today, will see that in demand for the nationalisation or socialisation of the means of production, etc. nothing else must manifest, but that which through the exploitation of the means of production must benefit the general public. I do not want to discuss the present-day experiments, which will perhaps be achieved to a certain extent. It will succeed when the means of production actually circulate — when the totality does not own the means of production. The "totality," after all, is only something abstract and can only carry out something based on some majority decision. Therefore, it must freely circulate as, for example, intellectual property thirty years after a person's death. Then it can, of course, be administered by the spiritual organism. Achieving the demand for the socialisation of the means of production can still intervene in the freedom of the individual.

If what I spoke about today is implemented, there will be no waste of individual human capacities. For thirty-five years, I have always endeavoured in the field of the social question, to think things through to the end, not to pursue theories, but to find what is viable within life. If you think through what I have said today, you will see that it is possible to simply continue in the direction I have indicated at every point of the current social order. Therefore, what I have stated is the opposite of any utopia: it is something immediately practical.

It is somehow possible to bring about what I am calling for, whether one starts in Russia, where today things have progressed to a certain degree of destruction, or here in Switzerland, where the old ways continue. Even in the most diverse institutions, one can separate cultural, economic, and legal life. One has to reverse, as it were, the machine that ran everything in the last few decades. Thus, for example, can the monopoly position of individuals be restricted if the relationship of one individual to another is under the control of one limb of the social organism only, namely the constitutional state? A monopoly position cannot come about, for as I shall also show in my book, what a person receives as a manager can be determined from the outset. At the same time, that which arises through marketing either has to be put back into the enterprise or given to the general public, i.e., someone else who can administer it.

All the harm, which arise from the present stance on private property, will be eliminated in this way. However, in my arguments, one should note that my proposal will achieve the same goals others aspire to with inadequate means. That is what I would like to say in connection to the first honourable speaker. Indeed, he has made a point that is justified. You see, he was describing people who talk about the individual state as an organism in a similar sense that science defines an organism.

With this, he succumbs to a wrong way of thinking. Comparisons must be correct; When one regards the individual state as a cell, the whole organism must be the entire economic world.

The mistake in thinking impairing this truth is when people think of the spatially limited as a totality. This direction of thinking would immediately cease if one saw that one could not compare the state with an organism but with cells assembling themselves. So, without going further into this, I would like to express this truth: the whole earth has become unified regarding labour today. But this is justified in a different sense from that which I have explained. As I have said, I have not spoken theoretically but out of direct engagement with the relevant issues.

Of course, we must agree with the second speaker when he says that the love of one's neighbour must become the fundamental notion of humanity. But I would like to draw attention to one thing. I always consider it more fruitful when you discuss something rather than raising opposing points. You see, loving one's neighbour has been spoken of for two thousand years. But, nevertheless, I would ask you to consider the last four or five years! So perhaps it is a question of not just abstractly talking about neighbourly love but finding concrete ways to make this love of our neighbour possible. And here I would like to agree with the honourable speaker. You see, one of the most important, most beautiful, that is to say, most significant sayings of the Gospels, of Christ Jesus, is this: "I am with you always, even unto the end of the world." That more or less would be the correct translation. Today it is time to realise that in the most Christian sense, this is true.

We do not only have to look for Christ in the Gospels, but the Christ also who was, as it were, entombed in the Gospels. We have to look for the Christ who is alive, who walks among us. We have to listen to what the Christ proclaims anew every day. I believe that one who understands the Christ in the right way can recognise the signs of the times anew with each new age. And I think that today Christ speaks to us so that we must not stand still, not even with the morals of the past regarding loving one's neighbour, but that we must also progress towards new conceptions of life. That is what I would like to consider. I recently heard a speaker in Berne, a Catholic priest who spoke very effectively.

The man spoke very similarly to our second speaker. He also said: Neighbourly love must prevail; above all, Jesus Christ must lead the modern social movement. — I would like to say that nothing could be more self-evident than this. This gentleman — in Bern, I mean — spoke very effectively, but I remembered that I had read these remarks in my schoolbooks forty-five years ago — they remain words. That gentleman used the exact words. I had to think that, between the version in my textbook and what the man said today, there occurred the terrible catastrophe of the world war! — it is necessary today to rethink, to approach things differently from before.

Did we learn anything at all? Shall we continue in the same old rut, again and again, saying just as our forefathers used to "love your neighbour?" Despite preaching that you should love your neighbour, they could not prevent the terrible days that followed. It is not a matter of preaching neighbourly love! In various meetings, I have stated repeatedly: If there is a stove in the room, and I speak similarly, as it has now become customary for people who speak out of a bourgeois worldview about all kinds of ethical decrees, including the love of one's neighbour, then I should declare: The stove has to warm the room. But even if I speak out: Dear stove, it is your duty to keep the room warm, it is your sacred duty — and I repeat this over and over again, the room will remain cold! So, I can save myself the trouble and simply put wood in and light it. That is acting practically. Then the room will soon be warm.

Often, there is talk of forming associations in commercial life, how fraternity should prevail on a grand scale and be established; when we talk about how the social organism should be structured, we are talking about something concrete. Everything is already in there, including neighbourly love! But the mere talk of love for one's neighbour is not the kind of thing that can achieve anything in the complicated circumstances today. And when they say: Jesus Christ should be the leader — of course, he should be the leader. But what matters is not what one says but what one does. That is what matters, not merely emphatically calling: Lord! Lord! — he is already present! — but what matters is that one actually follows him.

When people object that the great spheres of life must form a unity, and one cannot quite imagine how these can be separated, then I would like to point out to you that it is nonetheless necessary to take this step forward in the field of social thinking, which unfortunately natural science for its part has not been able to take in its own domain. In my book, "Of Riddles of the Soul," I pointed out how I had been able to find out how the human organism is threefold in the course of thirty years of spiritual research. Firstly, there is the nervous-sensory organism, centred in itself and which, through the sensory organs, has a relationship with the outside world; Secondly, there is the so-called rhythmic organism, consisting of the respiratory and the heart organism. Thirdly, there is the metabolic organism.

All the activities of the human organism are contained in these three limbs, centred in themselves. Precisely because of this, they work together to form such a powerful unity that each member has its centre in itself. It is precisely through being centred in itself that living unity comes about. People tend not to think scientifically in this field; It is far from my mind to play with analogies like Schaffte or Meray, but I would like to point out that healthy thinking finds this threefold division challenging.

Concerning the social organism, we must not theorise about it but put it into practice.

I cannot see why it should be hard to imagine that a cultural organisation administers itself, so to speak, independently within itself. In turn, the constitutional state functions autonomously within itself. Lastly, the economic state independently directs itself within itself. The higher unity only really comes about in living cooperation. Whereas if one introduces a unity from the outset, be it directed towards economic life, legal life, as in this old constitutional state, or cultural life, as it was in the old theocratic institutions. These three members intervened with each other. They do not impede each other when they work together as a living unity and function autonomously; only the independence must be implemented correctly.

The other day a listener in Basel responded that he could not imagine how it was possible, that there must be justice and right in all three members. — Yes, certainly law and justice must be in all three limbs, just as the air must be in all three limbs of the human organism, altered in its materiality. Still, for this reason, it must be processed in itself by the respiratory and cardiac system, must be specially prepared in one element. This makes it particularly effective for the other sections. In this way, the proper unity comes about so that one member produces and develops what the others need in the right way. This is the basis of a living organisation. That is what humankind will have to come to terms with, for that is what matters.

That is what I have to say to the objections made regarding this division of social life. What is essential is that precisely what lies unconsciously in the proletarian demands becomes possible. But it can only be realised through a conscious social will. It is of these various possibilities that I wanted to speak to you today, as far as it was possible in this short time.

THE HUMANISTIC BASIS OF THE SOCIAL QUESTION

Bern, 14 October 1919

Sixth Lecture

Spiritual life can penetrate the social sphere. But, on the other hand, abstract science, which the modern proletarian feels as ideology, cannot penetrate social life structures. Their thoughts, their ideas are too feeble, do not penetrate, do not descend, are abstractions that remain in the conceptual-unreal. They are indeed ideologies. The spirit need not stop at ideologies. The spirit can certainly penetrate so strongly into the ideas that these become, at the same time, forces containing reality. With such ideas alone, is it possible to immerse oneself in the social realm.

When it comes to realising practical-life ideas, total untruths are ultimately less harmful than half-truths and third- and quarter-truths. Absolute falsehoods are relatively easy to refute and will hardly last long in public life. But, on the other hand, half-truths and quarter-truths are extraordinary strong temptations given the complexity of life. The impressions made on the mind will be carried through life for a long time until, perhaps through arduous struggles and suffering, one realises they are half-truths and cannot be applied to life as they are. Any person who looks at modern life unbiasedly, especially after the difficult years civilised humanity has recently gone through, will have to confess that what I have just stated pertains to what is now and has long been called the social question. A significant number of half-and quarter-truths is being thrown together from all sides in this social question.

In my book "Basic Issues of the Social Question" (GA 23), I attempted to look, apart from the half-truths and quarter-truths of the programmes, at this modern social question and how it can move forward following reality. These 'core points' are worked out further

137

here in Switzerland, for example, in the "Social Future" published by Dr Boos. Before I go into my actual task for this evening, perhaps you will allow me to make a brief, very brief, personal remark, which is nevertheless related to the topic. I am aware of its imperfections. What I tried to put forward did not originate from any given political directions. It does not advocate any given political standpoint, nor does it want to enter the contemporary political field. It arose out of a sustained observation of life. It does not intend to promote any programme or abstract social idea. On the contrary, it is part of practical life, as it presented itself to me.

Because of personal circumstances, I have had the opportunity to know all classes and categories of people of the contemporary world. I became acquainted with them in their mutual demands, in their mutual misunderstandings, in their failure to work together. When I had the opportunity to touch on subjects like today's, it was always mainly related to spiritual science. So, I may declare that what I have to tell you is not influenced by any political party. My life led me on many paths, but never to political parties. And the result of decades of social observation out of spiritual-scientific knowledge will also prevent me from ever participating in any given party programme. Suggestions for practical implementation are at issue. The fact that I must express this in what seems more or less abstract propositions is self-evident. But these abstract propositions describe life experience only and can certainly be a basis for the practical shaping of life. Let us look at social life from the point of view which does not originate in some party programme but from a practical viewpoint. Let us look at social life as it has developed for more than half a century in the civilised world as it concerns us. We shall find that the concept of social life has been fundamentally different for more than half a century among the leading classes of humanity on the one hand and the great mass of the proletarian people on the other.

I was a teacher at a workers' education school in Berlin for many years. Thus, I got to know the way the broad proletarian masses think, and not only the way they thought but their inward perceptions, how they felt and how this expresses itself in what then crystallised into the social demands of the present and the future. What emerged from my

"Basic Issues of the Social Question" is the precipitation of my observations of the social question, a reflection based on the insights I gained. What emerged as a conscious idea, as an intended party programme in the demands of the broad proletarian masses, cannot possibly help improve the social situation. I recognised that the proletarian mass succumbed disastrously to half and quarter truths. That is why someone serious and honest about the social question who worked for more than half a century in this field cannot stop at what resulted from the work of Karl Marx and his followers. As I said, out of this realisation, I wrote my "Basic Issues of the Social Question" at a point in time when one might think that such truths, such insights, could be understood and confirmed in the objective. I wrote it when years had passed since the disaster brought about by the war, the so-called world war. But, of course, I do not refer to the war's outcome; I refer to the tragedy, the terrible murder humanity suffered.

In the early spring of 1914, in Vienna, I had to state that the social progress of the modern human being resembles a disease from a spiritual-scientific point of view, a kind of ulceration that could soon erupt horribly. I wrote this book when the stream of programmed Marxism was supposed to lead to a practical result in Russia. The dreadful failure of Marxism in Russia could have been seen as the first confirmation of the ideas expressed in the "Basic Issues of the Social Question." Since then, further proof has manifested. I need only refer to the failure of the Hungarian revolution, which crushed so much hope. Whoever is aware of the circumstances know that this German revolution is a terrible experiment in world history, showing without parallel the incapacity of the ideas produced during the 19th century in many social circles to create any practical organisation of the social sphere. Let us look at the impulses from so-called Marxism, founded by Karl Marx and Engels, as the modern proletariat understands them. It is genuinely not mere theory but lives in the feelings and sentiments of the masses. Marxism was the first to create in wide circles of the proletarian population what one might call disbelief in a spiritual world. More important than all the rest is this disbelief in the spiritual world on the part of the proletariat.

Ideology is the word that one might encounter if one has become accustomed *to not thinking about the proletariat but feeling and living with* them. Ideology consists of the entire spiritual sphere or at least ought to include it. According to Marxism, law, customs, morality, art, science, religion, all this ultimately rises like smoke from the economy, the only actual reality consisting of the relations and interactions of economic production processes. The proletariat saw what was presented to them as the fundamental reality under the influence of the personalities mentioned above. How people do business, how they take part in economic life, how they relate to the means of production in economic life — so it is hammered into them — all derive from mere material labour. What rises in them as ideas, what grows in them as moral ideals, what religion ultimately is, what science is, what art is: all of this has no inner spiritual reality, they say, but all this is like a mirror image of the purely economic reality. And looking at where this view originated from, one must say: this view is the heritage from the world view that emerged in the last three to four centuries under the influence of the guiding circles of humanity.

Ultimately, it is not true that modern social life has come about solely due to capitalism and modern technology associated with capitalism. With the advent of modern capitalism and modern technology, a specific world view has emerged that only wants to deal with the chemical, mechanical, and physical facts, which does not want to rise to an independent grasp of spiritual life. The technical complexity of modern economic life has made it possible for everything to be, as it were, flooded by the influences and impulses of economic life. The way current economic life was established out of technology, and in turn technology out of contemporary science, resulted in a world view that is purely scientifically oriented, a world view that consists merely in ideas, in concepts, that refers to the external mechanical, chemical, physical life. Modern life was powerless to grasp any other ideas or worldviews than those related to the launching of economic life and technical enterprises on the whole. No other thoughts were possible. Modern thinking could grasp the external mechanical processes and activate them in practical life. Through science, one could understand chemistry and physics. But from these concepts, one thing was left out, which is closest to the human being, namely the human being himself. One only understood human beings composed of material substances with mechanical, physical and chemical forces. But since the human being is also spirit and soul, he was not in truth understood. This worldview excluded the thought-world of humanity. Therefore, no one could adequately explain scientifically how physical processes come into being. No one could tell the contemporary human being how mental processes arise.

What is the human being in his innermost being? You see, the leading circles hung onto the heritage handed down traditionally from religion, art, old world views, and ancient customs. That is what filled the souls of the prominent contemporary circles. With the scientific worldview, what flowed as science into technology and further into the economy was experienced as meaningful. And so, a double current arose in the inner life of the soul: the one current far distant from his daily life, from religious questions, far from what forms moral principles, art and particular world views, far from inner life. Just ask yourself, how far away, for example, the modern businessman, merchant, industrialist, or civil servant, is from what he feels and thinks as a spiritual human being. Think how far removed his aesthetic feelings are from his practices in daily life, as expressed in his accounts and bookkeeping.

Two very different currents of life arose. As an inheritance from ancient times, the spiritual current cannot penetrate outer life. In the outward practice of life, the fortuities of everyday life are felt. Consequently, the inclination arises to regard the religious, spiritual-moral, and artistic life as hovering above practical life. It was the only way to retain any content of the soul. Next to inner spirituality — alien to life — ran outer practical life. The proletarian, called away from the old crafts, placed at the abstract machine — which has nothing whatsoever to do with what lives in humanity — could only develop his feelings and sensations while standing at the machine. He could not take over the old traditions, customs, laws, art, religion, and worldview wherein the leading classes lived despite the modern soulless and spiritless technical economy. The labourer was left with that which emerged from this economy. And so, he took over a worldview his

141

leaders formed for him: a worldview that is spiritless, soulless, an ideology. An ideology can be represented theoretically. A rule can be invented. With an ideology, one can even appear very clever. But you cannot live with an ideology because it hollows the soul out. The soul of the human being can only truly live if he does not believe his thoughts to be unreal, but if he can be conscious of what lives in them, connected with something alive and authentic — with a real spiritual world.

And so, there is much said in the socialist programme; It is unnecessary to consider this because what penetrates the consciousness is very different from what lives in people's souls in reality. That which genuinely lives in the souls of the broad mass of the educated population today is soul desolation. It proves that the modern worldview can be thought of but not lived. Here you have the first part of the social question. I know very well how many people, from their point of view, from their own understanding, say: "You are talking to us about the social question as a spiritual question. We are concerned with the unequal social conditions of the world. We are concerned that bread should be distributed equally among people." — Yes, but that is a superficial view that can only be held by those who don't penetrate the surface of things. The social question lives in the sensibilities, in the subconscious life of the modern proletariat. Try as much as you might to satisfy the purely material needs of this proletariat, if you conceivably could — I can assure you, you won't be able to –: The social question will have to arise in a new form. It will not be successful as long as intellectual life has the kind of relationship with the proletarian soul I have just described. For people believe that it comes merely from material interests. But, in reality, it comes from the hollowing out of the soul, from a life without content. Therefore, we must regard it as the underlying basis of one aspect of the social sentiments of the broader aspirations of the proletariat.

The second reveals itself when one has learned not to think and feel about the proletariat but actually to think and feel with them. Then, finally, one learns to recognise what it means for the modern proletarian to realise again and again, as is taught by Marxism: he is standing at the machine, working, and he receives wages for his work.

One pays for his labour, just as one pays for goods on the commodity market. The modern proletarian feels that human labour-power is not a commodity, that work should not be sold and bought on the market like a commodity! From this arises for him what he calls his class consciousness. He does not want human labour-power to be a commodity; he feels that his labour provides more than merely what is justified by economic life: the ruling classes he considers as capitalists who claim the surplus-value for themselves. And so, the connection between surplus-value and the inhumane buying and selling of human labour-power as a commodity is the second thing that drives the proletarian.

And the third, what is it? One realises that the leading circles are inclined to handle the social questions differently from the proletarian demands. Out of themselves, we have to admit, few people in the upper classes are really willing to go into the core issues of the social question, simply because those who occupy a superior position are always much less inclined to think about the situation than those who have to struggle to conquer a place for themselves. So, the viewpoint arose that they can expect nothing from the prominent, leading circles, that they must rely entirely on themselves to solve the social question. The overall ranks of the proletariat felt this intuitively in the subconscious rather than in clear consciousness. Thus, arose one of the most disastrous things in modern history. What emerged was based on words that are often spoken and often heard, but the more profound meaning is hardly recognised. For example, you probably know that the Communist Manifesto, which in 1848 launched the Marxist social movement, concludes with the words: "Proletarians of all countries unite."

Understandable to anyone acquainted with the modern proletarian movement that these words were spoken. This struggle is still built upon today. It forms the basis, not the momentum and impetus of an idea people want to realise in practical life. These thoughts are not based on faith in the power of the spirit but build on the external material connections of human relations, on the unspiritual. And in these words, the disbelief in the spiritual is distinguishable in the most disastrous way. The more these words take root in the soul and are assimilated thoughtlessly without realising its fateful significance for the history of the world, humanity must sail into unbelief in the spiritual. Because the human being feels connected with the material aspects of life, he believes that he belongs to a specific class; it eliminates what should move him inwardly, namely faith in the strength of the spiritual impulse. And so, we see how the proletarian calls, again and again, for something which will have a catastrophic effect. They call for the transformation of the means of production and want private ownership diverted into shared ownership and joint administration. The proletarian believe that salvation will come only when the individual no longer manages the means of production according to his interest in profit, but when the community, in which everyone can participate democratically, administers the means of production. The proletariat considers itself betrayed by the people who belong to the leading, upper circles. They realise that the top classes have no interest in and do not concern themselves with remodelling social life. They do not recognise what lives inherently in their call of many decades, that a proletarian dictatorship will simply replace old administrative and social relations with similar repressive ties.

But we must not look at these things from a party-political biased point of view. On the contrary, we must look at the situation with complete impartiality. Perhaps one can only look into the presentation of the demands in the many newspapers and books without prejudice if one also considers the counter-image. The wishes of the proletarian live in their souls consciously, whether they are correct or not. That is what matters. In genuine movements, it is not a question of the content of thoughts but about that which lives in the people's will. We must bear in mind that millions of people believe these concepts. It is not a matter of disproving issues in the abstract, one way or the other, but what is important is to come to the point where they can be applied practically in a way that is true to life. The upper classes did not have to struggle with life as a by-product of economic activities, or at least not the way the proletariat had to. They have not had to ask the same questions to fill their stomachs or find enough bread or money. The social question has not developed out of the practical interests of each individual under the influence of modern life because the leading classes have not had the same experiences as the proletarian world.

You can take it however you want, the great tempter or seducer Karl Marx or the brilliant, ground-breaking Karl Marx, it depends on your point of view. But unfortunately, a comparable Karl Marx did not manifest for the upper circles. Therefore, the impression is that the proletarian demands are justified. Of course, one can prove or disprove them, but other views are possible, which can just as well be proved or disproved, as the antithesis of these claims. You see, the proletarian interprets all ideas in art, morals, science and so on as a kind of mirror image of purely economic conditions, which he alone can survey. Human thoughts are, for him, only triggered mirror images of economic interests and production relations. You see, the proletarian interprets everything that presents itself as the human world of ideas in art, customs, science and so, like a mirror image to the purely economic conditions. Everything that people think and feel emerges from the economic relations of production — so says the proletarian. But, of course, it would be easy for the other side to prove the complete opposite with precisely the same evidence. Let us take just one example: it is child's play, to prove that this whole modern economic life, as we have it in the civilisation of the Occident and its appendage, America, that this entire human economic life, as it dominates the modern world, is a result of human thoughts, which in turn are born out of the spiritual world.

If we consider the conditions before the war, we can state that about four to five hundred million tons of coal are needed annually in the western world. For the mechanical use by industry and otherwise, these four hundred to five hundred million tons of coal is processed in modern economic life. To calculate this figure, I include all that is necessary, for instance, private property and so on. The technological power flows into everyday economic life and then becomes economic power. Therefore, one can calculate the millions of tons of coal processed in the machines. The important thing is the comparison between horsepower and human power. Suppose we now assume that

145

a human being works for about eight hours a day. In that case, a simple calculation will tell us how many people would have to work, were they to accomplish the same by human power, as is achieved by technical processing of these millions of tons of hard coal. The extraordinary thing is that the calculation shows that seven to eight hundred million people would have to work if they wanted to achieve through human labour what is accomplished with the energy that comes from these coals. You see, bringing coal energy into the economic life in this way stems solely and exclusively from the ideas that have developed under the influence of the cultural development of the Occident. A comparison with the economic conditions of the Orient shows this.

There are about, well, let us say, 250 million people who have within them the forces from whose heads sprung all the thoughts to picture this modern economic life. There are about 1250 million people left who have not participated. If one calculates the same daily working hours, you get a far lower figure than the one that indicates how much is produced by coal mining and coal processing in the mechanical field. But this only means that human thinking specifies modern economic life. And these human thoughts have indeed not sprung from matter; they are the result of the development of Western culture. And one can very well prove that through these concepts, through this way of calculating, the human forces of another 700 to 800 million are added to our 1500 million people on earth. So that in truth we are assuming that not only 1500 million, but more than 2,000 million people work. One can easily see that the social question has arisen because of the character of this modern economic life that sprung from the contemporary mind. The creator of economic life is the current spiritual disposition and by no means an ideology.

On the one hand, there is the proletarian concept; on the other hand, the usual opposing view can be proven just as well. In the same way, as one can calculate how many people work to generate surplus value in Marxist fashion, it can be proven scientifically that out of everything that the modern economy derives from the ideas of the leading circles, wages can be calculated. But this did not happen, and I am convinced that it was out of sheer carelessness. What I am about to tell you is truly not something abstractly invented. On the contrary, just as I have proved in the case of coal mining, you can ascertain from the facts of economic life that the opposite of what Marx proved, only in a limited way, is valid for surplus-value. Let's consider the structure that modern technology has imposed on economic life. First, we must recognise that what modern technology has inflicted on economic life originates from human thought. These ideas, in turn, have a spiritual source. A particular concentration of the means of production is necessary simply because of the advanced technology and must be engaged with and administered by individuals.

One can wonder what will happen when, contrary to modern economics and production relationships, where the means of production are in the hands of individuals, the surplus-value is to be administered collectively. Just see what comes of it! Indeed, one can abstractly assume what the leading classes have achieved so far, in ideas and structure of the modern economy, can be taken from them and administered by the community. But suppose one does not look at things out of sentimentality or emotionally but observes the dynamics of life without bias. In that case, a troubling possibility for the future of humanity could occur, similar to the situation the Japanese found themselves in in the mid-seventies of the last century when they took over the first warships from the English. The English offered them instructors for these warships, but they sent the English instructors away and wanted to manage on their own out of national pride. Then a stunning spectacle was seen from the shore, as the gunboats went round and round in circles and could not move forward, for the Japanese had not learned how to manage the boats. They did not know how to close and open the valve that lets out the excessive steam. And so, they could do nothing but wait until there was no steam left. When one looks at current social behaviour, one must fear what will unfold. The individual leaders of the leading circles handle things out of expertise, albeit with damage. Should this be taken over by those who theoretically judge and decide democratically what to produce, how to administer things technically, what can one expect to happen?

These are all things that do not depend on party programmes, derived from a party template but manifest to those who look at life in

147

a practical and unbiased way, who has the will to approach life practically and impartially. The first thing that will happen is what I had to draw attention to in my "Basic Issues of the Social Question" (GA23). That which is needed above all things for humanity in addition to the knowledge of nature, the creator of modern technology and thus, of contemporary economic life, is genuine knowledge of the human being. Yet, you hear from many quarters about the problematic worldview attached to the monumental building currently built in Dornach, called a "School of Spiritual Science." You would do well if you were to assume from the outset the hypothesis that what I call anthroposophical spiritual science is the exact opposite of what is usually said by those who do not know it. Spiritual science wants to add to science the spiritual basis for modern economics, namely the fundamental knowledge of the human being. Therefore, spiritual science is also called anthroposophy, human wisdom. Modern natural science quite rightly does not concern itself with the human being.

Regarding its knowledge of nature and of all that connects with mechanical, chemical, physical, technical life and economy, it leaves the human being, as it were, in the background as a spectator. But this is the fatal point. People apply natural science also to social concepts; one supposes one can penetrate social life with concepts beneficial to natural science, which has elevated natural science to a high plane. But to form authentic social ideas, the human being must dive into his inner being. There must be genuine consciousness of the human being. It is this consciousness that spiritual science wants to add to merely scientific thinking and, dependent thereon, authentic social inspiration. Spiritual science wants — which is why it is uncomfortable for so many people — to penetrate deeper into the human being than is possible with anatomy, physiology, and biology, with which one merely penetrates the outer aspect of the human being. Instead, spiritual science wants to penetrate those depths of human nature where not mere thoughts, but realities take shape, facts equally valid as are those of outer life and nature.

On the one hand, spiritual science truly wants to rise to spiritual insight and knowledge of the spiritual. But, on the other hand, it does not want to avoid practical everyday life. For spiritual science, it is

148

inconceivable that such a duality lives in the human consciousness as I have described for the modern merchant, astronomer or civil servant, who have their segregated religious, aesthetic life, which hovers above everyday life. Such a life is seemingly very spiritual. In truth, however, it is barren, and therefore it has resulted in disbelief. Consequently, the broad masses cannot expect anything socially beneficial from spiritual life.

There have been thoughtful and honest personalities who were honestly inclined to delve into social life — who regard spiritual life as basically utopian. Fourier and similar spirits drew up such beautiful programmes for structuring social life. But out of which configuration of thought and state of mind did all these social and socialist ideas arise? They arose from a worldview as alien to life as religious life is to the merchant in the account book. It is self-evident that beautiful ideas that are genuinely meant and well-intentioned can emerge, but these ideas do not penetrate real practical life. Spiritual science wants to ascend to the highest heights of the spirit. When descending into the deepest interior of the human being, thoughts are not alien to life but penetrate reality. While reaching the highest spiritual heights, they should simultaneously comprehend how the account book reveals the relationship of the employer to the employee. Weak and powerless were the thoughts of that spiritual life that has dominated human souls in the last three or four centuries. These thoughts were beautiful aesthetic, religious, scientific, and worldly, but they were not thoughts that reached reality or recognised anything valid for human social life.

Take anything like, say, a modern moral code, a code of ethics, see what it states about humanity, goodness, benevolence, charity. Current ethics and ideas about brotherhood are alien to human life. They do not produce answers for practical life, any more than modern philosophy, which lives in abstract concepts, as does contemporary intellectual life in general. Only spiritual science can, in fact, reach down into what philosophy and science generally bring to light these days. Please read about this in my numerous books on this subject. You will find that spiritual science has nothing in common with abstractions passed off as philosophical worldviews and the like. Instead, you will see that spiritual science must observe the human

149

spirit to find the underlying knowledge of his being. The human being is the most spiritual of all beings. Therefore, he must establish an understanding that ascends to the highest height of the spirit and, at the same time, descends into immediate practical life. If one only penetrates deep enough, cognition reveals a unity, not a duality.

But this requires a specific social structure. And I tried to hint at this social structure, to outline it sketchily at least, in my "Basic Issues of the Social Question." I tried to prove how it is essential that the administration of spiritual life be detached from economic life and from the life of the state, to which the administration of justice must be left; the spiritual life must be detached from all political and economic life. While economic life dictates spiritual life, spiritual life can't develop freely. As long as the economically powerful can advance their specific viewpoint concerning intellectual and spiritual education, an inner connection remains between spiritual life and economic life. Spiritual life thus, is effectively unfree. The development of this innermost human characteristic must bring about complete freedom. He who understands spiritual life knows that it can only develop on an absolutely free basis. Spiritual life is a product of the inner human being. Therefore, cultivating inner human life must happen in complete freedom. Schools and educational institutes must be managed independently with an independent administration, independent of economics and the state, free from political and legal life. It makes all the difference when the teacher of the lowest school class does not need to orientate himself according to what is supplied by economic life and does not have to be guided by the state's requirements for education. He must be allowed to follow spiritual impulses in education and teach corresponding to what he recognises as the spiritual requirements of the times.

If I were to characterise concretely, I would have to say: In the future, the entire spiritual life, including teaching and education, must be organised in such a way that those who teach, who educate, from the lowest to the highest levels, can administer the spiritual stream in which they are active because spiritual life forms an independent member of the social organism. It manages itself in a section of its own organism. If this is the case, then one will not experience that which so powerfully confronts one's soul in the following situation.

In Stuttgart, we have now tried through our friend Emil Molt's active involvement to found a school, which, at least in its inner spiritual constitution, is structured in the spirit just characterised. The teachers first needed to prepare themselves to let the school function as far as possible in a completely free spiritual life. We had to commence this way because many new directions are tried today. What we intend here can be achieved only when approached with an instinct for practical life, not theoretical ideas and the like.

It is an eight-grade primary school with a free teaching structure. It should achieve the same external teaching as the public elementary schools, the ordinary vocational schools and grammar schools up to the age of fourteen or fifteen. It teaches boys and girls at the same time. The aim is to assist the individual pupil in developing completely free. The individuality will be socially shaped not from an economic standpoint or the state's templates. But then you will see that you receive the regulations on what you must teach from grade to grade, already stating what the teacher must instruct at every stage. For someone who can think straight and contemplate life independently, it is clear that teaching and education must not be democratically determined day by day, hour by hour. That would be pedagogical short-sightedness. Instead, the educator must work with his professional and technical skills from out of spiritual life. It needs the expertise of those who can administer the spiritual sphere. People must deal with these things practically. Many things that appear practical today and cannot be imagined any other way turn out not to be what it seems to be if one looks at it impartially, following the inner laws of human development. Apart from freeing spiritual life with its specific administration, something else must also happen. I can only sketch this in short today. The independent state with the rule of law, that is, the separate state-political element has presently penetrated on the one hand spiritual life and, on the other hand, economic life. In the last centuries, what developed as legal life consisted mainly of economic life. The states' political constitutions drew them into this terrible war due to economic reasons.

To a great extent, the state was also the economic playing field. This situation would rise to the highest peak of impossibility if the Marxist programme led to a vast cooperative emerging from the state and the means of production commonly administered. There would not be anything new created, but that which has already caused substantial damage would increase to monstrous proportions. An independent legal life and the conception of law can only arise from an unfettered consciousness of rights. There must develop an independent state and legal field within the social organism that encompass all mature people capable of judgement. Spiritual life can never be administered democratically; expertise and specialist knowledge of the authoritative individual must oversee it. The administration of economic life cannot have a democratic basis either. The economic sphere itself must form the foundation. Economic life cannot be administered democratically. The person who runs his business in a specific field must be well-established and spiritually mature to manage the organisation. The responsible person must be well acquainted with the internal structures and act out of the economic sphere. It undermines decisions on what needs to be done in the factories or businesses when decisions are made democratically. Choosing what to do can only be fruitful after exploring the available possibilities with skilled expertise. Then he delivers the merchandise for the community with professional competence according to his abilities. However, he is not the only deciding factor; there remains the fact that every mature individual represents the democratic element, and there should be present a relationship from person to person.

In present-day socialist circles, the following is constantly stressed: The worker is separated from his product. He works on a product he barely understands or is only aware of a portion of that product. That is, without a doubt, true. The product is transferred to the market while he, as a human being, is in no way connected to it. On the contrary, he stays disconnected from what he produces without realising what he helps provide. But this is only the case as long as we do not have an independent social limb, alongside the economic life, in which the individual is part of a community of equals. This separate social sphere, where all rights are decided, this actual political life, is the content of state life. Here democracy can genuinely develop. But we need to cultivate this in practical terms. We cannot assert those who, in any particular economic area, have achieved worthwhile goals will also do outstanding work in the field of law, and therefore law questions can best be answered by them. No, this is not the case because the human being can only develop and become capable of judgment when he acquires actual expertise. Therefore, the judicial life must not be chaotically connected with economic life but must stand next to it. And the human being must establish a concrete relationship with other human beings based on the law.

He must develop an interest in the other people with whom he lives in the sphere of economics, where economic life comprises needs that have to be satisfied. Then, on the ground of the rights of the other, every human being will realise that all people are members of humanity. You participate in something because you belong. Nothing else determines your relationship with others. You are a part of humanity; you now learn to recognise yourself as a member of the state built on human equality, on democracy. This state becomes a reality for you. It becomes a reality by dealing first and foremost with labour laws. Labour laws will no longer be established within economic life. No longer will the worker be dependent on the economic power of the one whom he works for or with whom he undertakes the work. Instead, his rights will be established in a field where everyone is equal.

And other conditions will have to be settled on the appropriate ground. I can only characterise all this in general terms. You will find more details in my "Basic Issues of the Social Question" (GA23). Then economic life, the genuine, unified economic life, remains. Commercial life will differ from contemporary situations; consumers and producers will form associations. These associations will have to determine needs and prices and the value of goods transformed by human labour into commodities. Economic life will not decide the worth of human endeavour; that will be the task of legal life. Based on economic life, the corporations will only have to concern themselves with just prices. Expertise and professionalism will establish prices; for what he produces, the individual receives as much of corresponding goods as serves his needs until he has produced the equivalent of what

153

he exchanges for his labour. I will soon arrive at the primary status of economic life; if I state it like this, it seems a little paradoxical, but nevertheless, it defines the basic concepts.

Above all, just prices must be established. No joint administration, or common administrative ownership, will achieve social equilibrium. Only by determining the relative value of the commodity through human reason flowing out of the actual management of economic life can the just relations be determined. Dryly, paradoxically and trivially expressed: if I made a pair of boots today, this pair of boots must cost so much that I can acquire goods for making another pair of boots, including all that which is necessary for the unemployed, the sick, the invalids, and so on. These are the primal elements of economic life. The above can indeed be achieved when economic life is entirely detached from the other two social limbs: independent spiritual and legal life. As I said, I could only briefly sketch these things out for you, but they have been developed from actual practical life, from a conception of life as it should be. That was why, while that terrible war raged, I advised many people: we can only counter this frenzy by ideas that have grown on a spiritual basis. Therefore, we have the choice, I said, to speak now of such human concepts as a starting point for the betterment of the earth, or we will experience cataclysms and social revolutions.

It was not easy to accept reason. So came the revolution. But these revolutions have their peculiarities. Revolutions do happen in the world. One of the greatest revolutions was the one that took place with the advent of Christianity. What kind of revolution was that? It was a spiritual revolution. The conditions of spiritual life were transformed. Something new must arise through a metamorphosis in the development of humanity, and it can only manifest out of spiritual impulses. The Christian revolution had a spiritual nature. The legal life and economic life were a consequence of the spiritual upheaval. Therefore, this upheaval was significant. Those familiar with the development of Christianity know how profound the spiritual turmoil brought about by Christianity was. But let us now consider an upheaval of legal and political relations: We find such disruptions in the French Revolution or the continental revolution of 1848. Study these revolutions, and you will discover: they achieved some goals and altered some matters. They substituted some issues for the old, but many demands were not addressed and left unsolved. Some earlier requirements were resolved, but three elements of human life remained. One can follow the upheavals in the spiritual, political and legal spheres; the French Revolution and the Revolution of 1848 stemmed from the Christian transformation. Currently, they want a revolution in the economic sphere. The economic playing field can mechanise itself but cannot transform itself. Anyone familiar with historical connections in the world knows that the spirit fertilises all life. When legal relations are transformed, something spiritual remains in social relationships.

It is an illusion that the transformation of outer circumstances can happen out of itself. In present-day Russia, a world-historical law takes effect. It occurs whenever there is a purely economic revolution. Such an economic revolution must be the gravedigger of modern civilisation unless it takes up again something genuinely spiritual. Lenin and Trotsky actually are the last to consistently build on what has lived for decades in the Darwinism of the masses. Of course, one could consider the ideas as mere economic ideas. Still, attempting to apply them practically, at the very moment when one wants to introduce it into life, one becomes the gravedigger of civilisation. And under the influence of such ideas, only death could spread in the European East. We have to realise that we need something quite different in our time: a renewal of spiritual life.

I wanted to emphasise particularly strongly today that we need to develop a free spiritual life as an independent limb of the social organism based on the spirit. Out of this spirit, a real social future will emerge. No one must expect something to come from a new revolution. People want an economic revolution. An economic revolution can only destroy; it cannot build. Today the world is ripe for a new spirituality. That is what an impartial person ought to declare. He does not rely on party demands or programmes but looks at life objectively and honestly. What people call the social question is usually poorly understood. The enlightenment of the broad masses is necessary for human development — those who can have to enlighten

155

the general masses through their inherited education. Otherwise, passions define the demands. It prevents them from seeing what has to happen in the interest of humanity and the social future. In my "Basic Issues of the Social Question" (GA23), what I attempted does not follow any party-political templates. On the contrary, it observes and recognises humanity's world-historical development. Whoever wants to start from commonly shared means of production is ignorant of this development.

Even if it were possible to introduce common ownership of the means of production, it would not be feasible as it would destroy all individual initiatives. Moreover, it would not pass down to the next generation even if they were to introduce it for the present one. And from the protest of the new generation, the same demands would again arise. Therefore, not ideas from a one-sided reality but only those drawn from the outset from the fullness of life will suffice today. And the images I have presented to you of the threefold structure of the social organism also consider the development over time, not merely of the people presently occupying the same space. Therefore, this approach can much better influence spiritual life in its most essential areas –schooling and education, and the social organism — providing the appropriate power to the social organism. Today you hear again and again from the socialist side: Let us establish a standard distribution of the means of production, introduce compulsory labour, and so on, then we will affect the social structures so that people will work of their own accord. Well, it will achieve nothing. Humanity will only be willing and eager to work if spiritual life kindles the individual faculties of people, which can only happen if we educate the human being taking account of his complete individuality. The same goes for the threefold structure of the social organism. It underlies the practical most comprehensively; it can only be functional because it is based on spiritual science, where nature must be recognised, and the human being must consciously recognise himself in his actual being.

In conclusion, I would only like to emphasise that what you can read in detail about the future organisation of capital, labour and economy and so on, in my "Basic Issues of the Social Question" (GA23) and elaborated there is, as I have already said, still a feeble attempt at this time. It is not some contrived programme but derived from practical life, so it must therefore be a feeble attempt. Those who say: one cannot understand "Basic Issues of the Social Question" simply lacks the instinct for the reality that is necessary today if one genuinely sees the practical things in their fundamental truth. It is not a question of merely professing a social-scientific idea, but it is a question of affirming those attainable ideas instinctively. Then, when one attempts to realise such ideas, one will not claim that they are perfect from the beginning,

One must emphasise: the aim is to introduce the movement for the threefold social organism. How it will work exactly, in the end, will be revealed when transformed and put into practice. Therefore, I have often mentioned that it is possible not one stone may remain upon another of the specific statements I make. But it will stimulate the practical application of the underlying principles; perhaps something entirely different will emerge, but it will work. That is what matters, not programmes, not preconceived ideas. No matter how clever such ideas are or how long they were applied, one must work towards the reality of practical life! To work out of life itself! Not working randomly, but from the great, all-encompassing ideas out of which all great constructs, including social ones, have arisen. Hopefully, that is how everyone will think about such questions.

I want to use a comparison to express what I mean. Recently, someone in a studio where one usually only deals with sculptural work created a model of a chair. On the one hand, this chair had to satisfy our sense of beauty, as is our intention for the Dornach building; but on the other hand, it should be as cheap as possible. The least costly, in addition to the appropriate design, is the aim. So, we had made a model. When we handed this model to the person who had to make the chair, we said to ourselves: This is the model, but now the practical design begins, and possibly what comes out, in the end, will be quite different from the model. But it will be effective because we planned to create a functional model. I want the book "Basic Issues of the Social Question" to be seen in this way. Everything you will find there are suggestions on a future social structure. For example, for Switzerland's social future, this book and our other ideas are only intended to be a kind of model; But it should be a practically conceived model. If one understands it in this sense, it will be practically applicable. Perhaps it will look quite different, but it will only be effective if practically applied out of the primary impulse.

A tripartite social organism could, I think, most easily be realised — forgive me for expressing this here, especially those who are not entirely used to these ideas. I want to say it nevertheless — here in this country, which is rightly proud of its old democracy, it could work exceptionally well. Because the democratic element works well here, it is easier to discover how spiritual and economic life can be appropriately disentangled. — As a further development, the idea of Threefolding arises. If one is serious about these ideas, especially if one lives in a democratic community, it will be easier to understand what is necessary for the Threefolding of the social organism to come about. The threefold structure of the social organism is attacked from the left and the right, from all sides. Nevertheless, the ideas I propose on Threefolding are needed if one is serious and honest about the social question. Unfortunately, however, it has come to pass that I am personally attacked in the most foul-mouthed manner by the very leaders of the socialist parties of all shades.

But what is at stake is that three great ideas, genuinely and honestly meant, have arisen. One concept is liberalism, the other is democracy, and the third is socialism. Naturally, if one sincerely believes in these three ideas, one must not mix them or let one be overshadowed by the other two. One must realise: the independent spiritual life must radiate into the whole organism. In free human development, the liberal element must prevail. All men are equal before the law in the political state. That is the democratic element. And the fraternal element must prevail in economic life. The valid basis of the social structure is at stake. One should not disavow the blessings of the more recent development of humanity, namely liberalism, democracy, socialism. We should not fight it one-sidedly or accept it blindly; one should discover how liberalism radiates within independent spiritual life across the other social spheres. In the actual constitutional state, democracy, which in turn illuminates all other social aspects of life, must prevail; in that economic life, concerned only with the production, circulation and consumption of goods and the determination of just prices, socialism belongs and, in turn, permeates everything. Then, when one sees through this, one realises that total errors are less harmful than half-truths or quarter-truths because one sees through them more quickly.

However, the flooding in of quarter, third truths often occurs in contemporary social movements. And by adhering to what is a partial truth, one erroneously believes one comprehends life in general. But the whole of life is not gripped until there is a living interface with the truth. Universal truth will not reveal itself in abstract ideas or realities. It can only be grasped in the living interchange of ideas. Then, the complete truth necessary for social life will emerge out of the half and quarter truths. And one will realise that it needs less work to combat total errors than correcting half and quarter truths. I wanted to emphasise this today, especially regarding the fundamental necessities of the social question in humanity's present and immediate future.

* * *

Dr Roman Boos points out that here in Switzerland, too, the danger in the economic field is immense, and creative efforts, which Dr Steiner has only been able to hint at in his remarks today, are vital. (A discussion does not seem to have taken place).

Concluding remarks on the discussion

Rudolf Steiner:

> My concluding words will be very brief. First, I want to emphasise that some might remark I spoke a great deal about the three limbs of the social organism. But it is not what matters to those who want social reform. For them, the social question is, above all, an economic question. Note the whole attitude of both the lecture and the impulse for the Threefolding of the social organism. You can see it at least in part: It does not present a ready-made

programme, but the basic idea that the social organism itself, that is, human social life, should be structured in a certain way. So, there are separate administrations for economic, democratic, political or legal life and an independent administration for spiritual life.

Now, of course, one can easily say: You are separating the whole of human society, which must be a unity, into three areas. But precisely through the independent administration of the three areas, the correct union of these fields becomes possible. It is not a question of renewing, as some have believed, the pre-Christian Platonic worldview of a learned class, a soldiering class and the class that provides nourishment. No, at that time, humanity was divided into three classes; so that the first belonged to one, the other the second, the third to the third class. We should avoid dividing humanity into categories instead of being deemed a unity. Therefore, not humanity as such, but a structuring of human life is the intention. Anyone who stands in the world is involved in all three regions in a certain way. He occupies a position in spiritual life in so far as he takes part in spiritual life in one way or another. He stands within all matters of law, as does every mature human being, either directly by some referendum or indirectly by representation or something similar. Furthermore, he has credit through knowledge or expertise in a particular economic field, in which he is incorporated by association. The whole of economic life is structured in itself.

Various objections show how little people understand the basic idea. For example, in one journal, there appeared a lengthy discussion of the Threefolding of the social organism, saying: Yes, he wants to replace one parliament by three — a spiritual parliament, a legal parliament and an economic parliament — what matters is that only what every human being is capable of judging can be decided in a democratic parliament, specialist knowledge is not required, technical and professional education should not be taken into account. Well, there is no separate parliament in the spheres of spiritual life and economical life; it is just the other way around. It is a question of applying parliamentary issues honestly by limiting them to the appropriate area. One can thus see that the very nerve of the matter has in reality been little understood to this day. But if one realises the root of the issue, one will understand how these ideas are envisioned out of practical reality. Anyone who believes in any programme, be it ever so beautifully devised, to structure economic life in a particular way, may think himself very clever, does not think realistically.

But the one who speaks out of practical life is the person who says: Humankind must administer the social organism from three areas; then, a healthy social structure will come about. People will experience this through the threefold social system. What is essential is not that one says: we must solve a social question. Today we cannot yet solve it, but tomorrow it will become possible — one person says it one way, another the other way, but that's the way a lot of people think. No, such ideas are entirely unrealistic. That is the point: The social question has come to the surface for humanity; we must create a social structure that solves the problem. However, it is a question that will keep coming up continually. Today the conditions manifest in this specific way; we must solve these problems at this time, one way or another, not tomorrow. And if tomorrow other questions arise, then we will need to solve them again; other issues will occur, and people will have to continue solving problems from within the social structure. So, it will be an ongoing process. The solution has to be tackled from day to day. One cannot say we found the answer today and will continue to do it the same way in the future; we must keep on asking: How must we structure society in a social sense at present. Whoever does not consider the provisional characteristic inherent to human issues does not understand the actual reality.

People assume they can think today, but they think most unrealistically. They believe, for example, that social life will acquire a social structure through a transformation of economic life. That would be like assuming that the individual human organism obtains its form by what it eats and drinks. No, the human organism has an inner regulating faculty. It undergoes a specific transformation at the age of the change of teeth, and at the age of sexual maturity, it undergoes another transformation. Transformation processes occur from within the human organism, but new ideas also arise in the course of historical development. Today this development has reached a point at which we must tackle the Threefolding of the social organism!

In conclusion, I want to say the following to show you how things are meant. You see, anyone who follows my writings will know that I am not in the habit of mocking anyone when I experience something like this. I know best of all how worthy of consideration is that which even the simplest mind can put forward. But let us take the following. In a discussion, someone countered — where people think they are particularly revolutionary, they often respond according to a specific template. Therefore, I do not need to elaborate on the content — but this response boiled down to something like this. 'Look, ladies and gentlemen, we do not want to — he was speaking from the standpoint of the most radical slogan creators of the Socialist Party — we certainly don't want to abolish intellectual activity, we want it to continue to exist. For you see', he said, 'I am a shoemaker, I know quite well that I cannot do the work of an official functionary; so, we have to hire people who can carry out such functions when we take on leadership.' — A glorious thought! The good man believed that he could not be an official functionary, but he could be a minister and decide on the structure of the state. He quite naturally assumes this. But, unfortunately, these kinds of simple fallacies nowadays occur everywhere, underlying everything. It demonstrates such approaches cannot lead to anything fruitful.

I have recently heard the following from another side. Someone wrote an article that essentially condemned the whole structure of the threefold social organism to the ground. In one of my lectures a few weeks ago, an American came to me and said: 'I have read this article; it denigrates everything the way it was written. Thus, there must be something to it! And therefore, I obtained the book', that's what he said. — You see, sometimes derogatory articles have their positive effects, too. When he came to me, the man was already completely absorbed in the threefold idea. He said to me: Do you believe that this idea of Threefolding, in an absolute sense, can now apply to the entire human future? I said: No. We went through a phase of historical development, which has led to this unified state. In Austria, economic life, legal life, spiritual life, especially in the form of ethnocultural life, became wholly integrated.

I have often spoken about it. The administration in Austria in the 19th century inevitably led to the Bosnia and Herzegovina affair in the 20th century. Nothing else could possibly come of it. First of all, the annexation of Herzegovina was negotiated. Thus, a purely economic matter, namely the construction of the Saloniki railway, was accomplished. The result was chaos, in that a strictly spiritual element, namely the contrast between the Slavic and Magyar ethnic groups, was added. And out of the terrible turmoil of the peoples of the East, the three regions were being knotted together. But they are pressing towards a unified state. Now the time is ripe for separating the three limbs. Other conditions will arise in the not-too-distant future. Human affairs are alive and evolving. It is never finished. People want things to be valid once and for all, always and everywhere!

The uncomfortable thing about such ideas is that they cannot be conceived abstractly, like programmes; one can introduce a programme, then it's done. But, no, that's not how the social organism works; ideas born from the spiritual world reckon with intellectual, legal, and economic life in a tripartite system. And therefore, they can also only be valid for a particular epoch. Whoever works with such impulses is aware that they will have to replace the structure with something else at a given time. They take development seriously, seeking the answers for the needs of their age. I wanted to show a practical result. It cannot be absolute, as in the case of other programmes of the present. It emerges out of the present time in the most eminent sense. People may judge in the most diverse ways once the ideas offered are studied thoughtfully and in a living way. It is not a question of pedantically carrying out what is written on some page; reality must be utilised practically. Then none of the details of my proposed ideas might remain; no stone may be left on the other. But out of such a lively grasping, there will come into being that which can heal.

These ideas come forth out of actual practical life for practical life. No one should infer that a political program or some concept of development is meant with the threefold structure of the social organism. This Threefolding of the social organism should be received without any emotional mindset. It would like to be understood unbiasedly, as it is meant unbiasedly. Some say: Yes, this threefold structure of the social organism would work well, but it would have to come about at the very end; Before that, everything would have to come apart; we need dictatorship first. — If one thinks like that, then, in reality, one does not want the practical, but rather that which arises only from abstract demands emerging from a specific mood of soul. One does not want social Threefolding, as presented here, but merely wishes for something that seems fascinating. But if anyone seriously wants to attain something in life, they must come to view life without prejudice and with an overview of the whole.

Spiritual Science (Anthroposophy)

And The Conditions of Culture in The Present and The Future

Basel, October 20, 1919

Seventh Lecture

If you get on the streetcar here in Basel at Aeschenplatz and drive out to Dornach, then take the little way over Dornach, you will come to a hill on which rises the Goetheanum building, which is to become a School of Spiritual Science. Although, as can be noted in a pleasing manner, an extraordinarily large number of visitors have recently been coming day after day to see this building, it must be noted that if somehow in the outside world, for example in the context of newspaper articles, answers are given to the questions of what will actually be done inside this building once it is completed, these still today generally — exceptions of course taken into account — represent the opposite of the truth. All sorts of things are said about what will be done once or is already being done in this Dornach building. In any case, the answers that are given to the questioners are very far away from what the participants in the spiritual current, which is the basis of this Dornach building, actually set as their goal. For this goal arises from a careful consideration and observation of what I would like to call the cultural conditions for mankind in the present and future. And from all kinds of presuppositions, about which I will allow myself to speak this very evening, this spiritual movement, which is to find its expression in the Dornach building, is based on the conviction that today it is contained in the longings of wide circles that a complete recovery, a healthy further development of our human culture must take place from the soul of man, from that which man can grasp in his soul as his connection with the spiritual world. It is based on the conviction that, even in the face of the demands and pressures that express themselves in our social life, we must try from the spirit and the soul to find the impulses that correspond to the longings of a large number of people — and this number will become larger and larger.

Now it can be said, and this too is evident — I only want to mention it in passing — that now on Sundays and other days quite a large number of people from Basel and the surrounding area come out to see what we call our eurythmy performances in the provisional hall of our carpenter's workshop, where for the time being we have to hold these events until we can open the Goetheanum itself, and it is to be believed, It is to be believed that a large number of those who have already made the pilgrimage to Dornach for these eurythmy performances have gained the conviction that in this detail, too, an attempt is being made in a limited field to spiritualize something, to elevate something into the sphere of the spirit, which, under the influence of the materialism of the last centuries, is still being pursued today by our culture in a more or less materialistic, physiological and similar way.

This eurythmy is an art of movement of the human organism itself, which is brought out of the organization of the whole human being, the whole human being, which comprises body, soul and spirit. And apart from the fact that in this eurythmy a special new form of art is striven for, which cannot really be compared with what is often felt to be the neighbouring arts, it can also be said that underlying these endeavours towards the spirit is what I would like to call the animation of the possibilities of movement of the human organism, which in gymnastics, for example, are conceived merely in an outwardly physiological way, in a purely material way. The human being is to perform movements, and therefore this eurythmy will one day also receive a spiritual-pedagogical value. In addition to the artistic movements, the human being is to perform movements which are not merely derived from the anatomy and physiology of the human being as in gymnastics, but which are derived from that which can live in the moving human being: Spirit and soul.

Well, it is difficult not to be misunderstood when one appears before the world today with a thoroughgoing spiritual or soul current. One would like to say that misunderstandings are actually whistling out of every hole. And so, it can happen that, for example, in some places some misunderstandings concerning spiritual science itself have already been cleared away, that this spiritual science is even allowed to speak into social questions. However, we again committed the clumsiness, as we believe to be correct, but as others thought, of giving eurythmy performances at the same time in individual places where I had to speak about spiritual science and social questions. And behold, immediately the judgment asserted itself: How can a spiritual endeavour be worth anything which at the same time has dance exercises performed?

Well, I could easily add to the list of misunderstandings, which, as I said, come from all corners, because the world still often judges today as if everything that is to be done in the Dornach building is something obscure, something dark and mystical. One hears so often today, when there is talk of spiritual endeavours, that here or there, even in very many places, all kinds of mystical things are being done. That the movement which is to be connected with the Dornach building has nothing to do with such obscure mystical movements, could be taught to those who are trying to see clearly and truly in such things by the fact that the one who stands before you and speaks to you as of his cause, of the cause of this Dornach building, of this Goetheanum, can refer back to a book written as early as 1894, "The Philosophy of Freedom." And if someone reads this "Philosophy of Freedom," I think he will not get the impression that through this "Philosophy of Freedom" something of obscure mysticism, of rapture or the like is to be brought into the world. And I may say that, after all, everything that is to form the main content, the main impulse of this spiritual-scientific movement of which I have to speak, is permeated by that longing of contemporary humanity which expresses itself in the urge for such a way of life within which the individual human being can, on the one hand, fulfil his social duties, but can, on the other hand, be a free being as a single, individual human being.

By way of introduction only, I would like to point out a phenomenon which is connected with something very familiar to you. And if I take the starting point in my considerations today from a politician, then you do not believe at all that I will make it my task today even remotely to speak about the political culture of the present. I would like to speak about the cultural conditions of the present and the future in a much broader sense; but I would like to mention one characteristic that can show us how the call for freedom works its way out of the cultural aspirations and cultural ideals of the present, as it were, only in such a way that it is truly not taken deeply enough. And to take it deeply enough, to deepen that which is humanity's longing for freedom, is intimately connected with the conception that spiritual science has of the cultural conditions of the present and the future.

Those who have heard my lectures here this year and earlier, these honoured visitors, who remember how I spoke during the time in which one saw in Woodrow Wilson, one may say, a man revered by all the world, to whom one looked up, to whom one attached numerous hopes for the future, these honoured listeners will not hold it against me, if I, who in the times when this man had many followers, freely expressed my opposition from a certain point of view, if today I take as my starting point the special conception of freedom, the special call for freedom, which sounds out from the political world view of Woodrow Wilson. One must believe, after all, that the strong, otherwise, as I think, quite incomprehensible impression which Woodrow Wilson has made on the world up to now, where the matter ends, is based precisely on the fact that all program points, everything which has gone out into the world from this man, is finally based in a certain way on the impulse of human freedom. Let us see how this man worked before he became President of America, let us see what made him great as President of America. We will find that it is his conception of a possible social arrangement of human coexistence in which man can have his freedom in a democratic way. Woodrow Wilson saw how within the life of America, just in the last decades of the 19th century and in the beginning of the 20th century, those great accumulations of capitals in the hands of a few people have developed. He saw how the trusts and so on were formed. And he saw, how thereby the rule over other humans gained individual few capital-strong humans. There he started his contemplation and effectiveness. First of all, he asserted the impulse of freedom. Against the accumulation of economic-political power in the hands of a few, he demanded a complete democratization of human state life. He wanted that every single human being had the possibility to make his abilities effective in human coexistence. He did not want that those who had once established themselves in some branch of industry or commerce could have monopolies against which the legitimate abilities of the weak could not rise. He wanted the causes of what was happening in social life to be sought in every single place, even the simplest. And he often expressed this. And it is characteristic of him that he has everywhere subordinated his political endeavours to the goal of freedom.

We only have to look at his extraordinarily significant writing "The New Freedom." One would like to say that on every page one finds how what I have just said comes true. I will quote only one of his most remarkable sayings before you. He said: "There is only one way to create a free life, and that is to make sure that a free and hopeful heart beats under every garment." — I really believe that what has had such a strong effect is this call for freedom.

Well, this call for freedom always sounded into the practical-political-social effectiveness. The book "Die need Freiheit" (The New Freedom) is actually only a collection of election speeches. There is no talk of a freedom that is only philosophically speculated, there is no talk of some abstract freedom of consciousness, there is talk of a freedom that is to be realized and realized in life.

Well, such a freedom which is to be realized and realized in life, I also tried to understand it by my book "The Philosophy of Freedom" written in the beginning of the nineties of the last century. But now that I have published a new edition of this book after a long period of hesitation, I can say openly that I believe that a truly practical living out of freedom is only possible if this freedom is not sought merely in external social and political life, but if it is sought in the depth of the human soul itself. And it is in the depth of the human soul itself that freedom should be sought out through my "Philosophy of Freedom." If one stops at the surface of mere social and political life or of external social life, one will very soon see that the realization of freedom is not possible at all if one grasps it only in this way. For freedom is something which must spring from the individual human being, which cannot be there if the individual human beings are not capable of realizing it, if the individual human beings do not first pour it into the social life which they lead together. But if one wants to appreciate the whole significance of what has been suggested here for the culture of the present, then one must overlook many things that are brought about by mere phraseology in the present, and one must try for once to speak seriously and honestly and truly about many things. The call for freedom is, I would say, present throughout the entire educated world. It is there today for those who only want to hear it, for the American, for the European, for the Asian world. And the question is only this: how can the consciousness of freedom be realized out of the life of the present?

You have to take a closer look at how a man like Woodrow Wilson, who was enthusiastic about the impulse for freedom, talks about freedom today, and how others talk about freedom today. It will sound strange to you, and I must confess that I have hesitated for a long time whether I will express the truth that I have to say here in such a harsh form as I will, because such things still shock many people today, because such things are still taken far too much according to the usual phrases, far too little attention is paid to what actually stands behind these things. Read the book "The New Freedom" by Woodrow Wilson, take up how he speaks about the social conditions of America and finally about the social conditions of the present civilization in general. What do you find in it? Actually, only criticism, criticism about how this freedom is not realized within today's civilization, how one must strive to realize this freedom within today's culture and civilization. There are sharp words in this direction of criticism in the book of Woodrow Wilson "The New Freedom." And if one stops at the criticism — and there is not much other than criticism to be found in this book — and now really seriously and honestly asks oneself: How does this criticism of freedom or also social criticism of Woodrow Wilson relate to the criticism that is asserted from other sides? —, one comes to a strange result. I have endeavoured, for example, to examine Lenin's and Trotsky's critique of freedom to see how this critique of freedom and social conditions relates to the critique of Woodrow Wilson in New Freedom, and I believe that he who makes such a comparison honestly and truly can say nothing else than: With regard to the criticism of social conditions and the realization of freedom in the same today, Woodrow Wilson agrees with Lenin and Trotsky, however different the consequences they draw.

One must be able to admit such a truth, even if one finds it quite understandable that despite this criticism Woodrow Wilson naturally comes to the opposite consequences as Lenin and Trotsky. And even if one is convinced, just like the person standing before you, that Lenin and Trotsky are the gravediggers, not the new founders of a social life, that hardly anything worse could come upon mankind than if the ideas of Lenin and Trotsky were to find their realization — but an important, a significant fact is expressed in what must just now be set forth; What must now be explained is the fact that from the most opposite party standpoints, from the most opposite social passions, people today come to similar criticisms of the existing cultural conditions and finally also to the abstract call for freedom. Only they understand this freedom in very, very different senses.

If one penetrates the fact that finally the true impulse of freedom can come only from the depths of the human soul itself, then one asks: What is the reason that in spite of all the politicizing and calls for freedom there is so much in Woodrow Wilson's book and also in his other books of which one must say that they are abstract, impractical truths which can never penetrate into reality? I believe that what Woodrow Wilson thinks of as freedom is precisely what keeps him from being a truly practical man for the soul life of the present. It is very characteristic how Woodrow Wilson explains freedom. He explains it, one would say, as if he had absorbed the whole sum of his concepts from the art of machinery. He says, for example: A ship moves freely when it is so arranged that its apparatus is exactly adapted to the movements of the wind, the movements of the waves, when it experiences no obstacles and inhibitions from the movement of the wind, from the movements of the waves, when it is carried along freely, as it were, without resisting what carries it along. — And so, a man would be free in the sense of Woodrow Wilson, who would be so adapted to the social external conditions that nothing in him would give obstacles and inhibitions to be carried along, so that he would feel, as it were, nowhere that he was dependent, that he was constrained, that he was disturbed in any direction. One needs to take only one sentence seriously, then one will find what meaning this view of Woodrow Wilson about freedom has. If we seriously and honestly compare man, who is to act freely out of the innermost impulse of his soul in some social order worthy of man, if we compare him with a ship which opposes the wind and wave forces as little as possible, then we completely ignore the fact that the ship is stilled by another force, that the ship must be held still by another force against wind and wave, that it cannot hold itself still, but that man, if he is to be free, should certainly not be merely carried along by the social forces, but that under certain circumstances he must be able to stop and also to oppose the forces which act upon him. The opposite of that would have come out here for a real idea of freedom, which is found as a kind of definition of freedom in Woodrow Wilson. And this we shall find that the vague call for freedom sits in many human souls today, but that what they consciously associate with the impulse of freedom is something different from what they unconsciously really strive for. This was already before my soul's eye when I conceived my "Philosophy of Freedom" out of the human spirit in the eighties of the last century. I saw before my eyes how the question: Can man be inwardly free or unfree at all? — How this question occupied philosophy and world view and religious convictions throughout the entire civilized development of mankind. If man is a being, a natural being, driven purely by natural causes, then he is not free. Or does a being live in man who possesses and uses that which he is as an outer bodily being only like an apparatus out of his own innermost impulses? If he were, then it could be said that he, this man, is a really free being. Is man free or is he not free? Is he one or the other by his nature and disposition? These questions stood before my soul. And whoever wants to approach these questions within today's scientific community must, however, give an account of how he feels about the different views that have asserted themselves here and there in the whole civilized development of mankind on the question of freedom.

Now the main thing seemed to me to lie in the fact that the question is usually posed quite wrongly, the question: Is man by his own nature and being a free being or is he not? It is wrongly posed. And as a wrongly posed question, it can never be answered with a straight yes or no. And so, you will find that my "Philosophy of Freedom" aims at bringing the whole question to another ground. However, that which I will now elaborate lies more than the foundation under what is presented in my "Philosophy of Freedom" itself. Just as the human being of today is a person in whom the right consciousness of freedom has actually only awakened, so this human being of today has developed out of earlier states of the human being. Today far too little attention is paid to the fact that the principle of evolution should be applied seriously and honestly to humanity. It is true that one thinks that in the quite distant past man was once a kind of ape-like being; then one says: Scientifically, it is not yet time to talk about how today's man has developed out of this ape-like being, out of this animal-like ape-like being that once climbed trees. It is a long, wide desert between the ape-being of the human being and today's human being. But even if one does not admit it, in essence one has the idea that once man has become man, his soul-spirituality has not changed very radically. I know that this is a disputable proposition. But if you look at the history of the development of mankind, as it is usually seen, you will find this statement justified. And whoever takes a closer look at the history of the development of mankind will find that, as man has developed, the consciousness of freedom has awakened in him, so that from the depths of the souls of men the call wells up: First of all, you must be able to act freely out of your own passions, emotions, feelings and emotions; you must live in a social condition in which you can be free. But on the other hand, this call is actually only present as such. Today, there is also not the consciousness of humanity which allows this call to come to its full significance in man himself. That is to say, man does not find enough of his own beingness in himself so that he can say of this in himself: yes, there is something in me which is a free being. In the course of the development of mankind we have ascended to a great development of scientific knowledge, and the last one will be the one who represents the spiritual science meant here, who somehow wants to deny the great progress of natural science — I have often explained this here — or who wants to object to the justified views of natural science. But as we have developed natural science in the newer times, this means that man of the newer times, of the last three to four centuries, can actually only understand himself as a bodily being. Out of the depths of the human being, out of the naturally given human consciousness, does not rise: you are just as a real soul, you are just as a real spirit — as rises out of the depths of the human being: there you have your arm, there you have your hand, they are made of flesh and blood and bones.

This is not only, I would like to say, a negligence of the world view. One completely misses what actually lies at the bottom of it if one merely criticizes what I have just said and sees in it merely a negligence of the world view, if one merely says: The people of the present are so comfortable that they believe that man is only a material being and that nothing spiritual and mental expresses itself in him. No, my dear present ones, one does not get further with such a criticism, one must rather realize, as man has developed, so he is at first — if he does not take in anything else into his soul than that which a today external view of nature and external natural science and the consciousness of time can offer — forced to feel himself only as a material being. In other words, if we let that which of the present culture the time especially loves, that which of the present culture the time especially produces as science, as art, as religious conviction, and also lets it have an effect in the schools, if we let that affect the man of today in such a way that he is permeated by it, then he will, if he is honest, have to become precisely a materialist. That is a harsh word. But it is, I believe, a correct word. Today one can be dishonest in a certain respect, can say out of some prejudices: I do believe in spirit and soul. — Then one is not serious about what time consciousness and scientific convictions have actually brought forth. And if one takes it seriously with these convictions, then nothing else remains than that man feels as a material being. Once he has developed in such a way that if he today merely abandons himself to his self-given conditions of life, he only comes to the belief that he is a bodily being. A bodily being can just as little be a free being as any other natural being. Therefore, one can say: If the present consciousness is taken seriously, nowhere such a thing as the impulse of freedom arises from this present consciousness. One can sound the call for freedom out of subconscious instincts, as Woodrow Wilson does. But one will arrive at wrong concepts of freedom, at a definition of freedom that says nothing about freedom and a free being, as again Woodrow Wilson does, if one is absorbed in the time-consciousness of the present. One must have the courage to step out of this contemporary consciousness that has taken hold of the widest circles, that has become popular. And one can say, just in the time when I wrote my "Philosophy of Freedom," one could feel quite lonely with such ideas, no matter where one lived on earth, within the contemporary culture. One can understand it if the special views of Woodrow Wilson grew out of the — world-historically speaking — young life of America. And when I look at my "Philosophy of Freedom" today — I may also speak openly about this — I know how justified those reproaches are which can strike the reader of this "Philosophy of Freedom" today. I know very well that if someone today reads the first thirty or forty pages of this book, he will say: Well, this clearly bears the eggshells of German philosophy, professorial terms, university terms, school terms.

Nevertheless, I have to stick to the form of this book and appeal to the present in such a way that I say: Just as one should not take the essence of man according to his suit, one should also not take my philosophy according to its wrapping in the concepts that had to serve it as such a wrapping out of the time and out of the education, out of the spiritual life within which this philosophy arose. Rather, something else seems important to me, which, I would like to say, came to me as symbolically during this elaboration of my "Philosophy of Freedom." At that time, while I was working on this philosophy, I was also working at the Goethe and Schiller Archive in Weimar. There, an American scholar worked with me for some time. He was working on a literary-historical treatise on Goethe's "Faust." It was very interesting to talk to this man, and whoever can see reality in symptoms, had American spiritual life in the midst of Central European spiritual life in the excellent American literary historian Calvin Thomas. But you see, there worked, I would like to say, like in an exact Central European office in the Goethe and Schiller Archive in Weimar all kinds of scholars, also American scholars. When the office hours were over, I could only use my leisure time to write on my "Philosophy of Freedom." But then I often had to say to myself: How close is that which in Calvin Thomas' head is American knowledge, American insight, to that which the European scholars also wrote in the same matter, and how lonely one is in the face of this cultural formation, in the face of the whole world with that which can be conceived from an independent spiritual life as a real idea of freedom. To a certain extent, one also felt lonely in the face of what could come out of America's — world-historically speaking — young sense of freedom as an idea about the impulse of freedom. And at that time, it was a matter of concern to me to bring the whole question of freedom, as I have already said, onto a different ground. I had to say to myself: The way man is, if he only leaves himself to that, if he only takes that, which first of all can fulfil his soul out of the consciousness of time, then he cannot know himself as a free being at all. That is why I put the question differently. And this other question pervades that which I recognize as the idea of freedom. I cannot ask: Is man free or is he not free? — but: Can man in the interior of his soul, after he has gone through that which arises for him, as it were, from nature and from his being, further develop his soul by taking his soul development into his own hands, and can he then awaken something sleeping in him in such a way that this actually deeper being in him then comes to the fore, so that through this awakening of a second man in him he first becomes a free being? Can man educate himself to freedom, or can he not? Can man become a free being or not? How does he become a free being? — This was the new question that had to be raised.

In this way, however, it was pointed out that the man of today, if he wants to come to the consciousness of the full human being at all, must not stop at that which arises naturally for man in his development, but that he must take his development into his own hands. However, this is a point of view that is quite uncomfortable for many people today. In order to make it plausible, one has to say the following to people: Look at a five-year-old child. Let us imagine that this five-year-old child is standing in front of a volume of lyrical poems by Goethe. This five-year-old child, standing in front of the volume of lyrical poems by Goethe, will do something with this volume of lyrical poems; he will tear it, perhaps bite it, or something else, but one cannot assume that this five-year-old child will do the right thing with the lyrical volume by Goethe. But the child can develop, the child can be brought up, so that later on he will learn to do the right thing with this volume of lyrical poems by Goethe. Well, how would it be if one would say to the present people: Leave yourself only to that which the consciousness of time gives you of its own accord, then you will relate to the actual mysteries of nature, to the actual mysteries of the world around you, as the five-year-old child does to the lyrical volume of Goethe. It has the whole lyrical volume of Goethe before it like a completely understanding human being, but of course it does not penetrate into that into which one can penetrate as a completely understanding human being. It must first be educated. Now the call for freedom presupposes in reality that man really has the great intellectual modesty to say to himself: Perhaps I stand before nature, before the essence of the world, as the five-year-old child stands before the volume of lyrical poems by Goethe. I must first take the development of my soul into my own hands, then, just as for the five-year-old child after five or seven years the lyrical volume of Goethe becomes something completely different, then the world becomes something completely different for me. Whereas before, when I only abandon myself to what comes of itself, I am an unfree being, another person awakens in me when I take my development into my own hands. And as this other person glows through me, warms me up, penetrates me, I become a free being.

Yes, this was expressed as the foundation of a human conception of freedom in my "Philosophy of Freedom," and it was not meant merely as a philosophical truth, but it was meant to show that by what man awakens in himself, by what he advances — as if he only achieves that which is given to him by himself — by developing himself in this way, he develops a previously dormant, hidden reality in himself, as it were. He creates something in himself that first brings him to freedom. As long as one theorizes, as long as one thinks out abstract ideas, these will be a matter of man's head. They will not particularly seize the whole man. Actually, everyone who has dealt with such things knows how shadowy the most beautiful, the most ideal abstract ideas live in people. It is different when not abstract ideas but life itself is to be awakened in man, when man is to go through something alive, through which something awakens in him that was not there before. This is a living thing that takes up the whole man, that is not only a matter of the head, but also a matter of the soul and spirit of the whole man. There one takes together all sensations, all impulses, there one takes together the whole human will life, there freedom becomes a real force in man, there freedom becomes something experienced. Then, however, when it becomes something experienced, man wants to develop it also in the external living together, then he comes from his experience of freedom, by living with other people, also to an idea of such a social structure of human living together, in which only freedom can be realized.

Therefore, in the second part of my philosophy, I tried to establish a moral doctrine of man, to establish a social outlook, which, I would like to say, would then have to emerge as a matter of course from the awakened feeling of freedom and sense of liberty. If one thus takes the impulse of freedom as something that is grasped alive in the deepest essence of man, then freedom is not an abstract idea, then the philosophy of freedom is not a mere philosophy, then that which is expressed by such an outlook on freedom is something that passes over into all man's actions, into all man's aims. Then it contains something that others call for when they speak of freedom, but that is found by those who do not stop at the world views of the present when they want to understand freedom, but who rise to that which lies dormant in man, and which can be awakened. That which can be spoken to humanity in this way, I would say, as a language of freedom, as intimately connected with the cultural conditions of the human present and future, now, however, required another in its further development.

And here is the reason why it was necessary to go over from the foundation of a philosophy of freedom to the anthroposophically oriented spiritual science. Take one of the main books of this anthroposophically oriented spiritual science, my book "How to gain knowledge of the higher worlds." There you will find a detailed description of the paths that the human being must take inwardly and spiritually so that this consciousness of the other human being, of the truly free human being, can awaken in him. There you will find how it is possible that man really comes to such a comprehension of his own being that the true form of thinking and also of willing comes before his soul. And in this connection, I may refer to something to which I have already alluded in one of the last of the lectures given here: Thinking and willing become something different for the one who enters the human being in the way described in my book "How to gain knowledge of the higher worlds." One learns to recognize by thinking how the being, which one then grasps as the higher human being, was already there before the human being entered into physical existence through birth or conception. One learns to recognize by the true form of the human will how man carries his being through the gate of death into the spiritual world. One learns to recognize, by really rising, by developing oneself to the truer essence of man, the eternal in man.

With this, however, only the paths are correctly drawn in detail which led man, I would like to say, to regard the "philosophy of freedom" as something self-evident; the paths are drawn to find the truly free human being. At the same time, however, this serves the deeper cultural conditions of the present and the future, which express themselves precisely in such calls for freedom as I have characterized them in the introduction to my lecture today.

What does man need, then, if he feels intensely all that he feels about a dignified existence, what does man need in terms of content for his innermost human consciousness? What I want to say will perhaps be best illustrated if I refer you back to the starting point of the spiritual human culture of the last three to four centuries. For it was a great thing when in the dawn of the newer development of mankind spirits like Copernicus, Galileo, Giordano Bruno and so on appeared. What did they do basically? They broke with the knowledge and world view traditions of the old time and directed the human view to the unbiased observation of the outside world. They wanted to dispel prejudices. They wanted to make clear what man can gain by observing the outside world. Gradually, however, something else occurred, that which I have already partly characterized. It has happened that an old consciousness of what man is in his innermost being has been destroyed by the newer observation. If one looks at the vast starry sky today, completely in accordance with our newer natural science, what is this starry sky? Something that we want to understand by mathematics and mechanics, something with which we only feel related to this abstract product of our head, mathematics and mechanics. And let's compare this with the consciousness that man had in older times when he looked up to the starry sky. He did not have the abstract scientific consciousness: Up there the stars circle according to mathematical-mechanical laws, but you, earth worm, stand here on this earth, come into being with the birth and pass away with the death, and that what you are, that has nothing to do with the course of the stars. If we go back to older stages of human consciousness, we find that in this older human consciousness lay the view: You human being, as you stand here on this earth, you are not only attached to this earth; that which works and lives in you as forces is connected with that which circles up there in the stars, and if you perfect your knowledge, if you become conscious of yourself as a complete human being, then you know that you are related to the animals and plants and stones of the earth, as well as to the whole world space of the stars. We have bought what we have learned mathematically-mechanically about the stars with the cutting off of man from the cosmos, from the world. If one now goes in the way as I have described it, through the way to the higher realizations, and reaches in oneself to recognize that human being, which has not taken its beginning with the birth or conception, but which was there in spiritual worlds before birth and conception, and which also now lives in us, and which penetrates through the gate of death into the spiritual world, then one learns, however, with this human being, only in a new form, not in an old, worn-out form, again to know his kinship with the whole cosmos; then man again becomes permeated with world-consciousness. His mere earthly consciousness is transformed into world consciousness. But then man has something which he needs just as a cultural condition of the spirit in the present and for the future. Mankind could never experience the moment without the deepest damage to its being, when it would be pointed to new external observations and the old spiritual life would be extinguished bit by bit. Man needs faith, the hint to the knowledge of something lasting, which can stand firm, as the outer observation of the world expands.

Thus, it is anthroposophically oriented spiritual science which, on its paths, shows man himself in such a way that he can again connect with his world consciousness to the whole cosmos, that he again knows himself with his spirit in connection with the world spirit. This is not just a theoretical idea, it is something that lives in the whole human being and that makes him, this human being, another being. In the present and in the future, we will be able to speculate a great deal about what social institutions should be established so that people can find a dignified existence in them. In recent times, people have even deluded themselves into thinking that such institutions can be invented. One will only arrive at institutions that give man a dignified existence if man is able to create such institutions out of his deepest spiritual-mental being. For this, however, it is not necessary to dream of a transformation of the external social conditions; it is necessary to seriously tackle a new spiritual culture, to awaken that which slumbers and sleeps in the human soul, and which must first be awakened so that man can know of himself that he is a free being. Today one completely overlooks what a deep rift there is in our spiritual culture. For many centuries, certain social powers have watched over the fact that external science should not speak of the spiritual and soul. This should be a matter of dogmatism. This was to be experienced by a mere faith, to be dictated by mere authorities what one should think about spirit and soul; because a monopoly was claimed by certain social powers for dictating what was to be recognized about spirit and soul, therefore science was pushed away to the mere material. It has a very peculiar effect on those who look deeper into the development of mankind when they hear today how official science believes that it pursues truths without prejudice and through this unprejudiced pursuit of truths finds out something which today is called science only and which basically wants to deal only with sensual facts. In truth, this has become a process of development, in truth, it is human research, which has capitulated to the monopoly of certain social circles, which wanted to deal only with what people have to think about spirit and soul. A science, as I have characterized it, as it leads to freedom, it leads at the same time to the fact that man can not only investigate about the physical, about his bodily, it leads to the fact that man learns to investigate also about the spiritual and about the soul. And if he learns to investigate about the spiritual and about the soul, he takes up stronger, more realistic concepts than those he takes up when he has to limit himself to the mere outer material. And so, one has tried to let flow into social thinking only that which comes out of the present consciousness of the time. And from this point of view, one believes that actually human ideas cannot reach into the social conditions, or one makes up highly wrong social ideas. In my book "Of Riddles of the Soul" — one of the last that I wrote, and which, like the others, is only the straight continuation of what you will find in my book "The Philosophy of Freedom" — in this book "Of Riddles of the Soul" I have shown how the truly anthroposophical ideas cannot reach into social relations, how the truly anthroposophically oriented spiritual science is not only able to speak abstractly about all kinds of spiritual-emotional matters, but how, by grasping the truly spiritual, it is at the same time able to grasp the human being, which is body, soul and spirit, in its entirety. And so, in these "Riddles of the Soul," I was allowed to point out, for example, how it is a great error in present-day natural-scientific physiology to speak of man as having sensitive nerves that go from the sense organ to the central organ, while from the central organ, in turn, to the muscles go the motor nerves. An abstract science, which speaks of spirit and soul only abstractly, will never dare, it will not even find the method, to say something about the sensual, which cannot be proved merely sensually. One can prove that there is only one kind of nerves, that there is no difference between sensitive and motor nerves, that such phenomena as the *Tabes dorsalis* (spinal dysphoria), which one cites to support the opinion that there are motor nerves, prove just the opposite of what one believes to be proved by them.

Thus, in this anthroposophically oriented spiritual science something is created which in turn penetrates into the whole of nature, which has thrust enough to penetrate into the whole of nature. In this way, however, this spiritual science may also penetrate into that which must especially interest the culture of the present. This spiritual science may penetrate into the structure of social life. And out of those experiences which man has with the higher man, only the really social

183

concepts can be gained. That is why we live today in such a confused time, live today in such confusion and chaos, because the people who deal with the solutions of the various questions of social nature are not able to dig deep enough in the human being itself to find those ideas which can really dominate social life. And so, one is at a loss in the face of the most pressing and burning questions of the present time, and one stands precisely before these most scorching and burning questions in such a way that basically no answer comes as a rejoinder from within the human nature.

One has seen, by following the world-historical development of man, how great transformations have taken place. Or was not one of the greatest transformations that took place in the course of the development of mankind the one through which Christianity emerged? Christianity, which first gave the right meaning to the development on earth, came up through a mighty transformation. It has left many things behind. Not all people recognized the truths of Christianity; but on the whole, Christianity was that which had a transforming effect on the old cultural elements, which basically brought forth the whole European civilization with its American appendage of civilization. One later experienced something like the French Revolution, for example. While Christianity was a purely spiritual transformation and achieved its goal to the greatest extent, one can say of the French Revolution, which was a political one, that it achieved something of its political goals, but that important and essential things remained behind, which were not achieved of the goals that were set. And now we experience in our time the longing of many people for a new transformation, for new revolutions. And we already see these revolutions at work many times. Sad experiences have been made by mankind. If it only wants to be impartial enough, it would have to realize that even in proletarian circles. Mankind has had sad experiences with the extreme social revolutions in Eastern Europe, in Hungary, and a great lesson of world history should be the failure of these social revolutions. And an even greater lesson, if people can learn anything at all from the events of world history, could be the sad fate of the German revolution of

November 9, 1918, a failing revolution. And if you look at everything that results from such facts, from the failed revolutions of Hungary and Eastern Europe, from the sadly fading German revolution, then you will see: Spiritual transformations, such as those given by Christianity, can take place in the course of human development; political ones, such as the French Revolution, only in part; economic revolutions, such as are now being attempted, are doomed to failure, can do nothing but destroy, can bring up nothing new, unless they are transformed into spiritual impulses of progress. One of the most important and essential cultural conditions of the present is that out of the correctly grasped impulse for freedom people should come to the conclusion that all the questions which are being grasped today must be considered in connection with the whole spiritual development of mankind, with a renewal of human spiritual life. And mankind should become clearly aware of this before the sad and dreadful doctrine of misery could come to pass, which would happen if what is happening to the decline of human culture in the East of Europe, what has happened with such sad symptoms in Hungary, what is petering out in Germany, were to continue in the way it has been grasped by those who have no conception of the real impulse of the spirit.

Even what is done economically is done correctly only out of the human spirit, and we live in an age where the old concepts no longer suffice, where we must find new concepts that can also create a new economic culture for the present and for the future. Woodrow Wilson rightly says: We have new economic conditions, people could not close their minds to the new economic institutions; but we think about this economic life with the old legal concepts, with the old outdated intellectual ideas. — But then, then nothing sprouts from that which is rooted in his soul, which could now master the new economic life.

That which is sought here as anthroposophically oriented spiritual science in what is communicated here will on the one hand reach up to the highest heights of human spiritual and soul life, but on the other hand it will also be strong enough to reach down to where the most everyday institutions of life must be grasped. How is it today? Spiritual life has gradually taken on a completely abstract character. Just think how the religious, the aesthetic, the artistic, the ideological conviction of, say, a merchant or an industrialist or a civil servant is formed. That is a thing in itself, which he experiences in his soul. It does not reach into the account book or into what he does in his office. In the field where he creates his spiritual ideas, the ideas and impulses are not created at the same time, which are then expressed in his account book. At the most, it says "With God"; but that is also all, by which the activity, which is expressed in there, is connected with what he carries through the world as an abstract life of spirit and soul. That is why, when people with good social opinions, such as Saint-Simon, Blanc, Fourier, appeared in more recent times, it was said: These are good moral ideas, but with good opinions one does not change the social conditions — this can be heard today everywhere where one speaks from the socialist point of view. And one is right. With such social ideas as Saint-Simon, Blanc, Fourier and so on had, one does not transform social life, because they arose from the consciousness of people that when one thinks and ponders about the spiritual, this spiritual is a thing for itself, which should not at the same time grasp the world. In the end, all spiritual life has become abstract. On the one hand, man takes the upswing religiously or artistically or ideologically into spiritual heights, if he takes it at all. On the other hand, he leaves himself, I would say, to the chance of life; in natural science, by working in laboratories, on the observatory and the like, and what he brings out there, be it in the social, be it in the scientific field, has no connection with the abstract spiritual life. Anthroposophically oriented spiritual science wants to pour out a unity of spiritual and material life over the entire human civilization. And from that which is formed in man by his seeing the higher man in himself, rising to the eternal, should follow the possibility of grasping the eternal, which lies beyond birth and death for man, but at the same time to make the ideas so strong that they can intervene in everyday life. For it is not he who is serious and true about the spirit who speaks of the spirit, but he who is serious and true about the spirit who pursues the spirit into its last drawing into material existence, for whom nothing at all remains of spiritless matter

186

even in the practical conception of life. That is what one could call the cultural conditions of the present and of the future, that people would have such a spiritual-soul consciousness.

Then people who are imbued with such consciousness will also create social and political conditions for themselves, as they are longed for by such people as Woodrow Wilson, for example. Today, however, the situation is such that one actually only criticizes, that productive ideas are not yet there, because one does not want to descend or ascend to the spirit. Today we see how from America — we have given the example of Woodrow Wilson himself, certainly an authoritative personality — how from America the social life of the present is criticized, and the call for freedom is heard. But one does not want to decide to rise to the real impulse of freedom. And we have experienced how in Europe truly beautiful, witty ideas about freedom and social conditions have arisen. But in European civilization it is peculiar to us that we are not able to bring down from abstractions, from philosophical heights, what we think and feel so beautifully and to introduce it into immediate life. And we do not yet understand it when people speak of such an introduction of real, not merely imagined ideas into political life. And if we look over to Asia, we have to do with another civilization, which is just as aptly critical of the social and freedom life of the present as America and Europe. One has only to read the beautiful arguments of Rabindranath Tagore and one will find how he who is at the head of the Asiatic culture takes it so far in criticism. He does not get so far in the productive, because he is not able to say to himself: New things must be striven for, if again there is to be talk of spiritual life. He wants to let an old spiritual life remain, to let it alone be effective.

Now, unfortunately, we have experienced in Europe that people have finally lost so much the direct connection between what they strive for in spirit and what everyday life brings them, that we now see numerous societies busy shaping Europe according to purely external economic aspects and trying to satisfy their need for soul, since the Christian religion in Europe is no longer sufficient, from Asia by all kinds of theories and so on. Such relations are not suitable to bring about a new development of spiritual life; they are the last decadent shadows of the old.

What is meant here as anthroposophically oriented spiritual science reckons with all this. It is quite the opposite of what is said of it. And the Dornach building, which is so often said to be symbolic, does not have a single symbol, but it should only be built, I would like to say, in a purely natural way, so that it is envisaged that this and that will one day be driven in it, just as one learns to recognize the nut in its shell, and if one looks at the shell that is around the nut, one finds that it is naturally shaped in such a way that it is appropriate to the nut. So, we wanted to create a new shell for a new spiritual life also architecturally, artistically, pictorially. Naturally, the construction was not performed out of abstract ideas, not out of a tricky aesthetic view. Often, I have used a rather trivial comparison in order to say only to some extent what I actually mean by this Dornach building. I think many of you know that in Germany, in Austria, or even here, certain cakes are called Gugelhupf, and then the form in which the Gugelhupf is baked is called the Gugelhupftopf. Now I said that one imagines that which is to be baked in this building as a Gugelhupf, as a cake, then if the cake is to be right, the Gugelhupftopf must be the right one. Thus, the spiritual life that is to be driven there must have the right wrapping, just as the nut in the nutshell has the right wrapping. Except for this basic principle of construction, everything is basically still misunderstood in wide circles today.

Well, I wanted to point out today, as in other numerous lectures that I have already given here in the same place, how the things that are to be done in the Dornach building and what is to be done in it really relate to the civilized development of mankind, in contrast to the numerous misunderstandings that arise, which must arise very naturally. From the few hints that I have been able to give, but which are intimately connected with the most important human longings for the renewal of culture in the present and for the future, one can perhaps see what is meant and intended by this building and its cause.

When the call is heard from America, as I have characterized it in Woodrow Wilson, the call for freedom: that humanity, that existence worthy of a human being, which can meet this call as its realization, as the right answer to the question that is being asked, is to be found. Some people today still easily bypass this. Out of dark, vague feelings one raises time demands. Out of a clear realization of the spirit the answers must be given. I must think how right Woodrow Wilson is in a certain respect when he points out how decisions should not be made in secret consortiums about the affairs of the people, of mankind. Woodrow Wilson wants decisions to be made in each individual family home, whether in the countryside or in the city, but especially in the schoolhouse. That is a beautiful idea, that the nurturing place of the spirit should be the place of origin for the formation of the ideas of the time. And it is a beautiful statement of Woodrow Wilson where he says: Our goal is the reality of freedom. We want to work to prevent private accumulation of capital by law, and to make the system by which private accumulation of capital was created impossible by law. And another very beautiful saying is: Inside the country, on the farms, in the stores, in the villages, in the apartments of the big city, in the schoolhouses, everywhere where people meet and are true to each other, there it is where the brooks and rivers spring from their original source to form only the mighty force of that stream which carries and drives all human undertakings on its course to the great common sea of mankind. — It is a beautiful idea to call people together in such a way that from all individual sources the stream can form itself for the liberation of humanity, and it is a beautiful idea to have the goals set precisely from the nurseries of the spirit, from the schoolhouses, which are to carry humanity forward.

But if you take what I tried to elaborate today, then perhaps this call for the schoolhouses, as Woodrow Wilson raises it, will nevertheless have to turn out differently. For I believe that only when a cultural life is cultivated in these schoolhouses which is permeated by a realistic understanding, by a humane understanding of the free human spirit and the human soul, only then will the right stream of human freedom come out of the schoolhouse. As long as we cannot plant the right understanding of freedom in the human soul, we may gather them in the schoolhouses, they will hardly find any realistic goals there either. These will only be found when we have the courage to bring into the schools a spiritual, realistic world view, an artistic view, a religious confession. For more important for the future of mankind than what the people of the present generally decide to do in the schools will be what comes out of the schools when we bring the right spirit into them.

THE SPIRIT AS A GUIDE THROUGH THE SENSORY AND SUPERSENSORY WORLD

I

Bern, November 6, 1919

Eighth Lecture

If you travel from here to Basel, get on the electric train at Aeschenplatz, and take the road to Dornach, you will find there on the neighbouring hill a building — which, however, is not yet completed, but already shows in its outer work the intentions which are connected with it — a building which is called, which is to serve as a free college for spiritual science, which is to represent outwardly that which is striven for by that spiritual movement which calls itself: anthroposophically oriented, spiritual-scientific movement.

Since the construction of the building has shown visibly that there is something like such a movement, one can hear and read many things about what this spiritual cultural movement is based on. Certainly, there are also many things, which still have to be considered as an exception, that contain accurate information about these endeavours. On the whole, however, it may still be said today that what is said or written about it in public is quite the opposite of what is really striven for by this movement. It is very often described as an unscientific, obscure, in the worst sense mystical movement. In particular, it is very often described as if it wanted to stand in opposition to this or that, to societies, confessions and the like. In truth, this movement and this building in Dornach, the Goetheanum, by which it is represented, wants to serve those longings, those aims, which today often dwell so unconsciously in the souls of men, in the souls of the broadest masses, which in many respects do not yet find the form to express themselves, but which are connected with everything that is to lead present and future humanity out of the chaos of culture, which can be perceived by every unbiased person, and from which every unbiased person must extricate himself in the present.

If we are to indicate from historical phenomena what, I would like to say, is the main nerve of this movement, then we may perhaps point to something that seems to be quite remote from today's man, which also seems to belong to quite abstract regions of thought and imagination, but which only needs to be developed for the most general and broadest human interests, in order to lead us into the midst of that which is necessary to today's culture for its renewal, for its rebirth. I would like to point out what Goethe aspired to out of the whole breadth and depth of his world view, which is still not sufficiently appreciated today, to point out what he aspired to as a knowledge of the living world in contrast to the dead, the inanimate, the inorganic world.

That which Goethe strove for as knowledge was closely connected with his entire spiritual striving, and he took the best of what his world view had as its content from the contemplation of art but extended that which he gained from the contemplation of art to really scientific knowledge, as he had to see it precisely in the sense of the breadth and width of his world view. Goethe let work on him, however, with reference to the plant world so dear to him and its observation, all that could be available to him in relation to the plant world from the science of that time; but one can say, nothing was sufficient for him to explain the essence of the secrets of this plant world from what he could find in the science of that time. And so he turned his comprehensive gaze out of the originality of his being over the whole plant world, as far as it was accessible to him, over all its forms, and sought a unity out of the variety, out of the diversity of the plants. He sought out of the diversity of the plant that which he called his original plant. If one hears define what he understood by his conception, it could seem abstract, but it is not so. Goethe understood by his Urpflanze a unified image of which every plant, whatever external form it may bear, is an image, a unified, ideal, spiritual entity, with which one can walk through the plant world, and which, as it were, reveals itself in every single plant.

Such a primordial plant — so Goethe wrote from Italy to his Weimar friends —, such a unified plant, which can only be created in the spirit, which cannot be seen anywhere in the outer world, that must be able to exist — so he said seemingly abstractly — how else could one know that a single structure is a plant?

But it is not so important what abstract opinion he had about these things, it is more important that he had the faith, the deep faith connected with the essence of things, which is expressed in the following words. He said and wrote about this primordial plant: If one has grasped it in the spirit, then it must be possible for one not only to compare and recognize with it the plant forms that are out there in the world, but it must be possible for one to inwardly spiritually conceive plant forms oneself, which, even if they do not exist, could nevertheless exist.

This is a weighty, a significant word. For what does a man want, a recognizing man, who wants to grasp such a spiritual idea? He wants nothing less than to awaken in his soul a thought which can lead him, I would like to say, to use his own expression: to invent the outer reality which can then come into appearance. So, he would like to become inwardly so related to what grows in the plant, what grows in the living entities in general, that he has inwardly in his own spirit, in his thinking, in his imagining, what reveals itself outwardly in growth as power. So, he wants to submerge inwardly with his whole being into the outer world. The striving is much more significant than what Goethe achieved in detail with it. As I said, if one characterizes it only in relation to the plant world, which may interest one, the other less, if one characterizes it only in relation to the plant world, what Goethe wanted, it could appear abstract to some. But in this kind of spiritual endeavour lies something that can be extended over the whole scope of human knowledge, of human world view.

Then one ascends from the consideration of the single, insignificant living being to that of the whole human being, the human being, who does not only contain in himself, if one ascends to his wholeness, that what today the external natural science observes, what often the materialistic sense of the time regards as the only thing about the human being, but who includes body, soul and spirit.

Goethe started from natural science. What is called anthroposophically oriented spiritual science proceeds on the one hand from Goethe, in that it would like to develop the world-view mentality, which processes such things in the spirit, lets such things reveal themselves, which are so really intimately related to reality, as Goethe's idea of the original plant is to the individual plant; on the other hand, this spiritual movement knows itself to be in complete harmony with the true natural-scientific mentality in our time, not with some obscure mysticism. And on the other hand, it is in full harmony with a real, honest and time-conditioned religious aspiration of the human spirit in modern times. In recent years I have often spoken here of the fact that anthroposophy, the anthroposophically oriented spiritual science, does not fail to recognize the importance of this natural science and its tremendous influence on modern culture; indeed, it appreciates this natural science much better than many of those who want to stand on the ground of this natural science. Whoever not only adopts the common prejudices about natural science and thus, believes himself to be a true natural scientist, but who with full consciousness delves into what natural science could do for the whole education of the human soul and spirit, must say: if this natural science, as it has developed for three to four centuries, but especially in the course of the second half of the nineteenth century, were to be considered a true natural science, it would be a natural science. If this natural science would fully grasp itself in its own essence, if those who practice it would fully understand its own nature, then this natural science would already proclaim of itself today what anthroposophically oriented spiritual science wants to proclaim. This natural science would speak of its own accord of the human soul and spirit, of that which has eternal value in the human being.

Why does natural science not do this, although it penetrates so conscientiously, with such penetrating methods into the outer sensual reality of nature? Why, on the other hand, does this natural science not rise, in the same way as Goethe did for the plant world, to such an inner processing of the idea of nature that one becomes one in one's inner being with the creating nature itself?

To answer this question, one must look back a little on the historical development of mankind in modern times. In natural science itself great, tremendous progress has been made. One only has to go back to what started with Copernicus, with Galileo, what has developed up to the most recent time, up to the present in natural insights. But one must at the same time consider how little this operation of natural science was actually completely free with respect to its entire operation, with respect to its entire work within the spiritual life of modern civilization. It was not, because in the course of the recent development of mankind, not one unified world-view developed which, besides the free, independent natural science, also tried to penetrate into the essence of the outer sense-world. In the outer sense world there were monopolies, monopolies for the knowledge of the soul and the spirit. The religious world views kept certain ideas about soul and spirit. And they brought it about that in public one conceded to them, more or less forced or free, that only they have something to say about the soul of man, about the spirit of man.

The naturalists, as well as other people, were under the influence of that which, I would like to say, asserted itself as a monopoly knowledge about soul and spirit. And they limited themselves, because they did not dare to ascend from the knowledge of the world to the knowledge of the world of the soul, to the world of the spirit, they limited themselves to saying: Yes, natural science has its limits; it must limit itself to the world of the senses alone.

Such a spirit as Goethe, who was certainly permeated his whole life by a reverent religious upswing in the feeling of a divine in the whole nature and in the whole world, he always felt the necessity to form his view of the physical, of the spiritual and of the mental in a uniform way.

Only one must look at the situation in which natural science found itself in a certain respect due to the pressure of the monopolies of knowledge just mentioned and look at what natural science can give man by its own power. Then one will understand such a unified striving for knowledge and spirit as was present in Goethe. Whoever does not let himself be oppressed, I would like to say, by the commandment, thou shalt not know soul and spirit, will undergo an education of his spirit precisely by the way in which the modern spirit tries to penetrate into the secrets of natural science. And this education then gives the stimulus to continue the development of the human spirit to higher stages of development than those which one simply has by being born as a human being.

But in order to understand such stages of development, one needs a certain intellectual modesty. This intellectual modesty, it is very necessary for the present man. This intellectual modesty must lead the present man to say to himself: You are not only a being, which perhaps in the development of the world order has developed up from lower organisms to the present perfection, but you are a being, which can develop itself further, has developed further in this life; so that the forces, which you received at birth, can experience a higher and ever higher formation.

You see, one must be able to say to oneself the following. One must be able to look impartially at the five-year-old child who has, say, a volume of lyrical poems by Goethe in his hand. This five-year-old child will truly not be able to do much with Goethe's lyric poetry volume, at least not what the adult person knows how to do with Goethe's lyric volume. He will perhaps tear up the volume or do something else with it. It must first grow up, then it will treat the volume of Goethe's lyrical poems in the right way. Its development must be taken in hand. For as a five-year-old child, everything that is in the volume of lyrical poems is before the eyes of this human being, but there is not yet the possibility that this human being can extract from this volume of lyrical poems everything that can be in it for him. Thus, the man of the present must learn to feel himself in relation to the whole breadth of the existence of nature and the world. He must be able to say to himself in intellectual modesty: You stand before nature in such a way that, by virtue of your present development, it cannot give you that which it truly contains within itself; One must be able to presuppose the possibility of taking one's development into one's own hands, so that one then, by attaining a higher stage of development than that which comes to one simply by birth, by then being able to treat that which one always has before one, which one believes to recognize — like the five-year-old child who does not yet know what to do with it — in such a way that it reveals to one all that which it closes up in itself in secrets. It is precisely the effort that one makes when using the scientific method today, the depth into which one penetrates, that can cause one to feel a power awakened out of the effort of the spirit, through which one undergoes such a development. It is not because of modern natural science that people are so reluctant to admit that man can undergo a development. No, it is due to the pressure which I have just characterized, and which one has only to look at without prejudice in order to be able to surrender freely to what lies in the scientific treatment of the world itself. Then one will feel that the soul is awakened inwardly, just by looking at nature in the modern sense, that forces arise in it which were not there before. As a rule, the natural scientists of the present day do not bring themselves to awaken these forces. But if they did, they would be able to proclaim that which is sought in the problem of the immortality of the soul, the eternity of the human spirit. Scientific thinking, scientific attitude, they can lead to an inner awakening of the human spirit. And this can then be continued, can be systematically trained.

How this is possible, I have often sketched from this place and described in detail in my book "How to gain knowledge of the higher worlds" and in the second part of my "Secret Science." One can continue in full self-education that of which one notices that it develops through modern scientific knowledge. One can apply to the spirit what is called meditation, concentration of the thought life, of feeling, of will. One can push the inner world of ideas so far, or at least the ideas one uses by observing stars, by working in the chemical-physical laboratory, by externally observing plants or people or animals, one can further develop what one uses there in inner spiritual power by devoting oneself to thoughts in such a way that one only wants to live in these thoughts until at least the thought brings the soul to grasp inner connections. These cannot be grasped if the soul is not given such an inner self-culture. An awakening of an inner soul culture is possible. One can indeed achieve such an awakening, so that the ordinary life one lives out, even in ordinary science, seems to one like a sleep from which one awakens. And from this awakening one can observe anew what surrounds one as a world.

This is the one thing that modern man can go through. If he will apply natural science in the right way, I would like to say in the Goethean way, he will come to a religious knowledge, to a real spirit knowledge.

But also, from the life of modern man himself emerges that which leads to such a path and, I would like to say, to a corresponding future goal.

Whoever looks at history externally, as it is usually presented externally today, does not have the real history before him. One must look at the historical life of people more inwardly. One must be able to compare, for example, how a man of the 9th, 10th century after Christ was in his whole soul condition, and how a man of the present, even if he is a most simple primitive living man outside, is like a man of the present; for even the simplest man today differs quite essentially from the man of the 9th, 10th century after Christ. I do not even want to go back further. People are definitely in the process of development. Today, the word development must not only be taken in the restricted sense in which natural science usually takes it. We must be able to take it in a much broader sense if we want to penetrate into the essence of the development of mankind.

One must be able to say to oneself that a number of centuries ago, that is, in the centuries I have just indicated, people were much closer to each other within certain associations. A man was connected with his neighbour before this relatively short time by the fact that he was related to him by blood, that he was related to him by tribe. This proximity, this closeness, which brought people together in associations a relatively short time ago, is no longer present in modern times. If one is unbiased, one can see this everywhere. Modern man is rather closed in himself; modern man has become much more, I would like to say, a loner of his soul. The people of the older times did not pass each other like the people of the newer times. The people of the newer times have become strangers to each other, have become more distant. But for this, I would like to say, something else arises out of a spiritual conscience than arose for man centuries ago. It arises — again one can see it, if one looks impartially into one's own soul and has a sense for such things, again one can perceive something like an inner voice —, something arises like an inner obligation: You shall now, since you no longer feel close enough through blood relationship, tribal relationship to those immediately nearest to you, be able to come close to him through your soul development. You should accept his will in a real love of man. In order to be able to live socially with him, you should not pass him by, but you should be able to absorb his will into yours, to make his thoughts your thoughts. You shall be able to think, feel and want with his inner soul condition in your inner soul condition. You shall be able to approach him spiritually-soulfully.

Just as the occupation with natural science represents a kind of awakening for the soul life, a kind of awakening in the ordinary consciousness, which one otherwise has in everyday life and in ordinary science, if one only looks at ordinary science correctly, so this ordinary science gives, I would like to say, inner social duties, which awaken more and more in man. It represents something that can be described

199

in contrast to this awakening — I will have to express it somewhat paradoxically now, but some of the truths that have to be assimilated into cultural life in the present must still sound paradoxical today — that can be described as a feeling that comes over us when we feel inwardly: spiritually and mentally we have to get close to our neighbour, we have to get involved in his will, his thoughts; it is something that seems like losing oneself in the human being. This losing oneself in the neighbour with his spiritual-mental, this devotion to the neighbour, that is actually the basis of the so often caricatured process of social feeling in the present.

And if one says: Natural science can awaken us —, this feeling, it brings, I would like to say, the opposite soul condition over us, a strange soul condition, if one can only understand it. But just as little as one becomes aware of the awakening from the natural scientific method, just as little one becomes aware of this feeling into one's neighbour. But it will take hold of modern people more and more. Then they will feel this, in contrast to the awakening through science, like a falling asleep, like a resting in the surroundings, like a passing over of their own soul into the soul of the other. And just as out of the natural sleep awakens, vividly awakens the mysterious life of the dream, so out of this devotion to the human-soulful, which will overtake modern humanity more and more like a duty of conscience, it can awaken out of this devotion, which, I would like to say, in a higher sense is that of a sleep, love, which expresses itself in such a devotion. It is a kind of sleep in the human environment; but out of it something like a dream rises from the natural sleep. And this dream from the natural sleep can be compared with what will emerge more and more from the real, not from the caricatured social feeling.

This dream will give rise to that which says to the human being: See, by living into the will that develops alongside your will, by growing together with the thought that develops alongside your thoughts, you will know how you are inwardly connected with this human being.

Just as Goethe felt something that was given to him by his idea of the original plant, which he had to describe as a living into the whole power of the plant world itself, so one lives into the environment, into the living environment of the human world, precisely through the most modern feeling. And again, out of this living into the human world, something awakens, which now arises like a new realization just out of the social life. One feels that one is connected with the essence of the other person. You feel that from the being of the other person something speaks in you like a dream, which testifies to you: you were already connected with this person in the past.

Out of this real experience, out of this genuinely modern experience, will grow for the newer humanity as an experience, as a real experience, that which has already grown up for individual privileged spirits, such as Lessing, for example. If one wants to be pedantic, even if in a higher sense pedantic, one can say: Lessing, such a man was certainly great, but in his old age, when he was already half-imbecile, he wrote his "Education of the Human Race" and there he came up with the crazy idea that mankind lives in repeated earth lives. But for those who are not pedants, but who can really look into the development of such a man as Lessing, who has risen further and further, it is quite clear that such a man was only the predecessor of all those who get to know this peculiarity, this tremendous experience, which will arise from the correctly understood social feeling, will emerge from him, full of life, like a dream; But it will be a vivid dream, not merely a dreaming, of being connected with people whom one meets again in earthly life, of being connected in earlier earthly lives, with the expectation that one will be with them again in later earthly lives. That which is the experience of repeated earth lives, it will just develop out of the correct social life and feeling of modern man.

Ordinary natural science has already come to the conclusion that it no longer wants to be purely materialistic, at least in the case of individual spirits. But when the ordinary natural scientist wants to prove that something of a spiritual nature lives in man, something that is not merely an expression of the body, then he does not turn to such phenomena that he can prove and present, as one presents phenomena of the laboratory, the clinic and the like, but he turns precisely to the abnormal phenomena of human life. And I would like to say that it has become fashionable to investigate the dream world, which wakes up so mysteriously from natural sleep, just when one tries to point out how man also has a spiritual and a mental in him. But this means to investigate everything that results from the phenomena of suggestion, hypnosis, somnambulism and mediumship and so on. Here too, while anthroposophically oriented spiritual science wants to draw from a healthy knowledge of nature and from a healthy experience of the human world, it is obvious to confuse it with that which wants to lean on such phenomena as hypnotism, somnambulism and the like for a real exploration of the human spiritual-emotional being.

In order to get closer to these phenomena, one can start from the world of dreams, one can point out how this world of dreams conjures something in front of the human soul in the time between falling asleep and waking up, since the human being is not fully bound with his spiritual-emotional life to the resting body. But the one who is able to study this dream world properly, will he ever come up with an answer to the question: What is this dream world? This dream world is something that leads man beyond his ordinary outer daily life. — Then all kinds of things would not have to interfere in this dream world — for the unprejudiced it is quite clear — which come merely from the lower, animal-like drives of the human nature.

Just consider what man is capable of doing in dreams, how he is inclined to the lower instincts, how he is often inclined even to the life of crime in what he deludes himself with in dreams. Man must say to himself: when he dreams, he is not transported into some higher spiritual realm, but on the contrary, he has wandered down into the subhuman realm. Truly, it is a dream itself when people today want to claim — quite willingly want to claim — that in dreams they are carried away into a higher world. No, in a lower world than the one we look into through our senses, we are brought by the dream. And only then, when such an influence is exerted on man, by seldom some suitable fellow-man, that he is put into the sleep-like state of hypnosis, one can bring it about that, I would like to say, even irresponsible influences are exerted on man, by working into a kind of sleep-like state. Then he looks at a potato for a pear and eats it for a pear, therefore, purely because it is suggested to him, this idea is given to him: this potato is a pear. And still completely other things can be given to him! It is only the extreme state, which exists also otherwise as, I would like to say, not a completely permitted state, where one counts on the damping down of the consciousness by the other person, and wants to talk ideas into him in, I would like to say, rape. For the one who works in the sense of true spiritual science, the question arises: What is the state of the soul in which a person is in a dream? What kind of state of soul is a person in when he is in such a hypnotic or mediumistic state — which is also similar to a hypnotic state — when in such a hypnotic state he can experience such influences from some fellow human being or also from other surroundings?

In hypnotic state it is indeed possible that thought transmissions over long distances can present themselves, they can be experimentally presented, proved. But the only question is, into which regions one brings a human being, with his whole human-bodily-soul-spiritual being, when one descends into these regions. One brings him then into a region which is a sub-human, which represents the animal in the human being.

In fact, man is screwed down, hypnotized down, profaned down into that which plays as animal in him. And just through this, one gets to know the animal in man, which is still something quite different from the animal of the animal series; but one gets into the region of the subhuman.

In contrast to all that presents itself, the anthroposophically oriented spiritual science meant here would like to lead one to reach the soul-spiritual in man by not damping down what is already in man in order to apparently feel something spiritual-soul, But to develop what is already there in the world of the senses to a higher perception by educating the thought, the will, the feeling through meditation, concentration, as it is described in my book "How to attain knowledge of the higher worlds?" is described. — Anthroposophical spiritual science wants to lead man beyond himself, to lead him in a healthy way beyond that which is already there in sense perception and ordinary science.

In this way it enters a region which is something new compared to the outer world of the senses. It is very important to realize that man becomes dependent when he is put into hypnosis, into a somnambulistic, medial state, or even when he is merely given over to dream fantasy, that he becomes dependent on his outer sensory environment in such a way that he is no longer dependent when he gives himself over to normal sense life; When we devote ourselves to sensual life in an awake state, our will can avert its eyes from something toward which it does not want to turn them, can even turn little attention to what it hears. In short, we are more powerful of our humanity through the will when we are in relationship with the environment through the senses. That which is placed there in the freedom of our will, which brings us into a free relationship when we perceive sensually in the waking state, becomes a compulsory relationship, as it is in animalism, when we are damped down in the waking state by hypnosis. There we do not discover what is actually spiritual in man, there we discover that of animalism in us which is otherwise veiled by our free spirituality; that which is otherwise veiled acts upward, becomes dominant over man. Man is organized down to the animal. Only one does not recognize — since man does not behave like the animal, but already expresses himself more spiritually — that it is nevertheless a question of a down-organization to animalism. What anthroposophical spiritual science wants, on the contrary, wants to raise the human being to a higher level of consciousness, and through this one recognizes only that which presents itself on a lower level of consciousness. For then, when man develops his spirituality, as I have described it in my book "How to attain knowledge of the higher worlds," then another relationship to the world occurs. But not that world presents itself which presents itself when we are hypnotized or when we are in a medial state or when we become somnambulistic, not the world of the ordinary sensual environment presents itself, but a new world, a spiritual world, a world which man did not know before, but which presents itself to him as a real one, just as the outer sense world announces itself to the senses as a real world.

You see, man can go through this development by ascending from the human into a superhuman, just as he descends from hypnosis, from somnambulism, into a subhuman. This development can be undergone, and man can thereby come up to a direct perception, direct experience of the spiritual. The spirit can thereby enter into the human consciousness.

Now one can say: Certainly, in such a book, as in this writing "How does one attain knowledge of the higher worlds?" is described, which development one must go through, in order to understand that this is really a true world, which one gets to know in this way, as I have described it. But not every person can become a spiritual researcher, not every person can enter this spiritual world himself, so that he can make communications from this spiritual world. However, the one who comes to that development, which one has always called the world beyond the threshold of ordinary consciousness, where one knew of the existence of a spiritual, a supersensible world, who enters this world, in which he has the spiritual around him as one has the sensual around him for the ordinary consciousness, makes his discoveries in the spiritual. With these discoveries he knows immediately, for example, that by what appears of man today, by having him in a hypnotic, somnambulistic state, by becoming medial, his ordinary consciousness is damped down. What appears in man as the subhuman, that represents in truth an earlier stage of man's development, and that which develops today as his sense perception, his intellect perception, that represents a later stage of development. And even this can be recognized — you can read it in the "Secret

Science" — that man today, if he is put into hypnosis, becomes in an abnormal way, as he was in his environment in a development of the earth world, which lies far behind what the geological outer science presents to us as earth development. One can just learn something about a much more spiritual-soulful state of the earth planet, in which man, however, was already present and perceived his surroundings in such a way, as he perceives his surroundings today, when his consciousness is damped down. We recognize something of the past of the earth, which was not in such a way as the Kant-Laplace theory represents it, but was in such a way, as a spiritual-soul being itself, in which the human being was embedded as a sense being. And on the other hand, one recognizes the man of the earthly future, where the earth will be more spiritual again, where the man will recognize by his natural constitution in such a way, as one recognizes today, if one develops the soul, as I have described it.

But these insights, although they are a need of the newer, of the modern man, they will at first, of course, I would like to say, be reached only by individual people, individual people will come into that region of life which lies beyond the threshold of ordinary consciousness. So many things are necessary if one really wants to come to these higher realizations. You see, I want to give you a simple higher knowledge. In this simple higher knowledge, however, the one who comes to it sees, for example, what the attainment of higher knowledge, the discovery of higher knowledge, is actually based on. In ordinary history today one does not know that basically the development of the whole humanity is just as internally conditioned as the development of the individual human being. Who would not find it ridiculous today to say that the human being who lives to be seven, fourteen, twenty years old and so on is always the result of what he eats and drinks; that which he eats causes the child to develop further and further from childhood, that is what makes him an adult. Every man knows that this is not the case, that man goes through certain stages of his development, which even lead him over certain leaps in natural development. We have such a clear jump, for example, around the seventh year, when the change of teeth occurs. Those who have a sense for such things know what tremendous revolutions take place in the human organism, for example, when sexual maturity occurs; later the changes are no longer so clearly and distinctly perceptible but are nevertheless present. There something develops in the human being, which jumps out of the depth of his being. But this is also the case with all mankind. And so it was about the middle of the 15th century of our post-Christian time, when mankind went through a leap in its development. The condition of the soul of mankind became completely different. Precisely what I have characterized today as the fact that man feels lonely in relation to other men, that he is closed in on himself, that he no longer feels as close to man through mere blood relationship as he once did. This becoming more independent, this becoming more personal has developed in such a way that the change of teeth, the sexual maturity occurs in the single human individuality, in the single human organization. Thus, out of the whole human development, something came in the middle of the 15th century. Such a content of knowledge can only come from the spiritual world. And only when one gains such a content of knowledge, as an inner fact of experience, one can also have a judgment about the realities of repeated earth lives, about the course of the spirit in human development, about the life of the spirit in natural existence and so on.

But all that one can do in order to attain such knowledge is: one can prepare oneself for it by meditation, concentration, by devotion of thoughts, sensations, will impulses, as it is described in "How to attain knowledge of the higher worlds? One can develop, can then say to oneself: You are now ready to receive higher knowledge; but then man has to wait. The nature of spiritual science does not refer to the fact that one can go off and gather knowledge; but one can only make one's soul ready; then it must wait. Then one must wait, I would like to say, for the moment that one feels like an effect of grace from the spiritual world; one must wait until enlightenment comes. That enlightenments from the spiritual world occur, occurs with one person and not with another person. Therefore, the truths are such that they occur in some people, who must communicate them to their fellow human beings. Even if such simple realizations occur, like those of the turnaround of the whole development of mankind in the 15th century, one must have come to know them today in the pure life of the soul. One must have learned to renounce the forcible conquest of the spiritual world; one must have worked only on the development of the soul in order to make oneself ready to receive the truths. Then they come, come at the appropriate moment. One must confine oneself to accepting them as such individual truths. One must only be clear about it: if one wants to draw consequences from it, as individual people do, then one only brings caricatures of the spiritual world. Let us assume that some man has made various inner discoveries; he comes to an idea; then he immediately builds a whole system out of it, a system of nature, a system of history, an economic or a social system, or something. People are not satisfied to make such single spiritual experiences, but continue to draw their consequences, to build systems on them. The one who is experienced in the spiritual world, he only works on his spiritual development, that he is ready to receive what is revealed to him. Then he again accepts such a single experience, waits again until another one presents itself to him. As in the outer sensuous reality also the new experience approaches, so one must wait, so one must always be filled inwardly with resignation, through which one can wait until the individual inner realizations arise. Otherwise, one often brings about constructions of fantasy. And because most of the people have only such blurred imaginations, therefore they think that the laws which come into consideration come out only from imaginations. In truth, however, no fantasy images come out when man makes an effort to advance. Only if he does not make an effort to gain ideas about the invisible, he comes to fantasy formations. But only if he strives to make all thoughts and development, all work in the spirit, aim only at the fact that the spirit becomes more and more perfect in its cognitive faculty, then he can come sufficiently far; if he has learned to wait, then the discoveries in the spiritual world result to him through that which is to be communicated in the spiritual world. — However, if his destiny is favourable, I would say, in this direction, and he learns to wait, he can come to discoveries himself. But above all, he can come to the point where he can recognize as truth what spiritual discoverers tell him, and that he acquires the judgments through such an inner development in order to see the truth of what the other gives him.

This is precisely the secret of the life that people will lead when the spirit becomes their guide in the world of the senses and in the supersensible world. This will be the peculiarity that human coexistence will become more intimate. Today we see an illusionary socialism, a misunderstood socialism, we see how people want to work socially, but more and more socially they actually distance themselves from each other. Then, however, when one will realize: You can develop yourself to be able to recognize that to which the other comes through the intimacies of his inner life, through which he makes spiritual discoveries, then you will be able to enrich yourself spiritually in living together with him. Then you will realize that just when the spirit will be the leader in the realm of man's senses, through this spirit also the social life will be able to receive its right meaning.

The penetration into spiritual worlds presupposes, if one really wants to go beyond the threshold consciously, that one becomes fearless in a certain sense towards the experiences of the spiritual world. The ordinary world of the senses lets us, I might say, be lulled into a certain sense of security. The one who crosses the threshold of the spiritual world from this sense world into the real spiritual worlds, which lie at the basis of our sense world, experiences that the comfortable, solid ground is no longer under him. The spiritual world does not have the same forces of heaviness and the like that this sense world has. Within the spiritual world man feels as if he were on a surging sea, and that security which one otherwise has through a firm standpoint in the outer sense world through ordinary life, this firmness, must be given by inner force through which one navigates the spiritual world.

The Liberation of the Human Being

Moreover, you must bear in mind that when one enters this spiritual world, one is at first not adapted to this spiritual world. One is adapted to a world as a human being between birth and death; one is not adapted to that which reveals itself as eternal to the human nature when one enters the spiritual world. One is adapted to the world of this world, to the world here. When one enters the spiritual world, after having evolved in order to enter it, one actually feels at first, as long as one is still in the body, not yet having passed through the gate of death, not yet adapted for the whole evolution. One often feels this as a burning pain, I would like to say. Many people shy away from this. Only if one prepares oneself well to experience the one as well as the other, can one grow beyond oneself, can one venture out into the open sea of spiritual knowledge, on which one must have the guide, the spiritual guide in oneself.

But for every human being it is already possible today, if he observes such things as I have presented them in "How does one attain knowledge of the higher worlds?", to see from his own conviction, not through considerations, to see that that is based on truth, is taken from reality, what the spirit-discoverers, the modern seers can really reveal to the world.

A human coexistence will result from the fact that we in turn can learn to see, if the other develops in himself the abilities to fully recognize what has been discovered. A living together in the spiritual will result, which will give the basic power for a life, as mankind will need it in the future, just when some structures in the social organism are to be overcome, which have emerged from old forces and which can only be overcome by new forces of the spirit, which develop from soul to soul.

Precisely because the spiritual will become a reality for people, precisely because of this, people will come closer to each other. You only have to consider whether one person discovers this or that in the spiritual world; that depends on the way his life is. It is not true that man knows different things about the external sense world, depending on whether he was born in Europe or in America or in Asia. So, even if he is a spiritual explorer, a seer, every person knows something different about the spiritual world. The other thing that he knows, that in turn is to the other person, who in turn knows something else, a supplement to his own knowledge. People will know separate things, different from the spirit. But they will be able to complement each other.

In front of a real spiritual knowledge, which is meant in such a way as it has been presented here today, it is truly not a disgrace or something degrading, if one person in a really social existence simply takes in what is transmitted to him from the spiritual world, what the other is able to discover. For it is not to be feared that any man who becomes a spiritual discoverer would shine through immodesty within his fellow-men's society. Just when one wants to penetrate into the spiritual world, one must first acquire that very much in the corresponding high strength, what I have called intellectual modesty, and one knows very well, just when one begins to know something of the spiritual world, how little one actually knows. This is not to fear that the spiritual cognisors become particularly arrogant. Those who speak of the spiritual world in phrases, who speak of the spirit without knowing anything about it, who speak of it by mere philosophical conclusions, they may become haughty. But those who penetrate the spiritual worlds know, moreover, how small they are as human beings in relation to this spiritual world that wants to realize itself through them, and they truly know that they should become neither haughty nor opinionated.

Now I would like to mention something else. If, on the one hand, it must be said that for the salvation of the future of mankind it is necessary today that those who have not yet discovered certain truths should listen to those who have discovered them, and that this is by no means something shameful or degrading to freedom, then at the same time it can also be pointed out that even he who can perhaps already recognize to a high degree, who is a seer, learns tremendous things from his fellow man. That is the strange thing, that in this direction one gains a completely new relationship to one's fellow man precisely through being a seer, precisely through the development of the soul-spiritual. It must be said that even in a simple, elementary way of life things can reveal themselves. We experience them, we have the sense to penetrate into that which reveals itself as mysterious soul-spiritual depths, for example, also through a child. If we do not interpret it symbolically, if we do not brood over it, but devote ourselves to it in love, we will be able to recognize it spiritually, so that later, when the seer has exercised such love for the simple, he will be gifted with the moment to recognize something great. And every great, real spirit-recognizer will be able to tell you about those moments where not by interpretation of what he has just seen, but how really just then, when this power has been released in him, he has experienced afterwards something else in some person, by choosing the spirit as his guide. One gets to know a person. That which he communicates to you out of his experiences, out of his experiences, perhaps as the simplest, most primitive human being, leads you into spiritual depths, if you are able to recognize correctly, to find the right connection. One makes the discovery that what people experience, what people experience, that this can lead to a revelation in every person.

Yes, over the whole wide circles of human beings, from every human being, whom we meet, if we choose the spirit as the guide of the sense world and as the guide into the supersensible world, from every human being, if he communicates his experiences and adventures to us, that which he has gained more from the world, can give us something, it can come to revelation in us something, which is absolutely necessary for his further development. We only often notice that people themselves, with their deficient powers, do not apply to their lives what they believe they have in their consciousness, in their conscious life of the soul; they think it is something highly unimportant, because people are inadequate to reach through their own power of judgment to see supersensible things. If one looks into the depths of the human soul, if one has acquired the sense in this way, as I have described it today, one can also gain so much as a spiritual researcher in the newer natural science, through the way natural science works in the clinics, on the observatories, in chemical and physical laboratories. If we accept what we are told about the work in the natural scientific workshops, then deep secrets of nature will be revealed to us. This is precisely what the researchers with their power of judgment often understand very inadequately from themselves, when they describe their work and their results, what they themselves do not quite reach with what they say about it, cannot be revealed in its depths. And precisely through what spiritual science does in this field, that which medicine today so often strives for, which it cannot achieve with its own means, will be spiritualized, which is connected with what I have described, that medicine and natural science can be fertilized precisely through spiritual science.

But social science can also be fertilized, if the spirit can become a guide through the sensual world and into the supersensual world. And one need not believe that what should be one of the basic forces of every human being as a religious element, through the knowledge of the spiritual life, through the fact that the spiritual life takes hold among us and the spirit becomes the guide of man in the world of man, would suffer! No, the opposite is just the case. Precisely that which the religious confessions themselves have sought, they have not been able to attain because of the needs that have arisen from healthy scientific life, by preserving old traditions. Thus, they could only achieve what they wanted to create as a belief in man's soul and spirit by means of dogmatic commandments, whereas in reality, when people will come to make the spirit their guide in the world of the senses, they will stand in the spiritual world with their soul life. But people who recognize the spirit, people who live with their ideas, with their feelings in the spirit, they will also be able to worship the spirit, they will be able to find the way to truly religious worship. Those people who do not know anything about the spirit, even if they count themselves to a "word religion," will not be religious people in reality. Those who have the spirit as their guide do not fear that Christianity could be damaged by the penetration of the spirit by modern spiritual science. Oh no, those show themselves small who say: no spirit knowledge should come, because it will undermine the religious feeling, it will undermine Christianity. He who really recognizes the spirit cannot think so little of the power of the Christ-impulse, which has really been working in the world since the Mystery of Golgotha. He must think much higher. He must think in such a way that he says to himself: whatever insights may come, the more one will penetrate into the spirit, the better one will learn to venerate that which can only be increased in its significance for mankind by recognizing it better and better.

It is not spiritual science that will hinder the real religious development of mankind, but the desire to stand still beyond real knowledge and spiritual progress will have an inhibiting effect on religious development. And it could be that in the not-too-distant future many people will realize where the obstacles to religious development actually come from. They come from the fact that the denominations no longer want to live with what is present in the innermost human being as a need.

You see, I only wanted to point out how the spirit can become the guide of man through the world of the senses and into the supersensible world.

Man learns to know that in him which is eternal and immortal, which passes through birth and the gates of death, precisely by developing the spirit in himself to which he belongs. He learns to recognize that he is a member of the spiritual world through his soul and spirit, just as he is a member of this world through his body.

Today, however, it is so that what I have characterized lives fully in the deep subsoil of the subconscious. The one who sees things through today knows how many people there are who have the longing for such a following of the spirit; but in the consciousness of people, it is often not so. In the widest circles there is still, I would say, an aversion, an antipathy to such spiritual leadership. But he who is in the midst of such a spiritual movement sees the way in which spiritual movements or external cultural movements have been met in the course of the historical development of mankind. And if today one is attached with heart and mind to the fact that something like the Dornach building, the School of Spiritual Science, the Goetheanum, should stand as an external representative — it is not yet finished, it is only under construction, but hopefully it will be finished in not too long — that something like this should stand as the visible sign of the spiritual movement which I have characterized to you today in the lecture, then it is necessary to remember historical things in the face of many a dismissive judgment.

Think what today's world would look like if at that time, when Columbus wanted to equip a few ships to sail westward to regions of which he really knew nothing, and the others knew nothing either, if the opinion had prevailed — you can read in history that it was very present, this opinion — which considered this intention of Columbus a foolishness, a madness! But finally, he won. Think what has become in the modern time by the fact that not the cleverness of those who refused Columbus the ships had triumphed, but that the "madness" of Columbus had triumphed. This madness of Columbus is for many people what anthroposophical spiritual science wants. Today it is still madness for many. But this madness does not only include that which is only a spiritual knowledge, no, this madness includes such a development of the spirit, through which one also becomes a really practical person, through which one becomes such a person that one can practically attack a voyage of discovery into real life. A real voyage of discovery into life is to be inaugurated by that for which this Dornach building is to be the outer representative.

May many people therefore see madness in what is to be undertaken with it. Whoever, out of inner knowledge, has connected his heart and mind with that which is to stand as a symbol for the fact that the spirit is to begin to become the leader in the development of mankind through the sensuous world and into the super-sensuous world, knows that out of this "madness" must develop that which many people, and finally all people of the civilized world, must seek, In order to get out of some of the chaos and confusion of culture which the unprejudiced feel today, in order to reach that which many people and many souls long for, long for more than the contemporaneity of Columbus India once longed for, long for that light which is to dawn on humanity so that it can really go towards higher cultural goals in humanity.

THE SPIRIT AS A GUIDE THROUGH THE SENSORY AND SUPERSENSORY WORLD II

Basel, November 10, 1919

Ninth Lecture

It is probably still considered in wide circles as the sign of a particularly enlightened spirit when one rejects the possibility of penetrating the spiritual, the supersensible world through human cognition. It can be said that in some circles of the scientific way of thinking there is already a front against this so-called enlightenment. But no matter how much this side may talk about the spirit and the supersensible world from this or that point of view, one cannot say that a really satisfactory way into the world of the spirit is even attempted or striven for in wider circles today.

That there is the possibility of penetrating into the supersensible world not merely through a vague, scholastic faith, but through a genuine and true continuation of that kind of conception which has made natural scientific thinking so great in recent humanity, is what anthroposophically oriented spiritual science, which — as I said here a few weeks ago — is to find its outer representation through the Goetheanum in Dornach, seeks to present to the world as a proof to be fathomed through the experience of the spirit.

If I am to explain from a different point of view than I have already done in numerous lectures here, how the path of this anthroposophically oriented spiritual science is, then I would like to speak today by way of introduction about something seemingly quite abstract, which may seem remote to some.

The Goetheanum did not take its name from Goethe for nothing. In a certain respect, Goethe's whole world view, his whole way of thinking, is the starting point for a new spiritual-scientific striving. And even if one can say that what one finds in Goethe is still a beginning, one can perhaps best illustrate the principles by starting from certain simple thoughts or ideas of Goethe. Well known in wider circles, but unfortunately still too little appreciated today, is what Goethe called his metamorphosis theory, in which we also find his idea of the original plant.

With this original plant Goethe does not mean a sensual plant structure of simple kind, as the correct today's natural scientist would have to say, but Goethe means with his original plant something which can be grasped and experienced only in the spirit. But at the same time, he means with this original plant something which is not to be found in any single plant, but which can be found in every single plant of the wide plant kingdom of the earth. So, he presupposes that — I would like to say — within every sensual plant there is an original plant to be grasped supersensibly, to be experienced in the spirit.

The same he imagines, although he has stated it less clearly, for the other, for the non-plant organisms. And if Goethe developed this idea of the primordial plant, in part precisely out of his artistic disposition, it must be said that his main striving was directed toward finding something scientific in the very best sense through something like the primordial plant, something that can be a guide to man as an idea, can be a spiritual guide through the whole wide world of plants.

When Goethe travelled through Italy to clarify and mature his world view, he once wrote to his Weimar friends, who knew well what he actually wanted with his original plant, that the image of the original plant had once again dawned on him, especially in the rich, bursting plant world of Italy. First of all, abstractly — one does not need to stick to the abstract, as we will see shortly —, first of all abstractly he says: Such an original plant must exist, because how else could one find in the whole manifold plant kingdom that every single being is really a whole plant? — As I said, this is expressed abstractly, but Goethe expresses himself about this original plant much more specifically, much more forcefully. Thus, he says, for example: If one has grasped this original plant in the spirit, then from the living image of this original plant one can make images of individual real plants, which have the possibility of existing.

One must only look in the right sense at what is actually said with such a word. Goethe, then, wants to arrive in spirit at an idea of the plant being, and he wants to have in spirit the possibility of forming mentally out of his original plant an entity which is an individual plant, but not like a plant which he sees sensually, but which, as it were, invents in addition to the sensual plants such a plant which does not exist sensually, but which would nevertheless have the possibility, if the conditions were there, of existing in sensuality. What is actually pointed out there? It is pointed out that man can immerse himself in sensual reality through his soul and in this immersion in sensual reality experience the spiritual that is in sensual reality in such a way that he grows together with this spirit that weaves and lives creatively everywhere in nature.

That is precisely the great thing about Goethe's world view, that it aims at this immersion in reality, and that it is convinced that if one immerses oneself in this reality, one comes to the spiritual aspect of this reality, so that one discovers the spirit of reality, which can then be one's guide through the whole confusing variety of the sensual itself.

Now one can extend what Goethe aimed at to the whole world surrounding man and to man himself. The anthroposophically oriented spiritual science makes it its task to extend this type of conception in the widest circle to all that which man encounters from others and from himself. It is thus the opposite of all unclear obscurantism, the opposite of all unclear mysticism. It strives for what Goethe claims for his world view: to submerge into the spiritual world with mathematical clarity, with mathematical transparency.

Now this spiritual science feels itself in harmony with the newer natural science, although it goes far beyond the natural science of the newer time. One only has to go through this natural science to see how this spiritual science must sprout out of this natural science itself. Let us look at what this newer natural science actually strives for. It sees its actual aim in finding such a knowledge of the things surrounding man, of the mineral, vegetable and animal world, yes, of man himself, in which nothing of any subjective feelings or ideas of man himself speaks. This natural science, especially on its newer standpoint, that of experiment, on which it has rightly placed itself as natural science, seeks to investigate nature in such a way that the individual phenomena and processes of nature themselves reveal their essence, their laws, that man weaves nothing into that which he calls knowledge of nature from that which he finds in himself.

In this way, what has appeared as natural science for three to four centuries, but especially in the 19th century, differs from the knowledge of nature of earlier times. Whoever follows this knowledge of nature of earlier times knows that people carried into the natural phenomena what they had formed in their ideas and, so to speak, took out of the natural phenomena what they had first brought in. That this should not happen, that man should let nature speak to him in a completely unbiased way, that is the endeavour of the newer natural science.

But one cannot do otherwise, if one does research on nature, than to let the spirit do the research. One cannot but apply what one has in oneself as a life of thoughts, as a life of ideas, and what is of a spiritual nature, to the context of natural phenomena. Now one can take a twofold path. One path has been taken by the ordinary natural scientific world view of recent times; the other, however, is the path that anthroposophically oriented spiritual science would like to take.

When natural science forms its ideas, these ideas, which are to be gained from nature as purely as I have described them, then it can, I would like to say, look at itself with these ideas; then it can ask itself:

What essence, what value do the ideas have which we apply to external nature? — The newer natural science does not do that. The newer natural science restricts itself to recognizing everything about nature that does not give an answer to the question: What is man himself? — That is the characteristic of all, one may say, insightful natural scientists, that they say: Yes, we can investigate many things about the physical world outside of us and in us — the question is not answered by that: What is man himself? — And again and again one must emphasize: By striving to know nature, natural science presents a world view in which man is not inside as soul and spirit. Natural science, honestly standing on today's standpoint, has no answer to the question of soul and spirit.

One must answer the question why this is so historically. Natural science itself does not know why it does not advance to the knowledge of soul and spirit, why it stops in front of soul and spirit in spite of its admirable results about the outer nature, why natural scientists appear again and again who say: Yes, if natural science would speak about soul and spirit, it would exceed its limits. — One believes to speak unbiasedly about nature. One does not speak impartially, because a burden, a pressure is over natural science, actually over the way of thinking of the newer natural research, what has been established for centuries as a certain way of thinking. And this pressure consists in the fact that from certain confessional currents a monopoly was claimed over the truths of soul and spirit.

If we go back a few centuries, we find that in the very time in which the newer natural science had its early red, the religious confessions claimed their monopoly to dictate the truths about soul and spirit. Before this monopoly claim the natural science of the newer time retreated. The natural science of the newer times has penetrated with magnificence into the outer nature; but not because one had recognized by this penetration into the outer nature that one could not ascend to soul and spirit, one has omitted this ascent, but because it was so firmly rooted in the unconscious human views that account must be taken of the monopoly claim of the confessional religions.

Therefore, this belief turned into an apparent proof that one cannot penetrate into soul and spirit.

Anyone who has seriously studied the natural scientific research methods of recent times, and who has then inwardly and spiritually processed precisely that which emerges as ideas about outer nature, with the exception of the actual essence of man, knows that the other path, which anthroposophically oriented spiritual science is taking, must be taken further into the future of humanity. If natural science would understand itself, if it would not live under the indicated pressure, then it would come to the Goethean principle precisely because it strives for a natural science which refrains from the subjective of man, it would grow together with the spirit which is spread out in the phenomena and facts and essence of nature. And the newer natural science, if it understood itself, would of itself choose precisely that which the anthroposophically oriented spiritual science must now claim for itself as a continuation of the natural scientific direction.

However, the inner power of imagination, the power of thinking, which can be acquired through natural science, must be supported by careful inner spiritual methods. And on the training of such inner spiritual methods rests all that by which the spiritual science meant here wants to find the way into the supersensible, into the spiritual world in general.

Today it is perhaps much too easy to imagine what is meant here by this way into the supersensible world. One thinks that something like an inner spinning is meant, a surrendering to all kinds of ideas, through which one weaves out all kinds of what the essence of things should be. One perhaps imagines that this is easy compared to the difficulty of the experimental method or compared to the methods used at observatories and in clinics. But if you read through something like I have tried to present in my book "How to gain knowledge of the higher worlds?" or in my "Secret Science," you will see that it is not a matter of some arbitrary spinning around in inner ideas, but of a strictly lawful, inner mental working of the spirit up into the spirit. For true spiritual science can never be of the opinion that one can penetrate into the spirit by external methods of experimentation, but true spiritual science must represent the opinion that only the spirit in man can find the spirit of the world.

What man has to do in his inner being, I have often described here in these lectures, in my books as meditation, as concentration. Today I would like to point out that this work of concentration, this work of meditation is a purely inner work of the soul. But where does this inner soul work strive towards? Where does this work only with inner soul forces, this devotion to the pure activity of the soul-spiritual in the human being's inner being, strive towards?

You know, by living in the world, we perceive the world through our senses, and then we process this world. This is also how natural science does it. Then we process this world by thinking about it, by revealing its laws, by imagining about it. But you also know that this imagining leads to something else, to something that is intimately connected with the health of our personal human being. This imagining about the world is connected with the fact that we can retain the impressions of the world, as we say, through our memory, through our power of recollection. Man so easily passes over this power of memory, this memory of man, because they are something so commonplace to him. But this is precisely the peculiarity of the real striving for knowledge, that that which is often commonplace must be understood by man precisely as that towards which the most important, the most meaningful questions must be raised.

When we perceive the world of the senses, form ideas about it, and after some time seem to bring them forth again from our inner being, so that we remember events we have experienced, then much unconsciousness lives in these memories, in this memory-acting. Just think how little you are actually master of your memory with your will, how little you can command your memory power, so to speak. Consider above all how little you are able, while you perceive outwardly, to think also of this memory. Or is it so that the human being, by looking out into the world with his eye, by hearing the sounds with his ear, that he at the same time takes care that there are ideas which make a recollection possible? No, in addition to the perceptions, in addition to the inner effects of the senses, man would have to consciously exert another force. In reality, he does not do that in ordinary life. I would like to say that the memory with its power runs alongside the outer life. But it is that which works there subconsciously, which, so to speak, co-determines all life in the outer sense-world, so that we carry this life along through our memory through life. It is this that is to be brought up from the subconscious as a force. In other words: We cannot bring up from the depths of our soul that which we so unconsciously exercise in memory power running alongside, by merely remembering our experiences, but by trying to bring up the power, which we otherwise do not know at all, which just runs alongside, as I have said, to such a conscious clarity as otherwise is only the outer sensual perception, by bringing up this power from the subconscious depths and weaving and living in that which otherwise is in the subconscious of the memory. If we use the power of recollection not for memory, not for recollection, but to make ideas and conceptions, which are otherwise just kept alive by the power of recollection, consciously present in our spirit, we strengthen something in our spirit by which, when the necessary time has come, we come to know an awakening quite different from that which we experience every morning. If one works again and again consciously in such a way, as otherwise only the memory, the memory power works, then one experiences something of a new awakening in the soul. One experiences something of an appearance of a completely different person in the soul than is the person who otherwise passes through the sense world. One cannot reach the spirit by theorizing. Every philosophical argument, which wants to reach the spirit by mere conclusion, has actually nothing else in mind than the word or the words of the spirit. The spirit wants to be experienced. And it can be experienced only by raising that which is otherwise subconscious memory, which lives in deeper layers of our human soul, so that it lives

224

in us with such a bright clarity, as otherwise that lives in us which we see through our eyes, What we hear through our ears, and that in this uplifting the conscious will lives as the conscious will lives when I turn my eye from this wall to that wall in order to turn my gaze away from what I see here and to look at what I can see there. By using my senses, the conscious will lives in this using of the senses. This will must fully penetrate this inner work of the soul, then one arrives at something which is a continuation of the ordinary activity of the soul of man, which relates to the ordinary activity of the soul of man in the same way as the waking life of the day relates to the life of sleep, from which at most the dream emerges.

That there is something like this in human nature, which can be brought up and which becomes a new organ of cognition, which becomes what Goethe calls the soul eye, the spiritual eye, that is what anthroposophically oriented spiritual science wants to prove by gradually living into such inner soul work. It will thereby say what natural science is not able to say, because it lives under the indicated pressure. But this pressure must fall away from the knowledge of mankind, because mankind longs for it — one can notice this longing, if one is only impartial enough for it.

Thus, you see that anthroposophically oriented spiritual science does not want to be some inverted mysticism, not something obscure, but a really genuine continuation of that which is known precisely in natural science. And especially those who have had an education in natural science will find it easier to concentrate and meditate their thoughts, for they are used to methods and ways of research which disregard the subjective aspects of man and go completely into the objective. If we apply to meditation what we have learned from natural science, we eliminate all human arbitrariness, we bring into meditation, into the inner work of the soul, something which is such an objective regularity as that of nature itself. Precisely by taking the way of thinking and imagining of natural science into the human being, the chaotic, the unclear self-knowledge, which is striven for with many a complicated and inverted mysticism, where one only always wants to brood into one's own inner being, is overcome. Against this untrained brooding into one's own inner being, there is that working in one's own inner being which, at every step of this working, proceeds as only the most conscientious natural scientist proceeds, in that he extends his power of judgment over that which spreads out before his eye or before his instruments.

That is one side. I would like to say it is the side that points to the awakening of special powers of cognition. The ordinary power of memory, however, will not be there in such moments when one wants to investigate the spiritual directly, because this power of memory itself has undergone a metamorphosis. It has become a spirit eye that can perceive the spirit. With the usual conclusions, which the today's common logic has, one cannot penetrate to the real spirit. Whoever wants to speak of a real advance to the spirit, must point to the really existing forces that lead to this spirit. And such a really existing power is the power of memory. Only this power of memory must be transformed, must become something quite different. Every other penetration into the spirit leads at the same time into darkness, because the human will is thereby eliminated, and with it the most important piece of the human being itself. Just as we call that which rises from, I would like to say, organic subsoil of our spirit fantastic, just as we do not call that which we do not have in our power a correct memory, so the true spiritual researcher will not accept for his spiritual research any soul content which he does not penetrate completely with the light of his will.

So much about one side, the imaginative life, as used by spiritual research. But something else in man can be used and must be used if one really wants to find the way into the supersensible, into the spiritual world. And just as spiritual science is challenged from the spirit of natural science by the way of imagination of the newer times, so spiritual science is challenged on the other side by human life in the newer times. If you follow the development of the human soul through the last centuries with an open mind, not with the prejudice of today's historian, but with an open mind, you can say to yourself that just around the middle of the fifteenth century a tremendous change occurred in the constitution of human souls, however only within the civilized world, but just within this civilized world. It is only a prejudice if one believes, looking only at the outer historical facts, that a human soul of the civilized world in the 8th, 9th century after Christ had the same inner constitution as the human souls of today. Certainly, there are also today retarded human souls, which more or less still stand on the standpoint of the 8th, 9th century; but they are just instructive, because they lead us also outwardly back to that time. But on the whole we can say: One only needs to really look at human life according to experience. A tremendous change has occurred, which since the middle of the 15th century has become stronger and stronger in its effects. If one wants to describe it in more detail, one must say: If one goes back beyond this point in time, one finds that man faced man in a completely different way than is actually the case today, and that is actually striven for by unconscious human forces into the future of mankind. Whatever one may say against it because of certain prejudices, something is striven for with regard to the relationship of man to man, which has taken its beginning in the designated point of time. In earlier times man was close to man by blood relationship, by tribal relationship, by all that which out of his organism made him related to the other man, or which made him related to the other man also out of the organic connection which expresses itself, for example, in sexual love. Do we not see, if we only want to see, that in the place of the old blood connection, in the place of the old clan connection, of the old family connection, of the old tribal connection, more and more that which works from man to man in such a way that it passes from the soul, from the willing soul of one man to the willing soul of the other man? Do we not see that the development of modern times makes it more and more necessary for man to approach the other man through something quite different from his mere bodily organism? We see that the consciousness of the personality has been growing since the time indicated, that man has become more and more inward and inward, and thus, more and more lonely and lonely. Since that time man lives with his soul life, I would like to say, more and more isolated in himself. The soul life closes itself off from the outside world. The blood no longer speaks when we face our neighbours. We have to make our inner life active. We must live ourselves over into the other. We have to be absorbed in the soul of the other. One misunderstands very much, often especially in those circles which today rightly believe themselves to be socialist, what one can call the social principle, the social impulse of the newer times. One sees it rising, this social impulse; but one still knows today in the fewest circles what it actually consists of.

It consists in the fact that more and more the impulse awakens in the man who has become lonely, to live over into other men through his soul-spiritual will, so that the neighbour becomes the one who becomes it through our consciousness, not through our blood, not through our organic connection. There we are facing people, and we have the necessity to live into them. What we call benevolence today, what we call love today, is something different from what was called that a long time ago. But by living into other people in this way, it is as if everything that pulsates in ourselves, that lives in us as will, were to absorb the will of the other. We step completely over with our soul into the other. We go out of our body, as it were, and enter into the body of the other. When this feeling becomes more and more prevalent, when this feeling, permeated with love, I would like to say, spreads over people as modern charity, then something emerges from this co-experience of the will, of the whole soul life of the other person, which is a real-life experience. Today, many people could already have this experience of life, if they would not let it be clouded by prejudices. Where it appears, one beats it back with truly not good reasons. One need only remember a person like Lessing. At the end of his life, when all that he could produce in the way of human greatness had passed through his soul, he still wrote his "Education of the Human Race," which culminates in the recognition of the fact of man's repeated lives on earth. There are higher philistines, as there are higher daughters, and they have their judgment ready about such a thing. They say: Yes,

Lessing was clever all his life; but then he became decrepit and came to such dubious ideas as those of the repeated earth lives.

But these repeated earthly lives are not an invented idea; they are what we experience when we do not stand opposite the other person by mere blood relationship or by mere organic belonging together, but when we can really live ourselves over into that which lives in his soul. There the spirit of one person comes face to face with the spirit of the other person, and experience shows that this spirit can say: that which forms a bond for your soul, for your spirit with the other person, did not come into being through this life. That which lies in the blood arose through this life. But what appears in the spirit as a necessity has come into being through something that preceded this life. Who really follows this development of the newer life of mankind since the middle of the 15th century — there is only a mist still spread over it for the widest circles of mankind —, he will come to the idea of repeated earth lives from the coexistence with men. And what there comes to the appearance, that appears, I would like to say, like a dream. I say "like a dream" for the following reason: When we fall asleep, we sleep into an unconscious. Then, out of this unconscious, this or that emerges as a dream. One can compare this falling asleep into the unconscious with the immersion into the souls of our fellow human beings, as I have just characterized it. Then out of this immersion, I would like to say, not actually figuratively, but very actually, out of this falling asleep into our fellow human beings also something emerges at first like the dream of the repeated earth lives and draws our attention to the fact that something like this must be sought in order to understand life, in order to find the way through the world of the senses. And that which shines out of social life like a dream becomes a complete certainty when we now form the human will in the same way as I have shown earlier for memory. But just as memory must become a fully conscious force, so the will, on the other hand, must shed something that directs it completely in ordinary life.

What, then, in ordinary life directs our will, our desires, our appetites? If our desires did not arise out of our organic bodily life, the will would have nothing to do, so to speak. Whoever sees through the will by experience knows that this will is based on desire. But we can also detach that which acts as the actual force of the will from our desires. To a certain extent we detach it in social life. But this only makes us aware of what is really important. We release it in social life by loving our neighbour, by becoming absorbed in him, not by desiring him like a piece of meat. We do not love our neighbour out of our desires, but we use a desireless will. However, this desireless will can also be drawn upon through a special training. This happens when we do not merely want what can be achieved in the outer world, what one or the other desire, but when we apply the will to our human being and his development itself. We can do that. All too often we leave ourselves to life as it carries us. But even when one has outgrown school, that is, when others are no longer in charge of education, one can still practice continuous self-education, continuous self-chastisement. One can take one's own spiritual being into one's own hands, one can undertake to achieve this and that. If life has led you to a certain point in time, you can decide to become knowledgeable in this or that area of life, to transfer your power of judgment to another area of life, in short, you can reverse your will. Whereas otherwise the will always works from the inside outward, as desire dominates the outside, the will can be reversed, turned inward. By practicing self-chastisement through our will, by trying to make ourselves better and better in one direction or another, we apply the actual desireless willpower. And that which you will find in my book "How to attain knowledge of the higher worlds?" and in the second part of my "Secret Science" is aimed, in addition to the other things I have already characterized, at man's applying such a culture of will to himself, so that he penetrates more and more, I would like to say, into himself with his will. But then, when these two forces work together, the power of memory brought out of the unconscious, which then grasps the human will, then man knows himself inwardly as spirit, then he knows that he has grasped the spirit inwardly in a purely spiritual way, then he knows that he does not carry it out through the organs of the body. Then he knows how spiritual action is in the spirit, then he knows what it means: soul and spirit are independent of the body.

One cannot prove that the soul and the spirit are independent of the body, because they are not in ordinary life. In ordinary life, spirit and soul are absolutely dependent on the body. But in us lives another person, who is independent, whom we can bring up from his depths. Then that which is eternal in man will show itself to us.

You see, there is not at all a wrong, intricate mysticism in this anthroposophically oriented spiritual science. There is in it absolutely that which can be expressed in a completely clear way, but which one only comes to if one really explains it to oneself inwardly and does not only say: You shall develop your inner being, you shall look into yourself, you shall find God in your own nature. — In anthroposophically oriented spiritual science, reference is made to very specific forces that are to be brought under cultivation in a very specific way. That is what is important here. In this way, however, this anthroposophically oriented spiritual science is in another way the continuation of modern scientific and social striving. In the field of natural science, one can no longer completely disregard the spirit. And so, it has come about that, because one did not want to remove the pressure which I characterized at the beginning, one also wants to prove today, with the same methods with which one, I would like to say, ducks under the marked pressure, that there is something in man like a spirit, like a soul. And this is what has occurred among those who do not see through the whole situation in the cultural development of the present.

It is to this striving for the spirit, which, however, moves in a wrong direction, that we owe all the hopes which are based on certain justified foundations, the hopes which some naturalists have with regard to hypnotism, with regard to the possibility that one human being, with his consciousness damped down, can implant some idea in another. We owe to this striving the hopes that some place on the investigation of the dream life and the like, and we owe to this striving to come to the spirit after all — because man cannot help but seek the spirit after all — the whole error of spiritualism.

What is actually sought in this field? Well, take something like it is the case with hypnotism or mediumism, what actually happens there? There, that which is the normal human consciousness, through which man stands firmly in the ordinary life, is damped down. By hypnotizing man, that which is his conscious ability in ordinary life is damped down. In a way, other forces, which perhaps come from the neighbouring person or from others, have an effect on the unconscious or semi-conscious or quarter-conscious person. There is no doubt that all kinds of interesting things come to light. Certainly, all kinds of interesting things also come to light through mediumism; but that which comes to light is achieved on the basis of a dulling down, a lulling to sleep of the ordinary consciousness. This is never aimed at in the research methods of anthroposophically oriented spiritual science. The research method of anthroposophically oriented spiritual science says: Man has advanced in his development to the consciousness which he has in ordinary life through his senses in the awake state; if one wants to recognize something new about man, one should not paralyze this consciousness, not dampen it, but on the contrary, lead it further, as I have indicated. One should increase the clarity, lead the sensory perceptions into the power of memory, by applying the will, which otherwise arises only from the dull desire to self-cultivation. Because one does not go this way, does not have the courage and perseverance for this way, one dampens down the will and believes that one thereby comes to a knowledge of the soul, of the spiritual in man.

But what is the result of depriving man of his other abilities? By putting man to sleep, one arrives at an external way of looking at man which does not show him as a spiritual-mental being, but shows him precisely in his sub-humanity, in that which makes him more like an animal than he is in ordinary life. This must be strictly emphasized, that by all these sometimes-well-intentioned research methods man is led down into the subhuman. If I hypnotize someone and give him a potato, but through the suggestive power make it clear to him that this is a pear, and he bites into the potato with the consciousness of biting into a pear, then I darken his higher consciousness in such a way, act on him in such a way as is acted on the instinct of the animal. Only that man, even in his subhuman nature, is not entirely an animal, but that his animal nature expresses itself in a different way. That is the essential thing. And if one looks for any thought transference in the asleep state or in lowered consciousness in general, then one has to do again with an instinctive activity translated into the human, that is, with a subhuman. Whoever conflates what anthroposophically oriented spiritual science wants to be with these things, slanders anthroposophically oriented spiritual science. For here it is not a question of leading man down from his ordinary state of consciousness into a sub-human state, but of leading him beyond himself, so that the ordinary consciousness continues to work, and a higher consciousness is added to this ordinary consciousness.

This is precisely what anthroposophically oriented spiritual science shows by its research method, that the human being we have here in the sense world is based on an animal, a subhuman instinct; and this instinct can be evoked, demonstrated, by putting the ordinary consciousness to sleep. If it expresses itself differently than in the ordinary consciousness, then precisely the spiritual science meant here can trace this other expression. It characterizes this other expression, which always takes place in hypnosis, in the mediumistic state, as a subhuman, as a descent into animalism. But it shows at the same time that that which lives as animal in man is not as in the ordinary animal. The method of research that I have spoken of here as that of the spiritual science meant here, knows that what comes to light through such experiments as hypnotism, as mediumism, is something that still lives in man today from earlier human states. Precisely because this spiritual science does not come to a subjectively coloured, but to an objective self-knowledge, it can gain a judgment about what that actually is, what appears through hypnotism, what appears through mediumism. This is something that does not belong to this earthly world at all.

If one pursues with the means of spiritual science that which spreads in the earthly world in the animal, in the vegetable, in the mineral kingdom, if one pursues it in its relation to man, then one finds that man, as he is now, is adapted to the earth precisely by the fact that he has his present consciousness. The states of consciousness which occur in lulled, not ordinary consciousness, which occur in hypnosis, in mediumism, are not states of consciousness, are not human powers, which could derive from the fact that man is adapted to the earth; this derives from such an adaptation which was peculiar to man before the earth became earth. And just by such conditions is rejected by the research on conditions of the earth itself, which however preceded the today's earth condition.

If one investigates further how the present state of the earth is connected with the animal and plant world, one sees that man carries something in himself which does not let him appear to be adapted to the present existence on earth, but that the animal and plant world is adapted to the present existence on earth. With this one then gains the outlook that man, however, existed in primitive states, which, if evoked today, are nothing but depressing his consciousness, before the present animals existed in their present form. So that we have to say: Man has not risen from the animal world, but man was present, however, with such states of soul and mind as we bring up, as they appear animal-like in the characterized states, before the earth came to this present planetary condition.

I cannot give you today the details which you can read in my books. But I wanted to indicate at least that just by pursuing some things on which today hopes are placed for the knowledge of the present nature of man, thereby a way is shown to gain the outlook into pre-earthly times and into the nature of man in such prehistoric times. In the same way, however, by the fact that we can evoke states of consciousness which lie above the present state of consciousness adapted to the earth, we are pointed to how we will live in these higher states of consciousness when the earth will no longer be our dwelling place.

These things open up to the inner seeing. You cannot say: You cannot prove these things, just as you cannot prove that camels exist. You must have seen them, or somebody must have seen them, then you know that there are camels. So, you cannot prove the supersensible with the ordinary power of judgment, which applies only to the ordinary world. One must show how one comes to see the supersensible. From this seeing of the supersensible results that which indeed works into the sense world, but which can never be seen in the sense world itself.

So, of course, one could now say: Yes, you show us how individual people succeed in making the spirit a guide through the sense world and into the supersensible world by means of supersensible vision. But can all people thus come to see into the supersensible world? — This is how it is with this matter: If you let that work on you which is described by me in the books already mentioned as an inner discipline, as an inner development which you take into your own hands for your soul, then you will absolutely come to see from your own power of judgment, from your own common sense, which is then just developed, that which the spiritual researcher can discover in the spiritual world. But just as there are individual researchers for physical research who seek out one or the other, and one must then accept what they have found, so there will be individual spiritual researchers in the future of the development of mankind who will research this or that in the spiritual world. For them, whether they can investigate something depends on whether in certain moments of life, for which they have waited, without their doing — for one can only make oneself a waiter through soul development — that which appears as a spiritual fact becomes recognizable to them. This must come, one could say, using a religious expression, as through a grace. This grace will occur for man as a spiritual researcher just as, let us say, for one man and for another this or that experience occurs in the sensual world. Thus, it will be that certain facts will always bring forth individuals from the spiritual world.

In order to bring forth these facts, various things are necessary; it is not only necessary that one has gone through what is written in the above-mentioned books, that one can completely understand what the spiritual researcher says, but something is necessary which can be described as a quality of man with "fearless" in a very high degree towards the spiritual world. People are so reluctant to penetrate the spiritual world because they are actually afraid of the unknown, just as man is always afraid of the unknown. The spiritual researcher must become fearless. And on the other hand, he must acquire the quality of the capacity for suffering, the capacity for pain; for a real discovery out of the spiritual world, it cannot be achieved without a certain pain, without a certain suffering. You will understand that this must be so if you simply imagine that the state of spiritual seeing is not adapted to the ordinary earthly conditions, nor is it basically adapted, as our soul is adapted to our organism which has become ill and is in pain. If one really puts oneself with the developed soul into the facts of the spiritual world, one is in a world for which one is not organized at first. One penetrates into a world that cuts there, that burns there. That has to be gone through. And one only gets to the facts when one really approaches them with the attitude that consists in using everything that the soul can develop, but that one then waits until in certain, I would like to say again, graceful moments the spiritual facts approach the people.

This should not be imagined as something that comes to you like a fantasy idea, but as an experience of a penetrating intensity in relation to the inner existence of man. I will only take this simple fact, which I have already mentioned, which can actually only appear before the human soul today through spiritual research, the fact that in the middle of the 15th century the whole human race of the civilized world experienced a turnaround — a simple fact. That one may express it as a scientific fact, may only come from the fact that one has worked on his soul, has worked diligently, that one has not wanted to conquer the spirit by arbitrariness, but that one has put himself through this work into an expectant state, until there has come that which reveals itself as such an apparently simple truth.

Then something else is necessary. There are people, I only remember for example the philosopher Schelling or others, who got one or the other impression from the spiritual world through special moments of grace. What did they do? They could not build up a world view fast enough when they received an impression from the spiritual world. They draw consequences from some impression they get from the spiritual world. They got an impression, then they make a whole system out of it, a whole worldview. This is what the real spiritual researcher must completely get out of the habit of doing. The real spiritual researcher must stop at this single fact which reveals itself to him, and he must continue to wait until another fact reveals itself to him. One must not, for example, when one has become acquainted with the fact which I have mentioned today, that the earth was preceded by pre-earthly conditions in which man has already lived, deduce from it a whole scientific system about the evolution of the earth, but must accept such a fact as an isolated, single fact and let other equally isolated, single facts approach, so that fact stands up after fact, rich or less rich. But one must wait for each individual fact; that is what matters. Even if spiritual enlightenments are the basis of spiritual research, these spiritual enlightenments occur only when fate predestines man to them. Just as one must not conclude from the northern hemisphere of the earth what is in the southern hemisphere of the earth but must investigate separately what is in the southern hemisphere of the earth, so one must not conclude from one corner of the spiritual world to the other of the spiritual world but must learn to wander around in the spiritual world, to grasp the details in their isolation. From this you can already see that what people can explore from the spiritual world will be distributed; they can learn many things.

Now you might say: Yes, but is there not a danger that those to whom such spiritual facts are revealed will become arrogant among men, that they will regard themselves as special creatures, towering above the rest? — This has already been taken care of. The first thing that must precede real spiritual research is absolute modesty, precisely intellectual modesty. Without developing this modesty towards the rest of humanity, one cannot make any progress in the field of spiritual research. The spiritual researcher knows how to communicate individual facts from the spiritual world to his fellow men, but the fact that he has the grace to communicate something that is revealed to him, he owes at the same time to the way he approaches his fellow men. The spiritual researcher is one who approaches even the smallest child with true reverence when he hears something from the spirit and soul hidden within the human being, even if it only cries out from the child's throat. The spiritual researcher is happy when he hears this or that from the experience of the individual human being. The experiences that people communicate to him are his school. He subordinates himself completely to it. He knows only one thing, he knows that what people experience, even if they are on the most primitive levels of education, is infinitely valuable, that only that which is usually man's power of judgment does not follow. If people were to judge correctly what they have experienced, they would bring forth treasures of soul and spirit from within themselves and from the subsoil of their being. It is to these that the spiritual researcher looks. Every human being is for him an equal being with sacred riddles in the soul, only that the upper consciousness, the faculty of judgment sometimes does not follow what is in the depths of the soul. Thus, the spiritual researcher in particular becomes a humble man, because in this respect he always has the spiritual equality of men before his eye, and because he knows that he has that which he researches in the spiritual world only because he is a man among men. Through this, however, he is predestined to work in the spirit for other people, who for their part, through meditation and concentration, can bring their souls so far that they accept what the spiritual researcher says.

You may reply that this is not very well arranged, that people should live side by side in this way, that one should learn from individual people what one can understand, but what one cannot explore oneself. I can reply to this in two ways. One is that this is a fact which one has to accept like any other fact of life, even if it may be desirable for some people in a different way. That is one thing I can say in reply. But the other is that he who foresees such a human future, a human future in which there are those among men who look into the spiritual world, and from this spiritual world reveal intimate matters to men, so that in this way the other men experience from their understanding what they can gain in the way indicated, he also knows that then most intimate relationships develop from man to man. And he also knows that it is precisely through this that the social impulses pass from soul to soul and through this that the real social life in the spirit is evoked, which today is believed to be achieved only by external means. Just think how people will be brought together, how they will represent a social structure in their living together, when people will face each other in such a way that one person accepts what the other explores as an intimate matter most important for him. Just through this, people will come close to each other in the future in the desirable way, so that spirit will work over into the soul of the next person, as it has been indicated. Those who can explore the spirit will be felt as a necessity for the other people. On the other hand, the whole humanity is also felt by the spiritual researcher as that in which he is rooted, without which he cannot live, without which he himself would not have the slightest sense with his spiritual research.

If today the social question has also been made into something that is merely outwardly materialistically conceived, then that which is anthroposophically oriented spiritual science shows — viewed just inwardly — that when the spirit becomes the guide through the sense world and out of the sense world into the supersensible world, thereby also in the social living together of men that structure is brought about through which man can in the future become for man what he is actually to become.

With this I tried to characterize for you today, again from a different point of view than I have done in the numerous earlier lectures, how through anthroposophy it is attempted to penetrate into the spirit, and how this penetration rests on the basis of developing the inherent powers of the human soul. This is what I am trying to represent — it will soon be two decades — in what I call anthroposophically oriented spiritual science. It is still said in many circles that this anthroposophically oriented spiritual science represents something of a striving for Buddhism or the like. In the last lecture I already indicated how this anthroposophically oriented spiritual science, which works out of the essence of man, out of the present essence of man himself, perhorresces that weakness of man which does not want to strive out of what is there, not out of what we have acquired in the newer natural science, but which for my sake wants to go over to the Orient, to India, and take from there that which was adapted for a completely different age and no longer fits into our present. We experience it again and again. A few days ago it could be experienced here again that people say: Anthroposophism, as they express themselves, also represents some kind of escape to India. If this is said especially by people who call themselves "Christian," then I would like to remind these Christians of something they may know: "Thou shalt not bear false witness against thy neighbour." For it is nothing else than bearing false witness against one's neighbour if one speaks of what is meant here as anthroposophical spiritual science as if it were something obscure, as if it were something of a search for humanity that has become purely passive and the like. Because humanity has become passive, because humanity can no longer come to activity through that which has been traditionally imparted to it through the centuries, a new spirit must be sought as a guide through the sense world and into the supersensible world.

To those who always speak only of the rehashing of the old spirit and perhorresce, as natural science was perhorresced in Galileo's time, that which appears as spiritual science, they should be told above all, especially if they want to speak from the Christian spirit: He who is serious about Christianity need have no fear that any discovery, even a spiritual one, will be detrimental to the true meaning of the Christ-impulse, to the religious veneration of mankind. On the contrary, religious life will be given greater splendour by the fact that people will again know what is spirit and what is soul, that they will not allow themselves to be dictated what is spirit and what is soul, that they will search within the soul for the way to the experience of spirit and soul. But this is what is striven for in that movement which has its outer representation outside in Dornach in the Goetheanum.

Through this movement, that is striven for which lives unconsciously as longing in numerous souls without their knowing it. One will not be able to get it out of these souls by a mere decree or dictate, but it will live in the souls as an aspiration, even if one were to bring it to trample down the actual representation of this aspiration. For just as man would die if he stopped absorbing new life forces in his thirty-fifth year, just as he could not go on living from that time on if he did not supply himself with new material life forces, so mankind cannot go on living if it only wants to process the old, the traditional, if a new spirit does not arise at the proper moment of time and weave itself into the development of mankind.

For that is what this spiritual science wants to present, to present clearly and unambiguously, not obscurantism, not intricate mysticism. It wants to show clearly that the spirit is the living, the right guide through the sense world and into the supersensible world. In the sense world we become directionless without the spirit. But if we develop the spirit as a guide through the sense world, then it does not prove to be an abstract idea spirit alone, then it proves to be the living spirit in us. And then we would have to cut off its wings, through which it wants to strive into its real homeland, into the homeland of the spirit, if we did not, after we have chosen it as a guide through the sense world, want to ascend through it, through its leadership into the supersensible world. For the spirit is alive. And if the belief can spread that the spirit is nothing independently living in relation to matter, what is to blame for this? Only this is to blame, that man kills the spirit in himself by his will, and thus, the dead spirit cannot grasp the living spirit. But if the spirit in man is enlivened, then the living spirit in man takes hold of the living spirit in the world.

The Liberation of the Human Being

APPENDIX

Editor's Preface: At the invitation of the socialist youth organization Münchenstein-New-World, Rudolf Steiner spoke on socialism in the village of Münchenstein, near Dornach, on April 10, 1919. The day before, he had spoken to the Basel student body on a similar topic (see the fifth lecture in this volume). Possibly this is also the reason why the Münchenstein lecture was not officially transcribed. The wording of Rudolf Steiner's remarks during the debate that followed the lecture is based on the plain text transcription of a stenographic transcript, the original of which is no longer available. Since the present manuscript contains gaps as well as inaccuracies in some places, it required detailed editing by the editors.

Question: Is it not a great mistake that social democracy denies the spiritual and soul and recognizes only the body?

Rudolf Steiner: Well, it is not so easy to deal with this comprehensive question in a few words, for the simple reason that what is often described and represented in the praised scientific circles as spiritual and mental life is actually not something that is in the process of ascent, but something that is basically going through its last phase of development, its last descent. When one speaks of the spiritual, one should not speak of the spiritual in general, but one should always be clear that the spiritual undergoes descending and ascending developments. And if today the common, usual spiritual life, which I have also characterized in the lecture, which is a result of the leading class in the last centuries, if this spiritual life is rejected, precisely this spiritual life, which has become so through the state and economic development, especially of the 19th century, then one can understand this. It is a question of finding a real spiritual life, a spiritual life that retains its own reality. And then I have to say that, above all, it is necessary today to fulfil the one thing I took the liberty of saying in my lecture: that we really learn from events....

It is just the peculiar thing that within the so often praised civilization people have found themselves who have spoken of love of neighbour, of love of God, of brotherhood, have spoken, well, out of the age of the so-called humanity. They spoke very cleverly, very reasonably, often in rooms with mirrored windows, in heated rooms. These were heated with coals, which were mined by children from nine to eleven, twelve, thirteen years of age, as studies have shown, especially in the rise of the social movement of recent times! These coals were mined in mines where naked men stood among half-naked women, where there was really no reason to respect any sense of shame, let alone any Christian ideas. One must really consider that it is not merely a matter of blurting out such a word as that of charity. By the correctness and importance of the emotional content one will of course always make an impression ...

It is better to be less understood and to present that which can serve the new age than to have to repeat the old over and over again. The question must be raised for all those who say: Keep only your old religiosity, keep also the former belief in God and the like — for all these it must be said: Well, after all, you have always wanted to bring this for 2000 years. How far have you actually come with it, if you so oppose that which wants to serve the time? Just think that you would have had enough time! Time has been left to you for 2000 years; now it is necessary that you recognize that a new thing has to break in over the tested and troubled mankind. This has to be said by someone who stands on the position that he may cherish the hope, because he stands on the ground of true social thinking, that a new spiritual life will be founded, which will really bring man together again with a living spiritual life, not with a dead one, which the old traditions and the like have already become.

Certainly, one can reproach socialism, if one wants, that it has taken little account of spiritual life up to now. But let us wait and see. The spiritual life, which today even resounds from our universities, cannot find any special preference among those people who want to have something human, who want to have a spiritual life, which in turn will give all people the consciousness that their physical man is connected with inner necessity with the soul-spiritual in man. Let us wait and see whether it will not be the socialistically thinking people who will be the next to turn to the actual spiritual life and will no longer stand uncomprehendingly against it! It cannot be said that in today's bourgeois circles one meets with special approval if one tries to bring this school of thought closer to them ...

People come and want to have programs. People have all kinds of wishes, beautiful goals for the future and the like. — Programs are as cheap as blackberries today! Societies are founded, programs are written and so on. But that is not what matters. What matters is that we grasp reality. I am convinced that if one can say how people must organize themselves in a healthy social organism — and I see something healthy in the threefold structure of the social organism — then people will find what they like. Then they will find the organization, the structure of the social organism, in which men can realize accordingly that which must come for mankind. Perhaps not one stone of what I have to say today will remain; that is not what matters. It depends on the fact that one touches the things somewhere like I mean it. Then perhaps something completely different will come out. It is a question of the suggestion to seriously do something somewhere in the realm of reality that is conceived out of the threefold structure of the social organism, out of life experience, not out of a grey theory, not out of an egoistic prejudice. That is what matters.

That is why my program is one that calls upon people, above all, to have again the possibility of realizing this in a certain sense. What I have just pronounced is essentially different from the usual programs. And that's why I think time will take its course, of course. And basically, what is so often pronounced today is not so very young. One of those who stimulated the most, Karl Marx, the socialist confessor, he uttered in the first half of the 19th century, when he was still young, something like the following words: Should all enlightenment and persuasion bounce off the obstinacy of the possessing class, let it be the most sacred duty on the part of the proletariat to charge against the bulwark of capitalism ...

One of the listeners made the remark: "The capitalist soul has no feeling for the proletarian soul."

Rudolf Steiner: This is an experience that can be made in abundance in the present day. Now various necessary things have been brought forward today. Above all, because the time has already advanced too far, it is not possible to go into every single one. So, I would just like to comment on some of the points that have been raised. Above all, it has been said that what I have said contradicts the Social Democratic program.

You see, whether such contradictions exist or not will not be decided by the wording of what I have to say today, I think, but will only be decided by the future. I believe that today, under the present circumstances, it is necessary for people to express completely out of their unbiased conviction what they believe they have gleaned from life, what is necessary for the further development of mankind. Basically, enough programs have been set up. That which must come, must come through people and their insight. That is why I think it is most gratifying — and this has been admitted and acknowledged from time to time — that although I have a lot to say that does not agree with any program, with any party of the present time, there are still people who listen to these things and who pay attention to them. And I believe that we will make progress precisely by simply listening, by not thundering each other down. One may not thunder with words at all; one may also thunder down the one who is inconvenient to one, by not saying it in words at all, but by being silent. This has also become a popular method in our time. Thus, I have touched on some of the points that seemed particularly important to me in this discussion.

Appendix

It has been said, however, that we still lack intelligent people. I think about the relations of intelligence to today's true progress approximately in the following way. Allow me to make this historical comparison: Christianity, which has had a great, significant influence on the development of mankind in the form in which it came into being almost 2000 years ago, developed from Asia through the highly developed Greek world, through the highly educated Roman world. There was the top of intelligence, but it has not seized these people! It has struck with the people who came down by the migration from the north, who were looked at by the Romans as the barbarians, who were looked at by the Greeks as unintelligent people. They had the unused intelligence; they had the new, the then young intelligence. The others have had the old, the withered, the fertilized intelligence. — This is what we recognize today again as the basis of the main movement of the present history: We live, so to speak, in a new migration of peoples. Those people who are considered to be intelligent today, sometimes talk about something highly unintelligent. They are talking about something that cannot possibly advance the times. We live in a migration of peoples, which only does not move horizontally, but which moves from the bottom to the top — even if the expressions are meant symbolically, they can still be used for it. It is just those people who stand out with unconsumed intelligence from the circles from which the previous civilization has been formed. Basically, there is an understanding in these souls for what the future must bring. I believe precisely in this unconsumed intelligence, because it is healthy, it is not decadent. I see a migration of peoples in the modern proletarian movement, a migration of peoples that is only moving in a different direction. And it will bring something into the world that will carry humanity upwards again for a long time to come.

This is what lets us look into the future, what gives us some hints. Even if today there are still inadequate and unhealthy things everywhere, even in the most hopeful movements, we will not have to be pessimistic, but it is something that makes us believe that those who can feel what the old culture has done wrong will finally bring about what must be brought about today: a spiritual life, a legal and economic life that is there for all people. And you will perhaps have noticed from what I have said that I am not thinking of dividing people further into estates or classes. In older times, a distinction was made between the educational class, the nurturing class and the military class. This is not the point. Precisely because the institutions that we have in the three-part social organism are separated from the human being, the human being himself is that which unites all three members. And he will have his representation in a democratic state system or will stand in it himself; he will have to stand in the economic life and in the spiritual life, that is, in the whole three-part social organism. The human being is that which uniformly encompasses the three areas separated from each other. That is what I have said with the words: "to make the human arm." And he will become free when we no longer swear by the abstract unitary state.

Interposed question: Yes, but there must be law and courts for all three areas, for example?

Rudolf Steiner: Of course there must be. But it is a question of the fact that precisely if something is to live correctly in all three areas, this must necessarily be produced in the one area. Just as the human head is a part of the whole organism and also needs the air, so it cannot itself breathe the air; the lungs must breathe the air. And the air is then communicated to the whole organism ...

Today one can have a certain hope that things will come true which have not yet come true. And for this reason, because so much harm has been done in the last few years, mankind must want to atone, if I may express myself in this way, must want to do something so that things which could not be realized so far, will be solved little by little in a possible way. That is what I would like to say here in conclusion.

NOTES

In February 1919 Rudolf Steiner's public activity for the threefolding of the social organism had begun with the collection of signatures for the appeal "To the German People and to the Cultural World" and with its publication. In the same month he gave those lectures in Zurich from which the fundamental writing "The Key Points of the Social Question in the Vital Necessities of the Present and Future" emerged.

These lectures are published within the Gesamtausgabe in the volume "Die soziale Frage," GA Bibl.-No. 328. The lectures of March and April printed in the present volume continue this lecture activity within Switzerland. On April 20, Rudolf Steiner went to Stuttgart and remained there — with short interruptions due to lecture tours to Tübingen, Berlin and Dornach — until the end of September. In Stuttgart he developed extensive public activity to bring about a fundamental transformation of public social life in the sense of the Threefolding. On April 22, the "Bund für Dreigliederung des sozialen Organismus" (Association for the Threefolding of the Social Organism) was founded, and in numerous meetings the founding of cultural and works councils was initiated. At the same time Rudolf Steiner, together with Emil Molt, the director of the Waldorf-Astoria cigarette factory in Stuttgart, prepared the foundation of the Waldorf School, which was opened on September 7, 1919. In view of the upcoming peace negotiations in Versailles, Rudolf Steiner, in connection with the publication of the memoirs of the German Chief of Staff H. von Moltke, made an attempt to make the background that led to the outbreak of the First World War accessible to a wider public.

All this was undertaken in a situation when all conditions had been shaken by the attempt of radical forces to continue the revolution. Then, in July, the opposite direction took over. The apparent stabilization, the establishment of "peace and order" gave the upper hand to those forces that were only interested in maintaining the existing conditions unchanged, thus making a fundamental inner renewal completely impossible. Emil Molt summarizes his recollections of the events of these months with the words: "The greatest intensity of action was required for two reasons: First, the chaotic situation resulting from the revolution had to be used before the situation became solidified again, and then, in terms of foreign policy, the negotiations in Versailles had to be influenced and the lie of war guilt had to be exposed. The lack of understanding and the resistance of our contemporaries was stronger than we suspected. The tasks into which we jumped with fresh courage and enthusiasm were in the end also greater than our ability and endurance." Molt then points to the goals achieved in spite of everything, such as the establishment of the Waldorf School. (See E. Molt, "Entwurf meiner Lebensbeschreibung," Stuttgart 1972, p. 160) In October Rudolf Steiner returned to Dornach. In the same month he gave the lectures "Social Future" in Zurich (GA Bibl.-Nr. 332a). The present volume now also contains the lectures he gave on the social question in Bern and Basel in October and November. Of these lectures Emil Leinhas, a close collaborator of Rudolf Steiner, gives the following account:

"On October 1, 1919, Rudolf Steiner returned to Dornach for a longer period of time. I was allowed to accompany him to spend a few weeks of vacation in Dornach. Soon after, Rudolf Steiner gave public lectures on the Threefolding in various places in Switzerland. The first of these lectures took place before a decidedly middle-class audience in Bern. On this occasion, together with Dr. Boos and to our mutual amazement, I was once again able to experience impressively how much Rudolf Steiner knew how to adapt his way of expressing himself to the respective audience; how he knew how to take into account the life situation and perceptive capacity of his listeners and to speak entirely from the hearts of those present. His way of presenting Threefolding to the bourgeois audience in Bern, which had neither experienced a world war nor a revolution, was quite different from the one we are familiar with from Stuttgart. This absolutely lively way of Rudolf Steiner's lecture, which arose directly from the present contexts, which was far removed from anything theoretical, which illuminated the same subject from ever new sides and thus, gained new perspectives from it, was quite incomparable. Rudolf Steiner never spoke from an abstract thinking, but — even with frequent repetition of the same lectures — always from an immediate spiritual experience. This was the basis of the extraordinarily sparkling and heartfelt effect of his lectures, no matter on which subject and before which audience he spoke." (Emil Leinhas, "Aus der Arbeit mit Rudolf Steiner," Basel 1950, p. 80 f.)

Textual basis: The lectures were co-stenographed by the professional stenographer Helene Finckh (1883-1960) and transcribed by her into plain text. For printing, a few unclear passages were compared with the original stenograph and appropriate corrections were made.

The titles of the lectures are by Rudolf Steiner; the title of the volume is by the editors.

Proof of earlier publications

Bern, March 11, 1919, in the journal "Gegenwart," 5th Jg. 1943/44, No. 8/9. as a single pamphlet, edited by F. Eymann, Bern 1944, 1946 (2nd ed.).

Lecture Basel, November 10, 1919 in "Die geistigen Hintergründe der sozialen Frage," vol. IV. (Appendix), Dornach 1951.

Works of Rudolf Steiner within the Gesamtausgabe (GA) are indicated in the notes with the bibliography number. See also the overview at the end of the volume.

To page .

13 *The Real Foundations of a League of Nations*: From March 7-13, 1919, the International Conference of the League of Nations took place in Bern, with Rudolf Steiner as a guest.

On the occasion of this conference, i.e., outside the official program, he gave a lecture on March 11.

March in the Grand Council Hall of the Bern City Hall he gave a lecture on fundamental aspects of a League of Nations, to which notable personalities were also invited. Personal invitations were extended to National Councillors J. Hirter and O. Weber, furthermore Baron von Wrangel, Dr. Hanns Buchli and Dr. Roman Boos.

13   *leading statesmen of Europe*: In his lecture of March 15, 1919 (cf. the volume "The Social Question as a Question of Consciousness," GA Bibl.-No. 189) Rudolf Steiner mentions the State Secretary in the German Foreign Office, Gottlieb von Jagow (1863-1935), in connection with this problem. He summarizes Jagow's statements there in the words: "Through the efforts of the European cabinets it has been possible to establish such satisfactory relations between the great powers of Europe that peace is assured for a long time to come in Europe."

14   *which can only be described as a carcinoma*: This statement is found in the sixth lecture of the cycle "Inner Being of Man and Life between Death and New Birth" held in Vienna in April 1914, GA Bibl. No. 153. Literally it says there:

"So today it is produced for the market without regard to consumption, not in the sense of what has been elaborated in my essay 'Spiritual Science and Social Question' [in 'Lucifer Gnosis 1903-1908 .' p. 191; editor's note], but one piles up in the warehouses and through the money markets everything that is produced, and then one waits how much is bought. This tendency will become greater and greater until it ... will destroy itself. It arises from the fact that this kind of production occurs in the social life, in the social connection of the people on earth exactly the same, what arises in the organism, if such a carcinoma arises. Exactly the same, a cancer formation, a carcinoma formation, culture cancer, culture carcinoma! Such a cancer formation is seen by those who have a spiritual insight into social life; they see how everywhere terrible tendencies to social ulcerations sprout up. This is the great cultural concern that arises for the one who sees through existence. This is the terrible thing that has such an oppressive effect, and which, even if one could otherwise suppress all enthusiasm for spiritual science, if one could suppress that which can open the mouth for spiritual science, leads one to cry out, as it were, the remedy to the world for that which is already so strong in the offing and which will become stronger and stronger.

"What must be in its field in the spreading of spiritual truths in a sphere that creates like nature, that becomes cancerous when it enters culture in the way described." See also the corresponding statement of Rudolf Steiner in IV, chapter of his fundamental writing "The Key Points of the Social Question in the Vital Necessities of the Present and Future," GA Bibl. no. 23; paperback edition TB 606.

16 *in a speech of Wilson*: Woodrow Wilson, 1856-1924, President of the United States of America 1913-1921, delivered the speech mentioned here before the Senate on January 22, 1917. He literally said: "Above all else, it says that peace must be without victory. It is not pleasant to have to say this. Allow me to state my own view of it and to emphasize that no other view has occurred to me. I am only trying to face the facts, without any gentle cover-ups. Victory would mean that peace would be forced upon the defeated, that the defeated would have to bow to the conditions of the victor. Such conditions could be accepted only in deep humiliation, in a state of duress, and at unbearable sacrifice; and a sore wound, a feeling of resentment, and a bitter memory would remain. A peace resting on such a basis could not last but would be built as on quicksand. Only a peace between equals can last – a peace which is based in its whole essence on equality and on the common enjoyment of a common benefit. Right sentiment, right feeling among different nations is as necessary to lasting peace as the just settlement of intractable disputes about territory or race or ethnicity." (From: "The Speeches of Woodrow Wilson," English and German, ed. by the Committee on Public Information of the United States of America. Der freie Verlag, Bern 1919.)

The idea of a League of Nations to be founded is also contained in the last of Wilson's 14 points of January 8, 1918.

17 *The Paris Events*: This refers to the Paris peace negotiations that began on January 18, 1919, with 70 delegates from 27 victorious states, and concluded with the signing of the peace treaty by German Foreign Minister Hermann Müller and Transport Minister Johannes Bell on June 28. The constitution of the League of Nations was adopted at the plenary session of the Paris Peace Conference on April 29, 1919.

21 *that the ownership of capital must be separated from the administration of capital*: On the question of ownership and the so-called "neutralization of capital," see in particular the third chapter, "Capitalism and Social Ideas," in the paper, "The Key Points of the Social Question," GA Bibl. no. 23.

Karl Marx, 1818-1883. On "labour power as a commodity," see the "Communist Manifesto," Part 1: "These workers, who must sell themselves piecemeal, are a commodity like every article of commerce and are therefore equally exposed to all the vicissitudes of competition, to all the fluctuations of the market.... But the price of a commodity, thus also of labour, is equal to its cost of production." More fully in "Das Kapital," 1st vol., 2nd sec., 4th chap. "Purchase and Sale of Labour Power," and 3rd sec., 5th chap. "Labour Process and Process of Utilization." – On the surplus-value theory, see "Das Kapital," 1st vol., sections 3-5 "Production of Surplus Value." On "labour power as a commodity," see also Rudolf Steiner, "The Key Points of the Social Question," GA Bibl. no. 23, at the end of chapter 1, and the essay "Marxism and Threefolding" in "Essays on the Threefolding of the Social Organism and on the Contemporary Situation 1915-1921," GA Bibl. no. 24.

25 *how is the utilization of individual abilities in the social organism justified?* In the shorthand it says, which is obviously due to a hearing error: "... in the human organism ..." See also the 1946 paperback version of this lecture by Prof. F. Eymann, p. 15.

28 *"Baghdad Railway."* The construction of the Baghdad Railway from Asia Minor via Baghdad to the Persian Gulf was entrusted to a company founded in 1903 in which the Deutsche Bank or the German Reich had a decisive influence, which led to foreign policy disagreements, especially with England.

29 *When the lowest teacher knows how to place himself in a freely organized spiritual life*: See Rudolf Steiner's essay "Freie Schule und Dreigliederung" (Free School and Threefolding), in "Aufsätze über die Dreigliederung des sozialen Organismus und zur Zeitlage 1915-1921," GA Bibl.-Nr. 24. There it says: "It should not be asked: What does man need to know and to be able to do for the social order that exists; but: What is predisposed in man and what can be developed in him? Then it will be possible to supply the social order with ever new forces from the

growing generation.... The growing human being should grow up through the power of the educator and teacher who is independent of state and economy, who can freely develop the individual abilities, because his own are allowed to rule in freedom." (2nd ed., Dornach 1982, p. 37/39).

32 *Just as economic life on the one hand is dependent on the basis of nature*: at this point some words, which are indicated in the shorthand but do not allow the context of meaning to be reconstructed, have been omitted. See the edition by Eymann, op. cit. p. 22.

38 *In recent years, I have often presented these ideas to people; I have also... summarized them in an appeal*: As early as 1917, Rudolf Steiner, after discussions with Count Otto Lerchenfeld and Count Ludwig Polzer-Hoditz, wrote two memoranda in which he commented on fundamental political questions in view of the situation at that time. The two personalities mentioned above addressed these memoranda to influential politicians, including the German Secretary of State Kühlmann and Arthur Polzer-Hoditz, the head of the cabinet of Emperor Charles of Austria. The memoranda were first published in: Roman Boos "Rudolf Steiner during the World War," Dornach 1933. Within the complete edition, see "Essays on Threefolding ...," GA Bibl. no. 24.

Rudolf Steiner's appeal "To the German People and to the Cultural World" was first published in March 1919 and signed by numerous personalities of cultural and political life. It was also added as an appendix to Rudolf Steiner's book "Die Kernpunkte der sozialen Frage," GA Bibl.-Nr. 23. On the collection of signatures, etc., see Rudolf Steiner's lectures of February and March 1919, especially of February 15 (1st lecture in "The Social Question as a Question of Consciousness"), GA Bibl.-No. 189.

38 *mankind would again be divided into the old three estates*: The formulation "nourishing estate, defensive estate, teaching estate" comes from Erasmus Alberus (1500-1553), similarly also Luther; it summarizes what Plato said in the "Politeia" about the estates; see the "Phoenician myth," according to which God added gold to the rulers (wise men) at birth, silver to their assistants, the guards, but iron and ore to the peasants and artisans ("Politeia" III. Book, 414 ff. Book, 414 ff.). See also Vincenz Knauer, "Die Hauptprobleme der Philosophie," Vienna and Leipzig

1892. The book is in Rudolf Steiner's library. There, in the lectures on Plato (p. 124), it says: "Just as the spiritual in the individual human being is divided into the rational, the irascible, and the concupiscible, so in the state we find three estates, which we can call, in accordance with a phrase familiar to us, the teaching, the nourishing, and the defending estates."

39 *Herman Grimm*, 1828-1901. The statement quoted here is contained in "Die deutsche Schulfrage und unsere deutschen Klassiker" (from: "Fünfzehn Essays," 4th series, Gütersloh 1890, p. 46/47). There it literally says: "The world is filled with the urge to reach an unknown goal, for the love of which the tremendous efforts are made that we are witnessing. It is as if all the peoples of the earth, each in its own way, felt that the prerequisite for a general spiritual struggle was to free themselves from the past as the dominant power and to make themselves fit to receive the new. Inventions and discoveries, mostly of an unheard-of kind and often accompanied by comprehensive instantaneous consequences, promote this state of our expectant marching on in closed masses. Where to? – It animates us a feeling as if the sacrifices made must appear later, each one as small, all together as indispensable. The goal is: to make the whole of mankind in its final formation a kingdom of brothers who, yielding only to the noblest motives, move on together. Whoever follows history only on the map of Europe, might believe that a mutual general murder must fill our near future; while he who studies it on the globe, may abandon himself to the certainty that rather the hour is approaching when the Germanic peoples, united in the same thoughts of highest spiritual striving, will open the way to the true goods of human life for all the uncounted millions of Asia and Africa and what else the globe harbours. Allow this thought, which does not seem to be in harmony with our immense warlike armaments and those of our neighbours, but in which I believe, and which must enlighten us, if it should not be better at all to abolish human life by a common resolution and to call an official day of suicide."

41 *Discussion*: after the conclusion of the lecture, Roman Boos – after a short pause – opened the discussion with the words: "Dearly beloved, the discussion is now opened. If anyone wishes to cast a vote, they are asked to perhaps come here. Short questions can be asked from the place of sitting. It is also possible, if someone prefers to ask a question in writing, that they do it that way." The votes of the discussion speakers, which

were mostly only incompletely taken down (presumably also for acoustic reasons), have been summarized by the stenographer afterwards according to their meaning.

42 *Teacher at a workers' education school founded by Wilhelm Liebknecht*: Rudolf Steiner taught history, speech exercises and natural sciences there from January 1899 to January 1905. See R. Steiner, "Mein Lebensgang," GA Bibl. no. 28, ch. XXVIII, as well as "Briefe," vol. II, 1892-1902, Dornach 1953, and Johanna Mücke, Alwin Rudolph, "Erinnerungen an Rudolf Steiner und seine Wirksamkeit an der Arbeiterbildungsschule in Berlin 1899-1904," Basel 1979.

43 *a number of corresponding older editors*: one of them, Emil Unger-Winkelried, was for a time editor of the "Vorwärts," later editor of various daily newspapers, and finally managing editor of the "Bremer Nachrichten." On his experiences as a student at the Workers' Education School and his encounter with Rudolf Steiner there, see: E. Unger-Winkelried "Von Bebel zu Hitler," Berlin 1934, p. 47f. Furthermore Konrad Donat "Lectures by Dr. Rudolf Steiner in Bremen," manuscript print, Bremen 1980.

44 *Lenin and Trotsky*: Rudolf Steiner speaks about the connection between the two representatives of Bolshevism and tsarism in various lectures. In the 3rd lecture of the volume "Spiritual and Social Changes in the Development of Humanity," GA Bibl.-No. 196, Dornach 1966, p. 265 it says: "That which was Russian tsarism is called today, where it has appeared in its truth, Lenin, Trotsky, Bolshevism. This is the concrete truth of what was then merely an illusion. Tsarism is merely the lie floating on the surface; but that which this tsarism really cultivated, as soon as it itself was swept away, appeared in its true reality." See also the question answer to Rudolf Steiner's 2nd lecture in the volume "Social Future," GA Bibl.-No. 332 a.

And Lenin just draws attention to two things in Marx: The idea of the dictatorship of the proletariat, through which the state finally reaches dissolution, is already contained in the "Communist Manifesto" in its substance: "Political violence in the proper sense is the organized violence of one class for the suppression of another. When the proletariat, in the struggle against the bourgeoisie, necessarily unites itself into a class, makes itself the ruling class by means of a revolution, and as the ruling class violently abolishes the old relations of production, it abolishes with these relations of production the conditions of existence of the class antagonism, the classes in general, and thus, its own rule as a class." In a letter to Wedemeyer of March 5, 1852, Marx calls this rule of the proletariat "dictatorship of the proletariat" and describes it as a transition to a classless (i.e., stateless) society. – Lenin takes up this idea in his writing "State and Revolution. The State Theory of Marxism and the Tasks of the Proletariat in the Revolution," Belp/Bern 1918. There he speaks widely about the gradual withering away of the state following the dictatorship of the proletariat, constantly referring to Marx and Engels. Also the "new type of man," which is presupposed for the future communist society, is mentioned there: "The state will then be able to die off completely when society will have realized the principle of 'To each according to his ability, to each according to his needs,' that is, when men will have become so accustomed to following the basic rules of social coexistence and their labour will be so productive that they will voluntarily work according to their abilities ... the higher phase of development of communism ... also presupposes a productivity of labour and a type of man far removed from the present one, from that hasty man who is capable of... Magazine of public supplies to damage and the blue from the sky to demand." (p. 147) A detailed characterization of Bolshevism can also be found in Rudolf Steiner's lectures "The Basic Social Demand of Our Time. In a Changed Time Situation," GA Bibl. no. 186.

45 *Each according to his abilities*: In the "Critique of the Gotha Program" (1875) by Karl Marx it says: "... after the forces of production have also grown with the all-round development of individuals, and all the fountains of cooperative wealth flow more fully – only then can the narrow bourgeois legal horizon be completely transcended and society write on its banners: To each according to his ability, to each according to his needs!" The originator of this "formula" is Louis Blanc.

46 *I spoke... Before a workers' meeting*: In Zurich on March 8, 1919. Cf. R. Steiner "The Social Question," GA Bibl.-No. 328. Steiner also writes about the receptiveness of the Russians for ideas like that of the "threefolding of the social organism" in "The Key Points of the Social Question," GA Bibl.-No. 23, Ch. IV, Dornach 1976, p. 153: "And the peoples of the Russian East would certainly have had understanding at that time for a replacement of tsarism by such impulses. That they would have had this understanding can only be denied by those who have no

feeling for the receptivity of the still unconsumed East European intellect for healthy social ideas. Instead of the rally in the spirit of such ideas came Brest-Litovsk."

48 *Adolf Damaschke,* 1865-1935. leader of the German land reform movement. Cf. his work "The Land Reform. Der Weg zur sozialen Versöhnung," Berlin 1919, See also R. Steiner "Soziale Zukunft," GA Bibl.-Nr. 332a, Dornach 1977, p. 178; paperback edition TB 631.

Pamphlet: Rudolf Steiner, "The Key Points of the Social Question in the Vital Necessities of the Present and Future," GA Bibl. no. 23; paperback edition TB 606.

49 *I heard this answered yesterday as the solution to the social question*: lecture by Prof. Johannes Ude (b. 1874), a Catholic theologian and social politician. In a speech at the League of Nations Conference in Bern on March 10, he said, "And since they will not dare to call the Christ a fool or a hypocrite, he can only have been what he himself said he was, the Son of the living God." Discussed in more detail in R. Steiner, "The Social Question as a Question of Consciousness," GA Bibl. no. 189, Dornach 1980, p. 138.

51 *Carl von Clausewitz,* 1780-1831, Prussian major general and military writer. His work "On War" was published in eight books after his death and was the standard work of military science for a long time. The work was also studied intensively by Lenin. The famous quotation can be found in the 8th book: "One knows, of course, that war is caused only by the political intercourse of governments and peoples, but usually one thinks of the matter in such a way that with it this intercourse ceases and a completely different state of affairs arises, which is subject only to its own laws. We, on the other hand, maintain: War is nothing but a continuation of political intercourse with the interference of other means. We say: with the interference of other means, in order to assert that this political intercourse does not cease with it, is not transformed into something entirely different, but that it continues in its essence, however the means of which it makes use may be shaped."

52 *Johann Gottlieb Fichte,* 1762-1814, "Der geschlossene Handelsstaat. Ein philosophischer Entwurf als Anhang zur Rechtslehre und Probe einer künftig zu liefernden Politik," Tübingen 1800. Rudolf Steiner deals with Fichte's writing in more detail in the 5th lecture in "Die soziale Frage als

Bewußtseinsfrage," GA Bibl.- Nr. 189. No. 189. Formulations in Fichte's writing that are related to Bolshevism are, e.g. the following: "The main results of the established theory are these: That in a state conforming to the law the three main estates of the nation [agrarians, manufacturers, merchants] are calculated against each other, and each restricted to a certain number of members; that each citizen is assured his proportionate share of all the products and manufactures of the country in return for his labour to be put to him, as well as to the public officials without visible equivalent; that for this purpose the value of all things be fixed against each other, and their price against money, and kept above it; that finally, in order that all this may be possible, all direct commerce of the citizens with foreign countries be made impossible. .. Furthermore, the task of the state has hitherto been conceived only unilaterally, and only in part, as an institution to maintain the citizen in that state of property in which he is found, by means of the law. The deeper duty of the state, which is to place everyone in the property to which he is entitled, has been overlooked. The latter, however, is only possible if the anarchy of commerce is abolished just as the political anarchy is gradually abolished, and if the state closes itself as a commercial state just as it is closed in its legislation and its judicial office." (Fichtes sämtliche Werke, ed. by I. H. Fichte, Vol. III, pp. 440 and 453.)

54 *What is the meaning of the work of the modern proletarian?*: Public lecture in Bern, held on March 17, 1919, at the invitation of the "Educational Committee of the Workers' Union Bern." Rudolf Steiner had spoken on the same topic to workers in Zurich a few days earlier, on March 8. See the volume "Die soziale Frage," GA Bibl.-Nr. 328. The first four of the six lectures printed there formed the basis for the paper "Die Kernpunkte der sozialen Frage," GA Bibl.-Nr. 23.

55 *League of Nations Conference*: see note on p. 13, as well as the first lecture in this volume.

56 *Speeches ... by a leading statesman*: See note on p. 13.

creeping cancer: See note on p. 14.

64 *Carl Vogt*, 1817-1895, naturalist, committed democrat, member of the Frankfurt National Assembly in 1848. "Physiologische Briefe für Gebildete aller Stände" (1857).

Ludwig Büchner, 1824-1899, physician and philosopher, representative of unrestricted materialism and Darwinism. Works: "Force and Substance" (1855), "Darwinism and Socialism" (1894). On Büchner and Vogt, see Rudolf Steiner, "Die Rätsel der Philosophie," 2nd vol., 1st chap. "Der Kampf um den Geist," GA Bibl. no. 18. 65 Rosa Luxemburg, 1870-1919. Participated in the Russian Revolution in 1905; considered a representative of the radical direction within the Social Democratic Party of Germany. Taught Marxist national economics at the party school. During World War I, she was almost constantly imprisoned for calling against the war. With Karl Liebknecht, leader of the Spartacists, who formed the nucleus of the Communist Party founded by Liebknecht on December 31, 1918. Rosa Luxemburg and Karl Liebknecht were assassinated in Berlin on January 15, 1919. – On the Workers' Education School, see the note to pg. 42. In Spandau, Rosa Luxemburg spoke on January 12, 1902, at the opening of the Workers' Education School there on the topic of "Science and the Workers' Struggle," followed by Rudolf Steiner speaking on the same topic. See W. Kugler, "Rudolf Steiner und die Anthroposophie," 3rd chap. p. 173 ff, DuMont-Dokumente, Cologne 1983 (4th ed.). – In a letter Rosa Luxemburg wrote to Rudolf Steiner on October 14, 1902, concerning his activity at the Workers' Education School, it says: "I always hear from time to time about your successes in workers' education. ..."

66 *How does one get to the point where "surplus value" does not remain a privilege but becomes a right?*: The shorthand at this point reads, "How does one get beyond that surplus value becomes a prerogative, not a right?" – Since this formulation can lead to misunderstandings, the sentence has been changed in spirit, which then corresponds, incidentally, to the similarly worded passage on p. 76. There it says: "And this right can only be made a right instead of a privilege ..."

What is to be done?: This question appears again and again, especially in Russian literature and revolutionary movement. In 1863 N. G. Chernyshevsky wrote his fundamental novel "What to do? From Tales of New Men." In his writing "What Shall We Do?" (1884-1886), Tolstoy confronts his contemporaries with the appalling misery of the urban masses. And Lenin's writing "What to Do?" (1902), which establishes the doctrine of the elite party, prompted Trotsky to flee Siberia and join Lenin.

72 *a modern, very important researcher*: Emil Du Bois-Reymond, 1815-1896, Secretary General of the Prussian Academy of Sciences. In an academic speech in Berlin on August 3, 1870, he said, "The Berlin University, quartered opposite the Palace, is by its charter the intellectual body regiment of the House of Hohenzollern." (From: "Speeches," Vol. I, p. 92)

76 *Call*: see the note to pg. 38.

77 *For this, however, people must first be in the right relationship to each other*: The words recorded in the stenogram do not permit a reconstruction here of the actual wording and thus, also of the context of meaning. The corresponding passage has been marked in the text by a square bracket. 79 Then the proletarian will not only redeem himself: Marx, too, held – in his own way – the view that the liberation of the proletariat meant at the same time the liberation of mankind. Thus, he writes in "The Holy Family" (1844/45) in the 4th chapter: "If the proletariat is victorious, it has by no means thereby become the absolute side of society, for it is victorious only by abolishing itself and its opposite ... It cannot abolish its own conditions of life without abolishing all the inhuman conditions of life of contemporary society which are summed up in its situation."

80 *Proletarian Demands and Their Future Practical Realization*: public lecture given in the large hall of the Kirchgemeindehaus in Winterthur on Wednesday, March 19, 1919, at the invitation of the "Committee of the Education Commission of the Winterthur Workers' Union."

League of Nations Conference: see note to pg. 13 and the first lecture in this volume.

Speech of a former statesman: See note on p. 13. 81 Of the creeping cancer disease: See note on p. 14. 82 Such as the German emperor: Wilhelm II has expressed himself in this sense on various occasions. See the collection of such sayings by Joachim Kürenberg, "War alles falsch? Das Leben Wilhelm II.," Basel 1940; ch. 60, "Der Kaiser und die Reichstagsparteien." Some examples: "For me, every Social Democrat is tantamount to an enemy of the Reich and the fatherland!" – "A mob of people, not worthy to bear the name of Germans .... May the whole people find in themselves the strength to reject these outrageous attacks! If it does not happen, well, then I call you to resist the highly treacherous mob, to wage a struggle that will free us from such elements!"

83 *Engelbert Pernerstorfer*, 1850-1918. Along with Victor Adler, one of the leaders of Austrian Social Democracy. During World War I, he was vice president of the Imperial Council. Rudolf Steiner reports about his meeting with Pernerstorfer in the 8th chap. of his autobiographical notes "Mein Lebensgang," GA Bibl.-Nr. 28. In the monthly journal "Deutsche Worte" edited by Pernerstorfer, XII. Jg. 1893 (Dec.) appeared also a short review of R. Steiner's "The Philosophy of Freedom," GA Bibl.-No. 4, written by Aug. Schroeder. (S. 795/6).

84 *as teacher of the workers' educational school founded by Wilhelm Liebknecht*: See the notes on pp. 42 and 65 (R. Luxemburg).

Materialist conception of history: it was formulated most succinctly by Karl Marx in the preface to his writing "On the Critique of Political Economy," 1859, where it is stated: "The general result which has arisen for me, and once gained has served as a guide to my studies, may be briefly formulated thus: In the social production of their lives men enter into certain necessary relations independent of their will, relations of production corresponding to a certain stage of development of their material productive forces. The totality of these relations of production forms the economic structure of society, the real basis on which a juridical and political superstructure rises, and to which certain, social forms of consciousness correspond. The mode of production of material life determines the social, political and spiritual process of life in general. It is not the consciousness of men that determines their being, but conversely their social being that determines their consciousness. At a certain stage of their development, the material productive forces of society come into contradiction with the existing relations of production, or what is only a legal expression for them, with the relations of property within which they had hitherto operated. From forms of development of the productive forces these relations turn into fetters of the same. Then an epoch of social revolution occurs. With the change of the economic basis the whole immense superstructure turns over more slowly or more rapidly. In considering such upheavals, one must always distinguish between the material upheaval in the economic conditions of production, which can be faithfully stated in scientific terms, and the legal, political, religious, artistic or philosophical, in short, ideological forms in which people become aware of this conflict and fight it out. As little as one judges what an individual is by what he thinks himself to be, just as little can one judge such an epoch of upheaval from its consciousness, but must rather explain this consciousness from the contradictions of material life, from the existing conflict between social productive forces and relations of production."

86 *the handmaiden of theology*: the origin of the expression "philosophia ancilla theologiae," frequently used in the Middle Ages, goes back to Peter Damiani (1007-1072). See also: Immanuel Kant (1724-1804), "Der Streit der Fakultäten in drei Abschnitten" (1798), in: "Sämtliche Werke," ed. by G. Hartenstein, Leipzig 1868, vol. VII, p. 344: "Also, one can at best concede to the theological faculty the proud claim that the philosophical one is its handmaiden ..."

a modern, famous physiologist: see note on p. 72.

88 *Vogt, Büchner and Luxemburg*: see notes on pp. 64/65.

92 *Class struggle*: see on this the first sentence of the "Communist Manifesto": "The history of all hitherto existing society is the history of class struggles."

95 *Austrian Imperial Council*: On the composition of the Austrian Imperial Council since 1867, see Rudolf von Herrnritt, "Handbuch des österreichischen Verfassungsrechtes" (1909), pp. 142 ff. The complicated form of the electoral law and its development are also described there. The author explicitly states that the principle of representation of interests was combined with the tax base, and that "primarily economic interests (were) decisive for the formation of the Reichsrat."

96 *The so-called center*: In 1870, on the basis of an appeal by Peter Reichensperger, the "Zentrum" was founded as a Catholic party and formed the opposition to the formation of the Kleindeutsch-Prussian Reich. After 1914 it gave itself the name "German Centre Party." During World War I, under Erzberger's influence, it joined with the "Progressives" and Social Democrats to form the Reichstag majority of the Peace Resolution (1917).

101 *In my soon to be published booklet*: "Die Kernpunkte der sozialen Frage in den Lebensnotwendigkeiten der Gegenwart und Zukunft" (1919), GA Bibl.-Nr. 23.

Whoever looks impartially at the economic seven: See also R. Steiner, "Nationalökonomischer Kurs," GA Bibl.-Nr. 340. On questions of currency see especially the 14th lecture.

102 *What one produces spiritually*: Works of intellectual labour were at that time subject to a protection period of 30 years, which has since been extended to 50 years in most countries, including Switzerland, and to 70 years in Germany. After expiration of this period, the right of the heirs is transferred to the general public, i.e., anyone then has the right to reprint the works in question.

105 *Discussion*: The votes of the individual discussion speakers have been preserved only in fragments. The summaries are from the editors.

107 *Waiting for a millionaire*: allusion to the social reformer Charles Fourier (1772-1837), who in the last ten years of his life stayed at home every day at noon so as not to miss the great unknown benefactor whom he had ordered to come at that time and who was to bring him the millions with which he wanted to establish the first "Phalange" – the production cooperative he conceived. See Werner Hofmann, "Ideengeschichte der sozialen Bewegung des 19. und 20. Jahrhunderts," Göschen Collection 1962, p. 57.

112 *in Bern*: See the first lecture in this volume.

114 *Proletarian demands and their future practical realization*: public lecture given at the "Burgvogtei" in Basel on Wednesday, April 2, in the evening at 8 o'clock. In January 1919, a meeting of the Workers' League had taken place in the "Burgvogtei" with over a thousand participants, who passed a resolution calling for the determined struggle of the working class for political power. After the general strike of 1918, fierce directional struggles had arisen within the socialist movement, with the Basel section emerging as one of the most radical. See Markus Bolliger, "Die Basler Arbeiterbewegung im Zeitalter des Ersten Weltkrieges und der Spaltung der Sozialdemokratischen Partei," Basel 1970.

116 *An English Enquete*: Report of the Children's Employment Commission of 1842. Friedrich Engels thoroughly evaluated it in his epoch-making book, "The Condition of the Working Class in England," 1845.

Statements of the former German Emperor: See note to pg. 82.

117 *Lecture ... in Vienna in the spring of 1914*: See note on p. 14. the senior foreign secretary of state: See note on p. 13.

118 *On Wilhelm Liebknecht and the Workers' Educational School*: See note on p. 42.

also within the political party: Can only mean within the educational system within the framework of the party, not in political actions of the party. Rudolf Steiner's continued work at the Workers' Educational School was made impossible the moment some leading party officials noticed that he was not teaching in their materialist-Marxist spirit.

119 *Karl Marx and the Theory of Surplus Value*: see note on p. 21.

120 Vogt and Büchner: see note on p. 64.

Ferdinand Lassalle, 1825-1864; founded the General Workers' Association in Leipzig in 1863. When he was charged with inciting the propertyless classes to hatred and contempt of the propertied classes, he delivered his widely acclaimed defence speech, "Science and the Workers," before the Berlin Criminal Court on January 16, 1863. There he said, among other things: "This is precisely the greatness of the destiny of this time, to carry out what darker centuries did not even think possible, to bring science to the people!" From: "Ferdinand Lassalles Reden und Schriften," Berlin 1893, p. 83. – On Lassalle, see also the biography by Hermann Oncken, 3rd ed. 1923.

Rosa Luxemburg and the event in Spandau: See note on p. 65.

122 *Word of the German Emperor*: See note on p. 82.

123 *Karl Marx on labor power as a commodity*: See note on p. 21.

124 *The Allerhalter*: See J. W. v. Goethe, "Faust," Part I, Marthens Garten. Literally it says there:

> Who may call him?
> And who confess: I believe him?
> Who may feel and refrain from saying:
> I do not believe him.
> The All-embracing,
> The All-sustaining,
> Does he not grasp and sustain you, me, himself?

126 *Austrian Constitution*: See note on p. 95. 128 Du Bois-Reymond: See note on p. 72.

Science as handmaiden of theology: See note to pg. 86. the League of Nations.... must bring into being a super-parliament: On March 11, 1919, at the League of Nations Conference in Berne, there was extensive discussion of the need for a parliament of nations. Mr. Mühlestein expressed himself most radically, calling for a unicameral system with deputies of the peoples. Cf. report in "Neue Zürcher Zeitung" of March 11, 1919. Whether Rudolf Steiner refers to Mühlestein's statements in his lecture cannot be determined with certainty.

129 *Deaf ears have been preached to*: See the note to pg. 38.

131 in my book, which will be published in a few days: See the note to pg. 101.

135 *Freedom, equality, fraternity*: Within the three-part social organism, Rudolf Steiner assigns freedom to spiritual life, equality to legal life, and fraternity to economic life. See also "Die Kernpunkte der sozialen Frage," GA Bibl.-Nr. 23, end of 2nd chapter; "Neugestaltung des sozialen Organismus," GA Bibl.-Nr. 330, 10th lecture.

137 *That he will become the liberator of all that is human*: see note on p. 79. 138 Willy Handschin, board member of the "Jungburschen," member of the "Old Communist Party," founded in Basel at the end of 1918, which advocated class struggle and the arming of workers. In March, together with Fritz Platten and Humbert-Droz, among others, he was elected to the Central Committee of the newly founded Communist Party of Switzerland. The founder of the Youth League, of which Handschin was a member, was Jakob Herzog, whom Lenin held in high esteem as a genuine revolutionary type. See M. Bolliger, op. cit. especially pp. 70, 137f., 242, 283.

Mr. Studer points to the ideas of Freigeld and Freiland: it is the free economy theory of Silvio Gesell (1862-1930), presented in his work "Die natürliche Wirtschaftsordnung durch Freiland und Freigeld," 1916. – Otto Studer, a musician by profession, was founder and leader of the Basel group of the Swiss Free Economic Association.

Hans Mühlestein, 1887-1969; native of Biel. Versatile and highly educated personality of unconventional, thoroughly independent, sometimes adventurous lifestyle. Poet, dramatist, scholar, translator of Renaissance poetry, author of scientific works on various subjects: Etruscans, Hodler, Peasant War, history of religion ("The Veiled Gods"), atomic physics and ancient Greek philosophy. As a social politician always on the side of the persecuted. In 1918 deputy of the USPD Göttingen at the Congress of Workers' and Soldiers' Councils in Berlin. At times close to the PdA. Like

Rudolf Steiner, Mühlestein points to the "petering out" of the German Revolution. See also the note to pg. 128. "Schweizerischer Bund für Reformen der Übergangszeit": This federation is described by Fr.

Schmid-Ammann in his book on the general strike in connection with the confused situation after the general strike (p. 375). 139 Ein Herr kam dazumal: It cannot be clearly determined which lecture in Bern this refers to. There is no mention of the free economy in the discussion of March 11; there was no discussion after the lecture of March 17. It is possible that the visitor was Fritz Schwarz, who at that time was the managing director of the Schweizerischer Freiwirtschaftsbund, based in Bern, and who was considered to be a knowledgeable representative of the free economy idea in Bern. 140 One must recognize: A short passage had to be omitted here because the manuscript text did not allow for a clear reproduction of the text. 142 "Von Seelenrätseln" (1917), GA Bibl.-Nr. 21. The fundamental presentation of the threefold structure of the human organism is given by Rudolf Steiner in the chapter "Die physischen und die geistigen Abhängigkeiten der Menschenwesenheit." Paperback edition TB 637.

Albert E. F. Schäffle, 1831-1903; national economist; 1862-1865 member of the Württemberg parliament. 1871 Austrian minister of trade. Authored numerous sociological writings, including "Bau und Leben des sozialen Körpers," 4 vols, Tübingen 1875-1878, 2nd ed. 1896, 2 vols.

C. H. Meray, "World Mutation. Creation Laws on War and Peace and the Birth of a New Civilization," Zurich 1918. The writings of Schäffle and Meray are also mentioned by Rudolf Steiner in the "Key Points of the Social Question," op. cit, Chapter 2, and in the lectures "The Social Question," GA Bibl. no. 328, pp. 27 and 118.

145 *Social Will and Proletarian Demands*: Public lecture, held on April 9, 1919, in the large lecture hall of the Bernoullianum in Basel. The organizer was the Basler Studentenbund. – On February 25, 1919, Rudolf Steiner had spoken to the Zurich student body on "The Social Will as the Basis of a New Scientific Order." See the volume "Die soziale Frage," GA Bibl.-Nr. 328.

148 *Marx believes that such a time is approaching*: "For decades the history of industry and commerce has been only the history of the indignation of the modern productive forces against the modern relations of

production. ... But the bourgeoisie has not only forged the weapons which will bring it death; it has also begotten the men who will wield these weapons – the modern workers, the proletarians ... With the development of great industry, therefore, from under the feet of the bourgeoisie is pulled away the very basis on which it produces and appropriates the products. It produces above all its own gravediggers. Its downfall and the victory of the proletariat are alike inevitable." (Communist Manifesto) View of older socialist thinkers: For example, Claude Henri de Saint-Simon (1760-1825), Charles Fourier (1772-1837), Pierre Joseph Proudhon (1809-1865), Louis Blanc (1811-1882), Robert Owen (1771-1858), also still Ferdinand Lassalle (1825-1864). Concise overview of their ideas in Werner Hofmann, "Ideengeschichte der sozialen Bewegung des 19. und 20. Jahrhunderts," Sammlung Göschen, 1962. Detailed texts in "Der Frühsozialismus," Quellentexte, edited by Thilo Ramm, Kröner, 2nd ed. 1968. See also Rudolf Steiner in "Neugestaltung des sozialen Organismus," GA Bibl.-No. 330, lecture of July 30, 1919.

155 *the two main points of this social-democratic ideal*: In 1863 Lassalle founded the "Allgemeiner Deutscher Arbeiterverein," which demanded as a "moral duty" of the state the breaking of the iron law of wages through state-supported production cooperatives. In 1868, Marxists August Bebel and Wilhelm Liebknecht founded the "Socialist German Workers' Party." In 1875, the two tendencies united in Gotha to form the "Socialist Workers' Party of Germany." The Gotha program contained the first two main points mentioned by Rudolf Steiner. It aroused the ire of Karl Marx because it did not agree with his materialist views (see Karl Marx, "Critique of the Gotha Program 1875"). According to this program, the party "strives for" "the free state and socialist society. ... Abolition of the system of wage labour, the abolition of exploitation in every form, the elimination of all social and political inequality." In 1881, after experiencing Bismarck's Socialist Laws, Kautsky worked out a new, purely Marxist program, adopted at Erfurt, which included the two later demands mentioned by Rudolf Steiner: "Only the transformation of capitalist private property in the means of production – land, mines and quarries, raw materials, tools, machinery, means of transport – into social property and the transformation of commodity production into socialist production operated for and by society can bring it about that large-scale enterprise and the ever-increasing productive capacity of

social labour will turn for the hitherto exploited classes from a source of misery and oppression into a source of the highest welfare and all-round harmonious perfection." See also Rudolf Steiner's remarks on socialist programs in "Neugestaltung des sozialen Organismus," GA Bibl.-No. 330, pp. 110f.; see also Horst Seefeld "Programme der deutschen Sozialdemokratie," Bonn 1963, and Eduard von der Hellen, "Das rote Programm," 1892.

160 *Chairman of the "Goethe Society"*: Georg Kreuzwendedich Freiherr von Rheinbaben 1855-1921; Prussian Minister of Finance 1901-1909, President of the Goethe Society 1913-1921. See also Rudolf Steiner "Historical Symptomatology," GA Bibl.No. 185, p. 129. – Rudolf Steiner is listed in the Goethe Yearbooks of 1892-1898 as a member of the Goethe Society residing in Weimar. 161 Oscar Hertwig, 1849-1922. His book on social life: "Zur Abwehr des ethischen, des sozialen, des politischen Darwinismus," Jena 1918. The barrenness of natural scientific way of thinking for social life proves itself e.g. in the following sentences: "In the series of the different levels of organization of the substance, each is equipped with its own modes of action. These are simpler in the case of the chemical atom and molecule, according to their position in the series of stages, and can therefore be determined more precisely by the methods of natural research and classified into fixed rules and laws. On each higher level, however, they gain visibly in complication, until finally they can hardly be overlooked in their immense variety, let alone be expressed in any fixed formula. It is then hardly possible to predict with which mode of action man or even human society will react to any change in their environment, to any intervention from outside." – Then he places the most diverse kinds of "forces" in one line: "... when one speaks of atomic, of molecular and cellular forces, of chemical and vegetative affinity, of the forces of plants and animals, of spiritual and moral forces of man, of the force of a state, etc.... we can, as has been proved before, only investigate the effects peculiar to the various stages of organization; we can try to bring them under general rules and to make their origin comprehensible to us from the organization of the substance and its relations to the environment, that is, from the given system conditions. From this point of view, man, with his history and culture, with his moral and spiritual forces revealed in them, fits into the system of nature just as completely and completely as any other natural object, and can be made the object of natural research. If, after these

preliminary remarks, I return to our subject, then it can be said without being misunderstood that actions in which we see the expression of moral powers find their origin in the community life of animals which are already more highly developed also in spiritual respects. They arise gradually and in the same measure as a certain feeling of togetherness and kinship comes alive between the originally isolated individuals who think only for themselves.... . (In the class of insects animal states are already developing in different forms of formation. The study of social insects, bees, ants, termites, allows us to gain many points of comparison with human relationships. In this view, the enormous differences that exist between mankind with its spiritual and moral world on the one hand, and the animal kingdom on the other, are not differences of principle, but only differences of degree." (pp. 35-37)

162 *Heinrich Friedjung*, 1851-1920; historian and political writer. Among other things, he founded the "Deutsche Wochenschrift," which Rudolf Steiner edited from January to July 1888. See Rudolf Steiner, "Mein Lebensgang," GA Bibl.-Nr. 28, ch. VIII. – In 1909 Heinrich Friedjung had accused members of the Croatian parliament "in sensational newspaper articles of highly treasonable connivance with the leaders of the Greater Serbian movement on the other side of the border. The plaintiffs were able to prove in court that Friedjung's accusations were based on forged documents provided to him by the Foreign Ministry in Vienna. Friedjung, who had exposed himself by his uncritical use of falsified material, was forced to retreat." See R. von Salis "Weltgeschichte der neuesten Zeit," vol. 2, p. 350. 162 Alois Freiherr von Aehrental, 1854-1912; Austro-Hungarian foreign minister 1906-1912.

163 *Count with the two trouser pockets*: Could not be determined.

170 *A principle of national economy*: This refers to Rudolf Steiner's "Main Social Law" in an essay. Here is its wording: "The salvation of a totality of people working together is the greater, the less the individual claims the proceeds of his achievements for himself, that is, the more he gives away of these proceeds to his fellow men and the more his own needs are satisfied not from his achievements but from the achievements of others." From "Spiritual Science and the Social Question," 1905/06 in "Lucifer Gnosis. Gesammelte Aufsätze 1903-1908," GA Bibl.-No. 34, p. 191 ff; also as single edition, Dornach 1977.

171 *"Die Kernpunkte der sozialen Frage"* (1919), GA Bibl.-. No. 23; for Schneider's example, see 5. 133f.; see also "National Economic Course," GA Bibl.-No. 340, pp. 44-46, 47f., 51-53, 66; also "National Economic Seminar," GA Bibl.-No. 341, pp. 42-45, 48.

173 *This, too, will be elaborated further*: See "The Key Points of the Social Question," GA Bibl. No. 23, III chap. "Capitalism and Social Ideas."

176 *Kurt Eisner*, 1867-1919; Socialist politician, journalist, writer; belonged to the extreme "Independent Socialist Party" and was imprisoned as an opponent of the war. On November 8, 1918, he proclaimed the Republic of Bavaria in Munich and became head of the government. On February 21, 1919, he was shot by Count Arco on his way to the opening of the Landtag. Rudolf Steiner spoke with him about questions of war guilt during the International Socialist Conference in Bern, February 3-10, 1919, which Eisner had attended as Bavarian premier. His lecture, "Socialism and the Youth," took place on February 10, 1919, at the invitation of the Basel student body. The conversation with Kurt Eisner is mediated by Hans Kühn, see his book "Dreigliederungszeit," Dornach 1978, p. 33 f. See also Rudolf Steiner "Die soziale Grundforderung unserer Zeit. In Changed Time," GA Bibl.-No. 186, 1st lecture; also "The Social Question as a Question of Consciousness," GA Bibl.-No. 189, 6th lecture (in detail). See also series "Contributions to the Rudolf Steiner Complete Edition," formerly "News of the Rudolf Steiner Estate Administration," No. 24/25, special issue "50 Years of 'The Key Points of the Social Question' April 1919-April 1969," pp. 14, 16, 23 ff. – Although Rudolf Steiner had never personally met Kurt Eisner before that meeting in 1919, there were some points of contact between them. Thus, in 1893, Rudolf Steiner published in the "Literarischer Merkur," XIII. jg. no. 4, Eisner's writing "Psychopathia spiritualis. Friedrich Nietzsche and the Apostles of the Future." See "Gesammelte Aufsätze zur Kultur- und Zeitgeschichte 1887-1901," GA Bibl.-No. 31, p. 467 ff.; on December 3, 1893, Steiner asked Kurt Eisner in a letter to "speak out publicly" about the "Philosophy of Freedom," which he had the publisher Emil Felber send to Eisner. It has not yet been possible to determine whether Eisner complied with this request. The editors of the book "Kurt Eisner. Die Halbe Macht den Raten," Renate and Gerhard Schmölze (Cologne 1969, p. 7). In the same book {p. 29) one can also read that Eisner had arranged Steiner's employment at the Berlin Workers' Education School. Similarly, Alwin A. Rudolph in his "Erinnerungen an Rudolf Steiner und seine

Wirksamkeit an der Arbeiterbildungsschule 1899-1904," Basel 1979, p. 40.

177 *Discussion*: No transcript of this discussion is available. Rudolf Steiner spoke the closing words at the request of the organizer. In later lectures, Rudolf Steiner mentions the statement of a gentleman in this discussion who declared that nothing could get better until Lenin had become world ruler. See "Die Erziehungsfrage als soziale Frage," GA Bibl.-No. 296, p. 32 f., and "Soziale Zukunft," GA Bibl.-No. 332, p. 66.

179 *real errors*: Here the shorthand transcription has some discrepancies, therefore the manuscript wording was not included in the running text. The shorthand transcription results in the following wording: "so we have methodical findings, theoretical inside, real errors, as I said, in this circle I may already draw attention to such things. You can find in every physics book defined for example: Impenetrability is the property of the body, so that at the same place and in the same time only one and not two bodies can be. – It is a definition which is not justified by anything, which is just taken out of the air. Epistemologically correctly thought, it would have to be called: One physical body is called that, at whose place at the same time, if it is at the place, a second one cannot be. There are at all only postulates for the conceptual faculty in these definitions. Today one demands only definitions. In reality there are only postulates, there are only characteristics in the conceptual faculty. The conceptual faculty as such must not be somehow dominant. This is less noticed in the natural scientific thinking, but it is fundamental errors laying in the field of social thinking ..."

183 *A Catholic clergyman*: See note on p. 49.

184 *In my penultimate book*: See note on p. 142.

185 *Schaffte or Meray*: See note on p. 142.

The other day a listener in Basel replied to me: See note on p. 138; Hans Mühlestein.

187 *The Spiritual-Scientific Basis of the Social Question*: public lecture in Bern, October 14, 1919, organized by the Swiss Federation for the Threefolding of the Social Organism and the Bern branch of the Anthroposophical Society, opened by Roman Boos. "Soziale Zukunft": journal published by the "Schweizerischer Bund für Dreigliederung des sozialen

Organismus" and edited by Roman Boos, 1919-1921. See "The literary work of Roman Boos. Bibliography and Biographical Note," Basel 1973, p. 39 f.

190 *I had to say it in Vienna in the spring of 1914*: see note to pg. 14 "that can only be called ..."

On the failure of Marxism in Russia, the failure of the Hungarian Revolution, and the failure of the German Revolution: see R. von Salis, "Weltgeschichte der neuesten Zeit," vol. 3, pp. 88ff, 24ff, 151ff.

205 *Francois Marie Charles Fourier*, 1772-1837; worked out a social system in which agriculture and industry were to be linked by productive association and all intermediate trade eliminated. He called the conceived productive cooperatives "phalange." See also note to pg. 107.

208 We have tried... through our friend Emil Molt. ... to found a school: This refers to the first Waldorf School in Stuttgart, which was founded in 1919 as a unified elementary and secondary school by Emil Molt, director of the Waldorf-Astoria cigarette factory, and Rudolf Steiner, who was in charge until his death in March 1925. More than 200 schools in Europe and overseas now operate on the basis of Steiner's study of man and the art of education. – See Rudolf Steiner's lectures on the art of education, within the complete edition in the volumes Bibl.-Nos. 293-311. See also Emil Molt "Entwurf meiner Lebensbeschreibung," Stuttgart 1972. – The foundation of the school was at the same time a first step towards the detachment of the school system from the state in the sense of the threefold idea. See also Walter Kugler, "Selbstverwaltung als Gestaltungsprinzip eines zukunftsorientierten Schulwesens, dargestellt am Beispiel der Freien Waldorfschulen," Stuttgart 1981.

Then, however, one sees that one gets hold of the regulations: probably refers to the fact that the educational authorities imposed obligations on the Waldorf School to have achieved the "teaching goals" of the state school in the third, sixth, eighth school year respectively. Rudolf Steiner said in a speech on August 20, 1919: "Bad teaching goals, bad graduation goals are prescribed by the state. These goals are the worst imaginable, and one imagines the highest imaginable on them. The policy ... from now on will express itself by treating man as a template, by trying much further than ever before to fit man into templates. Man will be treated like an object that has to be pulled by wires and will imagine that this means the greatest progress imaginable. One will improperly and as haughtily as possible set up such things as educational institutions are. An example and foretaste of this is the construction of the Russian Bolshevik schools, which are a veritable burial ground for all real education. We will face a hard struggle and yet do this cultural deed." From: Rudolf Steiner "Conferences with the Teachers of the Free Waldorf School in Stuttgart," GA Bibl.-No. 300/1, p. 61 f.; for the regulations of the educational authorities see in the same volume p. 26 ff.

214 *Lenin and Trotsky*: authoritative leaders of the Russian socialist movement. See also the note to pg. 44.

216 *Today you hear again and again from the socialist side*: What is obviously meant is the Marxist utopia advocated by Lenin, among others, according to which man is to be educated through social structures. In December 1918, the Council of People's Deputies had appointed a "Socialization Commission" headed by Karl Kautsky. In response, Rudolf Steiner wrote "Proposals for Socialization. Guiding Principles for the Threefold Work" and a little later the pamphlet "The Way of the Tripartite Social Organism," which was the basis for further Threefold Work. On March 6, 1919, the National Assembly passed a law that placed labor as the highest economic value under the protection of the Reich and included provisions for the "socialization" of suitable enterprises. In July, the Bund für Dreigliederung had to issue a statement against the abuse of the factory council idea on the part of left-wing radicals. See Rudolf Steiner, "Aufsätze über die Dreigliederung und zur Zeitlage. 1915-1921," GA Bibl.-Nr. 24, p. 424 ff. – The introduction of workers' councils and the socialization of "enterprises suitable for this purpose" was finally included in the new Reich constitution.

222 *A long discussion of this threefold structure appeared in a journal*: this refers to the essay "Die Dreigliederung des sozialen Körpers" (The Threefold Structure of the Social Body) by Prof. Philipp von Heck in the journal "Die Tribüne," No. 1, July 1919. A reply by Rudolf Steiner appeared in the same journal in issues 3/4 and 5/6; reprinted within the Rudolf Steiner Gesamtausgabe in the volume "Aufsätze zur Dreigliederung des sozialen Organismus und zur Zeitlage 1915-1921," GA Bibl.- No. 24, p. 444ff.

225 *Bosnia and Herzegovina affair*: In 1878, the hitherto Turkish provinces of Bosnia and Herzegovina were occupied and taken into administration by Austria-Hungary in accordance with Art. 25 of the Berlin Congress Treaty. Since then, the monarchy strove to turn the occupation into an annexation. In 1908, after agreement with the Russian foreign minister, to whom the Austro-Hungarian foreign minister Alois Freiherr von Aehrenthal promised in return an agreement to open the Dardanelles to Russian warships, Austria-Hungary declared the annexation of Bosnia and Herzegovina, which was supposed to be a step towards the realization of trialism – i.e. the unification of the Southern Slavs under the rule of the Danube monarchy.

230 *Woodrow Wilson*: See note to pg. 16.

232 *"The New Freedom*. A Call for the Liberation of the Noble Forces of a People," Munich 1914. The comparison of Wilson's social critique with that of Lenin and Trotsky is treated in detail by Rudolf Steiner in "Social Future," GA Bibl.-No. 332, pp. 17-20. – The following are some passages from Wilson's "The New Freedom," which correspond to the Bolshevik criticism (pp. 86, 144, 179): "The hands that reach out to seize our forests, that prevent or reserve for themselves the exploitation of our great power-giving rivers, the hands that reach out to the heart of the earth to seize those vast riches which lie hidden in Alaska or in other regions of our incomparable States, – it is everywhere the fist of monopoly. Shall these men continue to stand at the shoulder of the government and advise us how to protect ourselves – protect ourselves from them?.. . If I am not proficient enough to beat my competitors, I will tend to communicate with them. ' Let's not cut each other's throats; let's join forces. We fix production, thereby determine prices: and we dominate and thereby determine the market.' This is quite natural. It has always happened since there was privateering. It has always happened since power was used to establish domination ... There is scarcely a section of the country in the United States that does not know that special interests and special purposes run the government. This has happened through the wielding of those interesting people we call 'bosses' in politics. A boss is not so much a politician as a political business agent for special interests. A boss does not belong to any party, he is high above the parties. He has his deal with the boss of the other party, so that, whether head or tail, it is always we who must lose. From the same sources the two bosses get their income, and they use the contributions for the same

purposes. They are people who obtained the influential position on which they stand by secret machinations; people who were never elected, whom the people did not designate to govern, and who are far more powerful than they would be if they had been elected or appointed."

234 *He says, for example*: Wording of Wilson's Definition of Liberty, op. cit. p. 218: "What is liberty? One says of a locomotive that it runs freely. What does one mean by this? One wants to say that the individual components are so composed and fitted into each other that friction is kept to a minimum. One says of a ship which easily cuts through the waves: how freely it runs, and means with it that it is perfectly adapted to the strength of the wind. Direct it against the wind, and it will hold and sway, all the planks and the whole hull will tremble, and immediately it is (tied up). It becomes free only when it is allowed to fall off again and the wise adaptation to the powers it must obey is restored. The freedom of man consists in the proper interlocking of human interests, commerce, and powers. The necessary relations between individuals, between them and the whole human institutions under which they live, further between these institutions and the government, are now much more complicated than ever before. It may be tedious and cumbersome to talk about these things, but it is well worth the effort to realize what is actually causing all the present confusion. Life has become more complicated, it is composed of many more elements and parts than before. And that's why it's harder to keep everything in order and to find out what's wrong when the machine stops running."

240 *Calvin Thomas*, Professor of Germanic Languages and Literatures at the University of Michigan. See also Rudolf Steiner, "Historical Symptomatology," GA Bibl. no. 185, Dornach 1982, p. 128.

243 *One of the main books*, "How to Obtain Knowledge of the Higher Worlds?" (1904), GA Bibl.-No. 10; paperback edition TB 600.

246 *Through many centuries certain social powers have watched over it*: meant here are the councils of the Roman Catholic Church, especially the eighth Ecumenical Council of Constantinople. In the "Canones contra Photium," this council, organized against the patriarch Photius, stipulates under Can. 11 that man has not "two souls" but "unam animam rationabilem et intellectualem."

247 *"Von Seelenrätseln"* (1917), GA Bibl. no. 21. See the note to pg. 142.

248 *Tabes dorsalis*: spinal dysphoria. 249 Revolutions in Russia, Hungary, Germany: see note on p. 190.

251 *Saint-Simon, Fourier, Louis Blanc*: see note on p. 148.

252 *Rabindranath Tagore*, 1861-1941. Indian poet, philosopher and educator. He became internationally known for his work "Gitanjali," an English prose version of a selection of his religious poetry. In 1913, he received the Nobel Prize for Literature for this work. His criticism of modern Western culture appears primarily in the book "Nationalism," German 1918. Some sentences from this work (pp. 22f., 35 u. 42): "History has come to a stage where the moral man, the whole man, almost without knowing it, is giving place more and more to the political man and the business man, the man of limited purpose. This process, aided by the astonishing advances of natural science, is becoming more and more gigantic and tremendous, throwing man out of his moral equilibrium by letting the human side of his being prevail through soulless organization.... This constant, tremendous mechanical pressure of the inanimate upon the animate is what the world of today is groaning under. Not only the subjugated races, but you yourselves, who believe yourselves to be free, are daily sacrificing your freedom and humanity to the idol of nationalism, and are living in the dull, poisoned atmosphere of distrust, greed and fear which extends over the whole world. ... But may you say that it is not the soul but the machine that is most precious to us, and that man's salvation depends upon his bringing it to perfection in the art of conforming to the rhythm of the dead wheel?"

254 *Saying of Woodrow Wilson*: Literally, op. cit. p. 98f.: "The great crucible of America, the place where all are made Americans, is the public school. To it people of every race, every origin, and every station in life send, or ought to send, their children; and here all are blended together, are imbued with the American spirit, and are developed into the American man or woman. But we should not only send our children to paid teachers in this school, but we should ourselves go to school together in the same schoolhouse, so that we may feel more vividly and more strongly what American life is. And in confidence I would say that wherever you find a school board that might object to the opening of the school to public meetings of any kind, there you must look for the

politician who objects; for the remedy for bad policy is to talk with your neighbour. The exchange of ideas between neighbours brings to light the veiled things of our political life; and if we can succeed in uniting neighbours, so that they may speak out frankly all they know, then our politics, our municipal politics, our state politics, will become as manifest as they ought to be. For the greatest disadvantage of our politics is that it does not look the same on the inside as it does on the outside. Nothing, however, clears the air so much as a free debate."

258 *Original plant*: Letter from Goethe, Palermo, April 17, 1787: "In the face of so many new and renewed creations (plants in the ' Giardino Publico,' Palermo), the old cricket came to mind again, whether I could not discover the original plant among this crowd. There must be such a plant! How else would I recognize that this or that structure was a plant, if they were not all formed according to one pattern?" – Italian journey, chap. Sicily.

He said and wrote about this primordial plant: Goethe to Herder, Naples, May 17, 1787: "Furthermore, I must trust you that I am very close to the secret of plant generation and organization and that it is the simplest thing that can only be thought ... The original plant becomes the most wonderful creature of the world, which nature itself shall envy me. With this model and the key to it, one can then invent plants into infinity, which must be consistent, that is: which, even if they do not exist, could exist and are not picturesque or poetic shadows and appearances, but have an inner truth and necessity. The same law will apply to all living things." – Italian Journey, Second Stay in Rome, July.

260 *Nicolaus Copernicus*, 1473-1543; founder of the heliocentric world system. His work "De revolutionibus orbium coelestium" (On the Orbit of the Heavenly Bodies) 1543.

260 *Galileo Galilei*, 1564-1642; was the first to use the telescope he constructed as a means of astronomical research, and his modern physics laid the foundation for Newton's later celestial mechanics.

Monopolies on knowledge of the soul and spirit: Paul distinguished between the "psychic" (soulish) and the "pneumatic" (spiritual) man. The eighth ecumenical council (not recognized by the Eastern Church) in Constantinople of 869 declared that man has not two souls, but "one rational and spiritual soul." To this the Catholic philosopher Otto

Willmann, much esteemed by Rudolf Steiner, said in his three-volume work "History of Idealism," 1st edition Brunswick 1894, in § 54, Der christliche Idealismus als Vollendung des antiken (Volume II, page 111): "The abuse which the Gnostics made of the Pauline distinction of the pneumatic and the psychic man, passing off the latter as the expression of their perfection, declaring the latter to be the representative of Christians caught up in the law of the Church, determined the Church to the express rejection of the trichotomy." – This soul endowed with spiritual faculties is considered in scholasticism as "forma corporis" (form-giving power of the body). From here it is only a step to the modern scientific view that the soul is only a function of the body. Simultaneously with the rejection of the independent human mind, the Church took over the monopoly of the Magisterium and established the dogmas to be believed. Subsequent councils, especially that of Trent (1547-63), confirmed the Church's monopoly. Most consistently persecuted were all teachings that attributed an independent spirit to man (Cathars, Bogumils). Still the Jesuit Zimmermann says in his articles against Rudolf Steiner (Stimmen der Zeit, 1918, p. 561): "The consciousness of men in the past and present says throughout that they have no direct spirit vision ... We have no body-free thinking. Body and soul are connected to a unity of nature; the spirit in us, although inwardly independent of the body, nevertheless needs, as an inner condition of action of the bodily life and the organs, some in particular. A psychology which seeks to give the lie to these experiential convictions of the human race deserves mistrust from the outset." – In his third article Zimmermann declares "that the Church forbids such working of the human soul to find ways into the spiritual world." (Formulation of Rudolf Steiner in "The Basic Social Demand of Our Time – In a Changed Time Situation," GA Bibl.-No. 186, lecture of December 21, 1918)

261 *Such a spirit as Goethe*: See Rudolf Steiner "Goethes Weltanschauung" (1897), GA Bibl.-No. 6; paperback edition TB 625; see also Rudolf Steiner, "Goethe-Studien. Schriften und Aufsätze aus den Jahren 1884-1901," Dornach 1982, TB 634.

263 *"Wie erlangt man Erkenntnisse der höheren Welten"* (1904), GA Bibl.-Nr. 10; paperback edition TB 600.

"The Secret Science in Outline" (1910), GA Bibl. no. 13; paperback edition TB 601.

267 *Gotthold Ephraim Lessing,* 1729-1781; see "Die Erziehung des Menschengeschlechtes," Berlin 1780. The decisive question is asked in § 94: "... But why could not each individual human being have existed more than once in this world?" – § 96 "Why could not I, too, have already once taken here all the steps to my perfection which mere temporal punishments and rewards can bring to man?" – § 97 "And why not at another time all those which to do the prospects of eternal rewards help us so mightily?" – § 98 "Why should I not return as often as I am skilled in acquiring new knowledge, new skill? Do I bring away so much at once that it is not worth the trouble to come again?" – The last sentence (in § 100) reads: "... And what have I to miss? Is not all eternity mine?"

269 *when such an influence is exerted on the human being... that he is put into... hypnosis:* See Rudolf Steiner "History of Hypnotism and Somnambulism," in "Spirituelle Seelenlehre und Weltbetrachtung," GA Bibl. no. 52; single edition under the title "Das Suchen nach übersinnlichen Erfahrungen," Dornach 1972.

289 *natural science... would.... exceed its limits:* See Du Bois-Reymond's speech "On the Limits of Natural Knowledge," August 14, 1872.

See also note to pg. 72.

294 *what Goethe calls soul eye:* "I saw not with the eyes of the body, but of the spirit, myself coming towards myself, the same way, on horseback again ..." (Dichtung und Wahrheit, 3. Tl., 11. B.) – "The eye may well be called the clearest sense . ... But the inner sense is even clearer. ..." (Shakespeare and No End, 1813-16). – "We learn to see with eyes of the spirit, without which we grope about blindly, as everywhere, so especially in the study of nature" (Draft of an Introduction to Comparative Anatomy).

307 *Friedrich Wilhelm Schelling,* 1775-1854. See Rudolf Steiner "Die Rätsel der Philosophie" (1914), GA Bibl.-Nr. 18; paperback edition TB 610/611; chapter "Die Klassiker der Welt- und Lebensanschauung."

The Liberation of the Human Being

THE FUTURE AND ANTHROPOSOPHICAL PUBLICATIONS

The Internet is about choice, and choice means the freedom to choose. The Rudolf Steiner e.Lib believes this is what the future of publications — the dissemination of knowledge — is all about.

This publication absolutely falls into that category: the freedom to choose whether to just use the information we present on-line or use that information and purchase one of our other offerings, like a hardcopy of the book, or a softcopy version, like a CD or something for your Kindle. Proceeds from your purchases help us to continue these efforts to bring newly translated material to researchers and Rudolf Steiner aficionados all over the world. Freedom is a gift ... it is a gift of love. And as John Lennon wrote, "Love is all there is!"

ABOUT THE LECTURER

Rudolf Steiner

Born in Austria in 1861, Rudolf Steiner received recognition as a scholar when he was invited to edit the Kürschner edition of the natural scientific writings of Goethe. In 1891, Steiner received his Ph.D. at the University of Rostock. He then began his work as a lecturer. From the turn of the century to his death in 1925, he delivered well over 6700 lectures. His written works eventually included some fifty titles.

The philosophical outlook of Rudolf Steiner embraces such fundamental questions as the being of man, the nature and purpose of freedom, the meaning of evolution, the relation of man to nature, the life after death and before birth. Through a study of his writings, one can come to a dear, reasonable, comprehensive understanding of the human being and his place in the universe.

Among the activities springing from the work of Rudolf Steiner are the Bio-Dynamic Farming and Gardening Association which aims at improved nutrition resulting from methods of agriculture outlined by Rudolf Steiner; the art of Eurythmy, created and described by him as "visible speech and visible song;" the work of the Clinical and Therapeutical Institute of Arlesheim, Switzerland, with related institutions in other countries; the homes for the treatment of mentally retarded children; and new directions of work in such fields as Mathematics, Physics, Painting, Sculpture, Music Therapy, Drama, Speech Formation, Astronomy, Economics and Psychology.

The success of Rudolf Steiner Education (sometimes referred to as Waldorf Education) has proven the correctness of Steiner's concept of the way to prepare the child for his eventual adult role in and his contribution to modern society. Today there are some seventy Rudolf Steiner Schools in existence in seventeen countries including the United States, Canada, Mexico, and South America, with hundreds of thousands of children enrolled.

ABOUT THE TRANSLATOR

Ernesta Carsten-Krüger

Ernesta Carsten-Krüger was born and grew up in South Africa. In her early twenties, she attended a course for Waldorf education. It was like lightning struck when she first met the educational principles that flowed out of this pedagogy, and of course, Anthroposophy.

Nesta first worked with the youngest children and later with primary school children. A significant change happened when destiny led her to social therapy and therapeutic education. She and her husband lived and worked for 15 years with the Camphill Movement. We alternatively lived in South Africa, Holland and Northern Ireland.

Now retired and living in Holland again, Nesta is still involved with and is a mentor for people with special needs, which means taking responsibility for legal and other aspects of their lives. And retirement has afforded her the time to help us translate the untranslated lectures of Rudolf Steiner.

The Liberation of the Human Being

ABOUT THE ARTIST

Martha Liddle-Lameti

Martha Liddle-Lameti is an internationally recognized fiber/textile artist who creates two-dimensional fiber "paintings," as well as three-dimensional sculptures and wearable art. Her work can be seen in private, as well as public collections, including Memorial Healthcare of Owosso, Michigan.

Marti was born in Detroit and studied art at Olivet College in Olivet, Michigan, and Eastern Michigan University in Ypsilanti, Michigan. She taught art and fashion design at Owosso High School and as an adjunct professor for Kendall College of Art and Design in Grand Rapids, Michigan. Her current studio is on Sanford Lake near Midland, Michigan.

Marti holds a BFA from Eastern Michigan University and an MAT from Saginaw Valley State University in Saginaw, Michigan. You can see more of her creations by visiting Martel Designs on Facebook or marti_lameti on Instagram.